THE VERIFICATION CHALLENGE

THE VERIFICATION CHALLENGE

Problems and Promise of Strategic Nuclear Arms Control Verification

Richard A. Scribner
Theodore J. Ralston
William D. Metz

A Project of
The Committee on Science, Arms Control and National Security of The American Association for the Advancement of Science

In Cooperation with
The Center for International Security and Arms Control Stanford University

Birkhäuser
Boston • Basel • Stuttgart

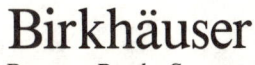

Cover design by Deborah Norris
Cover photo by Rockwell International

Library of Congress Cataloging-in-Publication Data

Scribner, Richard A.
The verification challenge.
"A project of the Committee on Science, Arms Control, and National Security of the American Association for the Advancement of Science in cooperation with the Center for International Security and Arms Control, Stanford University."
Includes index.
1. Nuclear arms control—Verification. I. Ralston, Theodore J. II. Metz, William D. III. American Association for the Advancement of Science, Arms Control, and National Security. IV. Stanford University. Center for International Security and Arms Control V. Title
UA12.5.S27 1985 327.1'74 85-13445
ISBN 0-8167-3308-1

CIP-Kurztitelaufnahme der Deutschen Bibliothek

Scribner, Richard A.:
The verification challenge : problems and promise of strateg. nuclear arms control verification; [a project of the Committee on Science, Arms Control, and National Security of the American Assoc. for the Advancement of Science] / Richard A. Scribner ; Theodore J. Ralston ; William D. Metz. [In cooperation with the Center for Internat. Security and Arms Control, Stanford Univ.]. - Boston ; Basel ; Switzerland : Birkhäuser, 1985.
ISBN 3-7643-3308-1 (Basel...);
ISBN 0-8176-3308-1 (Boston...)

9 8 7 6 5 4 3 2 1

ISBN 0-8176-3308-1
ISBN 3-7643-3308-1
Printed in the United States of America

To Paul, Amy and Mark
that their future may be more secure

and

to Herbert "Pete" Scoville, Jr.
who dedicated his life that all children
might have a brighter future.

AAAS Committee on Science, Arms Control and National Security*

Rodney Nichols (Chair)
The Rockefeller University
Anne Cahn
Committee for National Security
Roger Fisher
Harvard Law School
Mary Foster
University of California
Eugene Fubini
E. G. Fubini Consultants, Inc.
Noel Gayler
American Committee on East-West Acord
Sidney Graybeal
System Planning Corporation
Patricia McFate
The American-Scandinavian Foundation
Joseph Nye
Harvard University
Phillip Odeen
Coopers and Lybrand
William J. Perry
Hambrecht & Quist
George Rathjens
Massachusetts Institute of Technology
Condoleeza Rice
Stanford University
Herbert Scoville, Jr.
The Arms Control Association
Charles Zraket
The MITRE Corporation
William D. Carey
AAAS, Executive Officer
William T. Golden
AAAS, Board of Directors
Richard A. Scribner
AAAS, Committee Staff Director

* The Committe membership as of January 1985.

Verification Project Advisory Committee

Brewster Denny
University of Washington
Sidney Drell
Stanford University
Roger Fisher
Harvard Law School
Noel Gayler
American Committee on East-West Accord
Sidney Graybeal
System Planning Corporation
Bobby Inman
Microelectronics & Computer Technology Corporation
John Lewis
Stanford University
William G. Miller
Tufts University
Rodney Nichols
The Rockefeller University
William J. Perry
Hambrecht & Quist
George Rathjens
Massachusetts Institute of Technology
Herbert Scoville, Jr.
The Arms Control Association
Charles Zraket
The MITRE Corporation

Table of Contents

Preface

Avoiding the use of nuclear weapons is the most urgent and serious challenge facing the superpowers today. It calls for creative diplomacy and negotiations leading to nuclear arms reductions by the United States and the Soviet Union. In a tense world, however, arms control agreements cannot rest on trust alone. Each country requires independent assurances, i.e., verification of compliance.

As weapon systems advance and as each side seeks to minimize exposure and vulnerability of its military assets, the complexity of verification grows even as monitoring technologies become more refined and sensitive.

In dealing with the Soviet Union, an adversary whose system is closed and secretive, the United States is often presumed to be at a disadvantage in its ability to verify agreements. Furthermore, Soviet intentions have come sharply into question and the debate over the feasibility of verification centers increasingly on the likelihood of Soviet "cheating".

In recent years, the less-than-perfect ability to verify agreements with the Soviet Union has been cited as a reason to avoid arms control agreements altogether. The suggestion of such a drastic course underscores the seriousness of the problem and presents a dilemma for our open, democratic society. Many details of the means of collecting intelligence for verification are secret. How can a concerned citizen, without the knowledge of classified details, form a responsible opinion about the probable risks of a given approach to arms control to weigh against its intended benefits in restraining nuclear weapons?

In the fall of 1982, the AAAS Committee on Science, Arms Control, and National Security saw the need for better public understanding of verification and began formulating the elements of this book. Several principles guided the committee in this task: (1) Verifiable arms control agreements are in the best interests of all nations; (2) Under the best agreements there will always be some uncertainty about compliance; (3) The public should have the information it needs to weigh the risks of a particular agreement against its benefits; and (4) In evaluating whether to have an arms reduction agreement, it is important to compare the risks of noncompliance to those of not having a treaty at all.

Although the subject is difficult and complicated by the limits on disclosure, much can be done to inform citizens about the prospects and problems of verification.

This book aims to do that. Drawing on publicly available sources and the generous assistance of knowledgeable advisors, it explains how different types of verication work and what the U.S. has learned from its 20 years of verification and compliance experience. The information in this book is current as of early-to mid-1985. The principles discussed apply to existing treaties as well as to future ones. We hope this book will provide useful information for everyone who seeks a better understanding of this important issue.

R. A. Scribner
T. J. Ralston
W. D. Metz

Acknowledgments

We especially acknowledge the generous assistance of the advisory committee members (listed in full in the front of the book) and the members of the AAAS Committee (also listed in the front). Their wisdom, guidance, and encouragement not only made this work possible, but also improved the result immeasurably. Others who reviewed the drafts and gave much useful advice include David Hafemeister, Allan Krass, Michael Krepon, Mark Lowenthal, Christopher Paine, John Pike, Robert Scott, and Walter Slocombe. We especially thank Jack Evernden, Willard J. Hannon, and Milo Nordyke who struggled patiently to teach us about nuclear test monitoring. We are grateful also to many others, in and out of government who responsively provided valuable information and advice, and to the many scholars who have written about verification and arms control.

Our special thanks to Barbara Riley who typed most of the final draft and parts of earlier ones, to Mary Haddock who also assisted in the typing, and to Robin Eisenacher, Jacques Mitrani, Shelly Alpern, Wendy Frankel, and Jeff Levin who provided essential help in the final stages. We are especially grateful for the extensive and thoughtful editing done by Bea Scribner. Her help has made this work more accessible to a general audience. Finally, we recognize the many contributions of Kenneth Luongo, who collected pictures and graphics, secured permissions, and worked closely with us developing the captions. Ken also collaborated in producing the extensive glossary appended to this work, checking out facts and numbers and contributing in many other ways.

Early in the development of this project, we conducted a workshop which helped define the dimensions of our task and provided valuable guidance. Several of the participants joined our advisory panel. We especially acknowledge the contributions of Herbert "Pete" Scoville, Jr. Pete, to whom this book is dedicated, died before it was published. It was he who produced the first draft outline for this book and commented extensively on successive drafts. We will miss his wise counsel and support. Other workshop participants who provided useful comments and reactions included Robert Buchheim, Richard Clarke, Phillip Coyle, Paul Doty, Gerald Dineen, Henry Rowen, and Jeremy Stone. In addition, we especially acknowledge the essential assistance of Charles Zraket and his staff and partial support from the MITRE Corporation for the initial workshop. Without the continuing interest and encouragement of William D. Carey, AAAS executive officer, and the steady guidance of Rodney W. Nichols, chairman of the Committee on Science, Arms Control, and National Security, this work would have been much more difficult to accomplish. We also acknowledge the participation and contributions from several individuals at the Center for International Security of Stanford University.

We are pleased to note that this work was supported in part by a grant from the Alfred P. Sloan Foundation.

Chapter 1

Introduction

[A]rms control should be pursued because the peoples of the world expect it of their leaders. That is a reason of special importance in a democracy.

Report of the President's
Commission on Strategic Forces
(Scowcroft Commission)
March 21, 1984

The majority of American people have consistently favored restricting nuclear weapons through arms control agreements. Just as consistently, they have said they expect the Soviets to cheat.

Since the beginning of efforts after World War II to eliminate and control nuclear weapons, a central issue has been how to verify that the signatories to negotiated agreements comply with their obligations. The term "verification" has come to be used for the technological and intelligence processes used to determine "compliance."

That the U.S. must know whether negotiated agreements are being observed is taken for granted. Verifying compliance with arms control agreements is in most cases essential. The argument heats up around the questions of how much verification is enough and whether some weapons limitations are verifiable at all. Often, assertions about verifiability are shaped by political views, sometimes masquerading as technical judgments.

The complex and arcane nature of superpower negotiation, intelligence capabilities and arms control terminology puts the United States citizen at a disadvantage in understanding verification issues. This book seeks to inform citizens of the limits and possibilities of verification of nuclear arms control agreements between the superpowers.

Verification capabilities are part of a vast U.S. intelligence system. This system would operate to collect and evaluate intelligence about U.S.S.R. military capabilities independent of whether such information were specifically required by an arms control agreement.

Some people may wonder, then, why the U.S. needs arms control agreements if it is going to collect the information anyway. In fact, provisions of some arms control agreements actually facilitate the collection of required verification information. More fundamentally, verified agreements limiting nuclear weapons can promote stability and international security.

As the President's Commission on Strategic Forces (The Scowcroft Commission) wrote in their March 21, 1984 Report:

> (Arms control) can...make a substantial contribution to U.S. security. A nuclear conflict would be so devastating that we must, while protecting our freedoms and vital interests, leave no avenue unexplored which might reduce the chances that such a conflict would occur. The central purpose of our arms control efforts should therefore be to enhance U.S. security by increasing strategic stability. Increasing strategic stability reduces the possibility that a nuclear conflict between the two sides, one that neither wants, will occur. Given the stakes involved, this is of great importance.
>
> The very fact of arms control negotiations also has utility. The discussions which take place have, over the years, expanded the understanding of both sides about the strategic concepts, the priorities, the hopes and the fears of the other. While, on occasion, this dialogue can be trying, it may reduce the element of surprise and enhance the understanding of certain military programs or actions which otherwise could be dangerously misinterpreted.

Scope of the Book

This book provides an introduction to the technologies and processes of verification. What means are available to the U.S. to count Soviet nuclear missiles, submarines, and other weapons systems? When have verification capabilities facilitated or held back arms negotiations between the United States and the U.S.S.R. How do the superpowers resolve the inevitable differences that arise as they implement a treaty limiting a weapons system? These are among the questions answered in the following pages. The book focuses primarily on verification and strategic nucleare arms. Other important areas, such as verfication and chemical weapons, are discussed only as they may have some relevance to the focus of this work.

The first chapter provides an introduction to the technology, history and politics of verification, including an overview and a summary of some conclusions. Chapter two examines the principles and monitoring tasks of verification. It covers general approaches to weapons limitations, methods for maximizing verifiability, limits of monitoring, and risks and uncertainties. Chapter three presents information about U.S. and Soviet intelligence collecting and surveillance technologies. Its coverage includes satellites, radar, nuclear explosion detection, and other technologies and systems which the U.S. uses to monitor the military activities of the Soviet Union. The fourth chapter describes the next step of the verification process: analysis and interpretation of the data. In particular, it examines the process and capabilities of underground nuclear explosion monitoring.

Chapter five reviews twenty years of practical experience in verifying arms control agreements, from the Limited Test Ban Treaty of 1963 to the present mutual observance of the SALT II limits. It examines a special strategic arms negotiating authority the U.S. and U.S.S.R. have established to deal with questionable actions; what complaints or questions have arisen and how they were disposed of; and the overall compliance record of each superpower. Chapter six addresses several recent controversial compliance issues—public charges by both the U.S. and the Soviets—and their implications.

The seventh chapter asks how verification demands will be different in the future. It examines advances in weapons technology, recent and possible negotiations, as well as several new or alternative approaches, e.g., the freeze, for limiting nuclear arms. Chapter eight is a brief summary of the key verification findings and observations. The appendices include a comprehensive glossary of verification and negotiation terms as well as several key documents on compliance and arms control.

History—The Politics and the Technology

Efforts to conclude arms control agreements between the United States and the Soviet Union during the late 1950s and early 1960s foundered in part because the two countries could not agree upon mutually acceptable methods for assuring compliance. Two critical elements were missing, one technical and one political.

The missing technical component was a reliable, effective means to collect data about the other country's military activities on its sovereign territory in a mutually agreeable, non-intrusive manner. For example, in 1963 compliance with a treaty banning nuclear tests in the atmosphere, underwater and in outer space could be verified by our intelligence, but we lacked the capability to monitor underground testing. In other words, at that time, the U.S. could not verify a treaty banning underground tests. (Eventually the U.S. and U.S.S.R. negotiated and signed the Threshold Test Ban Treaty (1974) and the Peaceful Nuclear Explosions Treaty (1976), verifiable agreements that limited the size or yield of underground nuclear explosions. Furthermore, before the Comprehensive Test Ban Treaty negotiations were suspended by the U.S. in 1980, considerable progress was made toward resolving verification issues including getting the Soviets to accept a network of "in-country" tamperproof seismic sensors.) Similarly, no reliable means existed in the late 1950s for counting missile launch sites which, while sizable, might be located anywhere in the Soviet Union.

The Cold War. The overriding political problem was the hostile diplomatic and political relationship between the United States and Soviet Union during the "Cold War" period. U.S. proposals for overflights by aircraft (e.g., President Dwight D. Eisenhower's "Open Skies" proposal of 1955) or on-site inspection were rejected by the U.S.S.R. The Soviets feared that such activities would produce significant "bonus" information for U.S. intelligence not related to the treaty. Americans believed that the Soviets' reasons for rejecting the proposals hid more aggressive intentions. In the U.S., Soviet "good faith" was simply not a suitable basis for agreement.

Therefore, in addition to finding a reliable technical means to verify arms control agreements, it was also necessary to have a political climate conducive to constructive diplomatic exchange.

A major technical breakthrough occurred in 1957 when the U.S.S.R. placed Sputnik, an artificial earth satellite, into a long-term orbit in space. Ironically, this Soviet accomplishment demonstrated the technical solution the U.S. needed to "see" military activities on Soviet territory.

From the beginning of arms control efforts, verification has been as much a domestic political question as an international diplomacy and technical one. Those Americans primarily concerned about Soviet intentions and who believe that the principal way to ensure stability between the superpowers is to maintain the military superiority of the U.S. are usually skeptical that verification can be adequate. On the other hand, those who are more alarmed about the possible consequences of the superpower nuclear arms competition and who believe that the principal way to ensure stability is improved U.S.-Soviet relations are often more optomistic about verification capabilities. Such views shape positions taken in debates over possible arms agreements and the degree to which these agreements may be adequately or effectively verified.

NUCLEAR ARMS CONTROL AGREEMENTS*

Title of Agreement	Date Signed	More Common Name or Acronym
Nuclear Test Agreements:		
Treaty Banning Nuclear Weapon Tests in the Atmosphere, in Outer Space and Under Water	1963	Limited Test Ban Treaty (LTBT)
Treaty Between the U.S.A. and the U.S.S.R. on the Limitation of Underground Nuclear Weapons Tests (and Protocol Thereto) (unratified)	1974	Threshhold Test Ban Treaty (TTBT)
Treaty Between the U.S.A. and the U.S.S.R. on Underground Nuclear Explosions for Peaceful Purposes (and Protocol Thereto) (unratified)	1976	Peaceful Nuclear Explosions (PNE) Treaty
Weapons Systems Agreements:		
Strategic Arms Limitation Talks Agreements**:		SALT I Agreements
Treaty Between the U.S.A. and the U.S.S.R. on the Limitation of Anti-Ballistic Missile Systems	1972	Anti-Ballistic Missile (ABM) Treaty
Interim Agreement Between the U.S.A. and the U.S.S.R. on Measures With Respect to the Limitation of Strategic Offensive Arms	1972	Interim Agreement

Protocol to the Treaty Between the U.S.A. and the U.S.S.R. on the Limitation of Anti-Ballistic Missile Systems	1974	ABM Protocol
Treaty Between the U.S.A. and the U.S.S.R. on the Limitation of Strategic Offensive Arms (unratified)***	1979	SALT II Treaty

* As described in the 1982 Edition of **Arms Control and Disarmament Agreements,** U.S. ACDA. This table does not list the "non-armament" treaties (the Antarctic, Outer Space, Seabed, and Latin American Nuclear Free Zone Treaties), the nonproliferation agreements (the Nonproliferation Treaty, the U.S.-IAEA Safeguards Agreement, and the Nuclear Materials Convention), and the communication-confidence building agreements (the two "Hot Line" Agreements, the "Accidents Measures" Agreement, the Prevention of Nuclear War Agreement, and the Environmental Modification Convention).

** SALT I includes other agreements.

*** The SALT II Treaty has a Protocol to the Treaty, Agreed Statements, and Common Understandings. In addition, it has a Memorandum of Understanding Regarding Establishing of a Data Base, U.S. and Soviet Data Statements, a Joint Statement of Principles and Basic Guidelines for Subsequent Negotiations, and a Soviet Backfire Statement.

SALT I. By the mid-1960's, the political environment had improved and observation and sensing satellites were available. In 1967, President Johnson and Premier Kosygin held preliminary discussions on negotiations to limit nuclear weapons during an informal summit conference at Glassboro, N.J. Within five years, SALT I, the first Strategic Arms Limitations Talks, had been concluded, despite an intervening period of cool relations between the U.S. and U.S.S.R. due to the Soviet invasion of Czechoslovakia.

SALT I produced two agreements requiring ratification: (1) the Anti-Ballistic Missile (ABM) Treaty of unlimited duration, which restricts each country to two ABM sites (subsequently reduced to one each by a 1974 Protocol to the Treaty), and (2) an Interim Agreement which, for the first time, put a ceiling on the deployment of certain long-range strategic offensive nuclear weapons. SALT I set the stage for a decade of negotiations toward more explicit and detailed limitations on strategic nuclear weapons.

SALT II. The SALT II Treaty was signed by President Jimmy Carter and General Secretary Brezhnev in Vienna on June 18, 1979. Intended to last through 1985, it set limits on the number of strategic offensive nuclear missiles, warheads, launchers and delivery vehicles, and constrained the deployment of new strategic offensive arms. Although the U.S. Senate's consent has not been given and therefore SALT II has not been ratified, both the Americans and the Soviets have declared that they will adhere to the terms of the Treaty. During the SALT II congressional hearings, verification issues were of far greater concern than with SALT I.

START and INF. In June of 1982, President Ronald Reagan initiated START, the Strategic Arms Reductions Talks, which superseded SALT. These bilateral negotiations between the U.S. and U.S.S.R. sought reductions, as opposed to limitations, in the strategic arsenals of both sides. In his January 25, 1983 State of the Union Address, the President said:

> For our part, we're vigorously pursuing arms reduction negotiations with the Soviet Union...[We] insist that any agreement we sign can and will be verifiable.

The START and the parallel INF (Intermediate-Range Nuclear Forces) talks were halted in December, 1983. These negotiations were terminated by the Soviets in response to NATO's deployment of Pershing II and ground-launched cruise missiles.

Two of the major verification issues in SALT II, START and INF are (1) how to limit and count numbers of warheads when many intercontinental ballistic missiles (ICBMs) and submarine-launched ballistic missiles (SLBMs) carry more than one and some carry ten or more; and (2) how to limit and count cruise missiles which present a verification problem because of their small size, capability to be armed with nuclear or conventional warheads, mobility, and various (land, air, sea) deployment modes. These and other verification issues must be dealt with in any agreements that emerge from the new round of strategic, medium-range, and space weapons arms control negotiations begun in 1985.

The methods of verifying current treaties and possible future ones rely heavily on sensing instruments in space. These instruments, along with others on or in the ground were referred to in SALT I as "national technical means" or NTM.

Monitoring Soviet Military Activity: National Technical Means

NTM are the means used to monitor compliance with treaty provisions and are under the national control of individual signatories to an arms control agreement. They include photoreconnaissance satellites, aircraft- based systems (such as radars and optical systems), sea- and ground-based systems (such as radars and antennae for intercepting and/or collecting signals), and acoustic/seismic detector networks (for detecting nuclear explosions and calculating their yields).

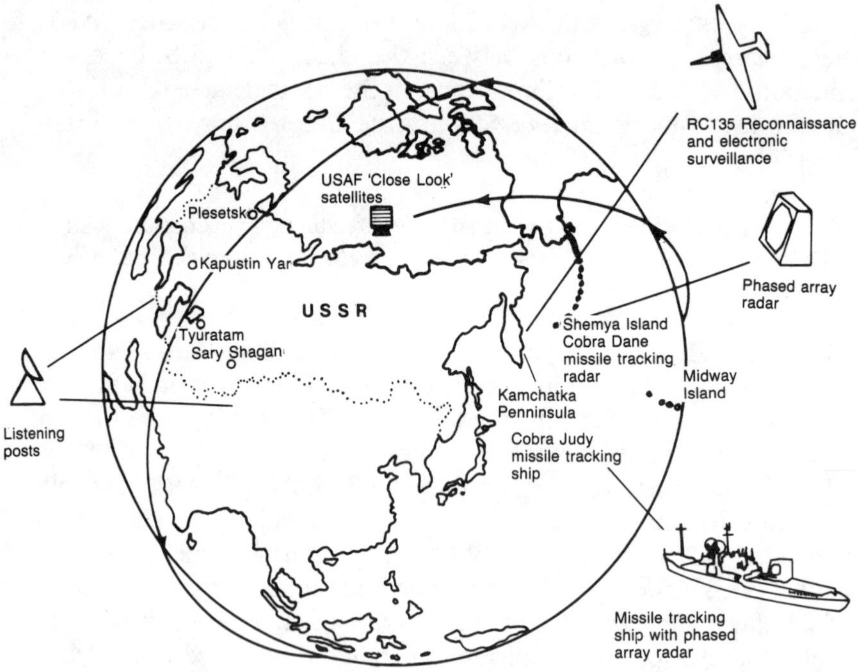

FIGURE 1. **Reconnaissance and surveillance systems for monitoring Soviet missile tests** are represented schematically in this illustration. Methods of monitoring are often redundant and complementary. This simplified drawing shows how the U.S. monitors Soviet territory for just one military activity, missile testing. Other systems monitor airfields, shipyards, troop maneuvers or unusual construction activity. The latest U.S. observation satellites combine the separate functions of area-surveillance photography and close-look photography. Various radars and listening posts around the world track Soviet ICBM and SLBM flight tests. Because the Soviets must test their missiles from west to east, the U.S. monitors the Pacific region. Large phased array radars on Shemya Island, Cobra Dane, and on board the U.S. Navy missile-tracking ship Observation Island, Cobra Judy, monitor and distinguish Soviet missile tests. The locations of major Russian missile-testing launch centers and target test areas are labeled. Only representative U.S. monitoring systems are shown; many others are omitted for simplicity. (AAAS)

While most information gathered by NTM is done by "remote sensing," other means include gleaning open sources and human intelligence. Whatever the source, NTM are unilateral means of verification. Sometimes information from on-site inspections is considered part of NTM. However, in practice, any on-site inspection arrangement, of course, requires the formal cooperation of another sovereign country. It is actually an example of a bilateral arrangement to assist verification. Multilateral means of verification, e.g., where an international authority oversees a verification process, have been proposed but not implemented for strategic arms limitations. This book deals primarily with unilateral means of verification.

The verification provisions of Article XII of the 1972 Anti-Ballistic Missile Treaty specify that "For the purpose of providing assurance of compliance...each party shall use national technical means of verification at its disposal in a manner consistent with international law," and that "each party undertakes not to interfere with the national technical means of the other party..."

VERIFICATION MEASURES AND APPROACHES

I. Unilateral Verification Measures

- A. National Technical Means, for example,
  1. Airplane and Satellite Surveillance
  2. Radars
  3. Electronic Signal Collection
  4. Seismic Monitors
- B. Human Intelligence

II. Bilateral and Multilateral Cooperative Measures

- A. On-Site Inspection
- B. In-Country Monitoring
- C. Other Cooperative Measures, for example,
  1. Agreed Compliance Forums
  2. Agreements Not to Impede and to Facilitate Verification
- D. International Verification Authorities

NTM Capabilities

The sophistication and observing power of the national technical means have improved steadily since the mid-1960s. Now both the United States and the Soviet Union have numerous kinds of technical sensors aboard satellites and arrayed around the world that are used for verifying arms control agreements. The capabilities of these instruments are a very important factor supporting both countries' confidence that they can monitor each other's military activities.

Counting Soviet Missiles. For example, at a certain point in the SALT II negotiations both sides agreed to exchange lists of numbers of strategic ballistic missiles. The Soviets listed 1,398 land-based intercontinental ballistic missiles (ICBMs). The U.S. counted 1,416 Soviet land-based ICBMs. The discrepancy, it turned out, was not in counting, but in the definition of operational missiles. Of the missiles counted by the U.S., 18 were at the Tyuratam missile test site, located in southwestern U.S.S.R. near the Aral Sea, rather than deployed in operational missile fields. The Soviets were not counting the "Tyuratam 18," but the U.S. was. The U.S. national technical means, however, had accurately counted all of the 1,416 missiles.

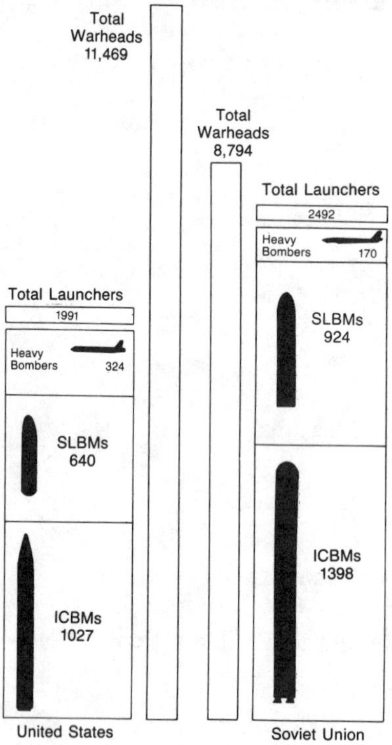

FIGURE 2. **Total U.S. and U.S.S.R. strategic arsenals.** This illustration depicts the asymmetry between the U.S. and Soviet strategic nuclear arsenals. While the Soviets have more launchers, they have fewer warheads and rely heavily on land-based ICBMs. Future arms control will move toward limiting warheads rather than launchers (as in SALT). Warhead limits are more difficult to verify than launchers. (Adapted from Understanding Nuclear Weapons and Arms Control)

Surveillance Satellites. From orbits of about 100 miles and higher, each of the superpowers has reconnaissance satellites observing the details of many activities and covering vast areas of the earth in a relatively short time. A single satellite in a "low polar orbit," for example, can cover the entire Soviet land mass within a day's time.

Some of the U.S. satellites can relay "real time" pictures of the Soviet Union back to the ground only minutes after passing over the U.S.S.R. Others pick up the heat of a rocket launch on land or sea. Still others are designed to pick up electronic signals (called telemetry) that can give information about Soviet missile development programs. The U.S. surveillance satellites used for monitoring include: (1) "search and find" satellites that take television pictures and photographs, and are designed to observe large areas of land and ocean; (2) satellites that have the ability to distinguish features, such as camouflage, that are not apparent in normal light; and (3) high resolution "close look" satellites (see figures 3 and 4).

The network of satellites is supplemented by an array of fixed and mobile radars and listening posts on the earth's surface that monitor activities at the perimeter of each superpower. An example of U.S. capabilities is the powerful long-range radar located on Shemya Island in the western end of the Aleutian Island chain of Alaska. Called Cobra Dane, it observes Soviet missile tests on the Kamchatka Peninsula. Another is the ship U.S. Observation Island, which has a similar radar and other listening devices and operates off the Soviet Pacific coast.

In addition, the U.S. has a network of aircraft and ground stations for seismic, acoustic, electromagnetic, telemetric, and radioactivity monitoring of Soviet nuclear weapons tests.

Monitoring Limitations

While these systems are extensive and their capabilities very high, they have limitations. For example, clouds can obscure some areas for days at a time, and the Soviets know when U.S. satellites are looking and when they are not. Of course, the U.S. also knows when Russian satellites are monitoring its territory. Fortunately, adequate verification does not normally require very rapid acquisition of data. Big changes, i.e., new construction or coordinated movements on a large scale, simply cannot occur overnight. And what might occur in a short time is very likely to be detected by our surveillance systems.

The capabilities, coverage, modes of operation, types of sensors, and limitations of the national technical means are discussed in more detail in chapter three.

Trust? No, Verify.

The negotiated provisions of an arms control agreement can be drafted to assist the verification process. Once the treaty is in place, verifying compliance includes monitoring the other country's activities and examining the flow of information, e.g., from satellite photography, electronic communication intercepts, and human reports of activities.

Assurance of compliance with treaty obligations is, thus, based NOT on trust, but on a country's broad intelligence capabilities including, in particular, its technical sensors.

The national technical means gives each signatory to an arms control agreement a great deal of current information on the other's activities.

This information allows it to test, challenge, and continually monitor compliance with arms control agreements. Because each country is able to rely on its own intelligence resources, each can have confidence that the information is trustworthy.

Verification and Acceptable Risk

No set of monitoring systems can be perfectly effective all the time. Redundant and complementary sensors, widely deployed, can synergistically increase the probability of detection to high levels, but never to 100%. Therefore, as the U.S. monitors U.S.S.R. military activity it must consider the risk that some Soviet actions may go undetected. The question is, what level of risk is acceptable?

Those who answer "none" essentially foreclose the possibility of any arms control measures. However, the risks of noncompliance should, among other considerations, also be weighed against the risks of not having any nuclear weapons limitations.

For those who believe that some risk is acceptable, the balancing considerations include the value of the limitation agreement; the likelihood that any action which could go undetected for even a short time would have little military significance; and the conviction that the U.S. would have early detection of significant and/or large-scale violations with time to negotiate a change or take suitable countermeasures.

This fundamental issue of verification and acceptable risk is discussed further in chapter two.

FIGURE 3. **An artist's conception** of the Agena D reconnaissance satellite. It is believed to be a search and find satellite. (Department of Defense)

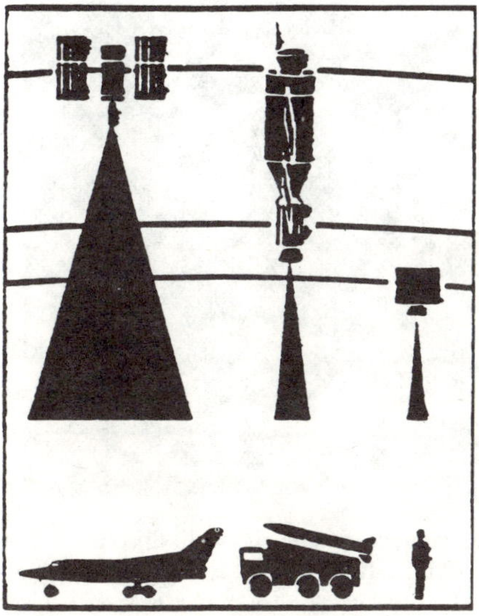

FIGURE 4. **U.S. reconnaissance satellites** have different ground resolution capabilities. This artist's conception portrays search and find and close look satellites and examples of the objects each is able to image clearly from space. (Physicians for Social Responsibility)

What Is "Early" Detection?

The strength of a verification program lies not only in its ability to detect possible treaty violations, but also to do so in a timely fashion.

It takes about ten years to develop a new weapons system to the point where it is reliable enough for deployment. An important question for judging verification capabilities is whether national technical means are sufficient to detect the development and testing of new weapons, or preparations to deploy new weapons, well before they would become operational.

Questionable activities, alleged to be violations of existing treaties, have occurred repeatedly. The interpretations of these situations are controversial. Selected illustrative cases are discussed in chapters five and six.

The record of detection is impressive. It shows that the national technical means picked up these activities long before the systems in question were operational—often years before. Early detection allows the United States time to resolve the matter by negotiations or to take appropriate countermeasures.

FIGURE 5. **The Teal Ruby space-based surveillance system**, shown in this artist's conception, uses infrared sensors to detect aircraft on earth. The U.S. is considering deployment of another satellite that will be able to detect cruise missiles. (Rockwell International)

Different Points of View in the U.S.

While powerful technologies are available to address the problem of verification, deciding what constitutes adequate verification is still an open question, as indicated at the beginning of this chapter. Some experts argue verification is straightforward, reliable, and assured by the means presently available. Others, including senior Administration officials, among them President Reagan, have said that present means are insufficient. The Reagan Administration has said the U.S. needs "ironclad" verification.

Three Views

Three distinct points of view about acceptable verifiability are the "Strategic Balance," the "Strict Constructionist," and the "Perfect Evasion" positions.

The Strategic Balance position holds that rough parity exists between the U.S. and the U.S.S.R., and that verification is adequate if it provides warning of new weapons development in sufficient time to allow for an effective US response and the prevention of a strategic imbalance.

This is, in fact, the definition of verification in the Department of State publication **The SALT II Agreement** (Select Document No. 12A, 1979). The idea behind this point of view is that in order to make any real difference strategically, violations would have to be so massive that early detection would be virtually certain.

The Strict Constructionist position holds that an arms control agreement is a legal contract and any questions, infractions, or minor violations are serious issues independent of their strategic significance.

A strict constructionist view tends to equalize all the elements of a treaty, so that minor violations have just as much importance as major ones. President Carter recognized this point of view by stating publicly that the United States would consider any violation of the SALT II Treaty to be a matter so serious that it could lead to Washington's abrogation of the agreement. The idea behind this view is that verification and compliance arrangements should not only protect U.S. security, but also they should instill confidence in the American public that the agreements are functioning fairly and effectively.

Under strict constructionist interpretation, the burden of verification can be much greater than the strategic balance position, since the resolution of even relatively inconsequential ambiguities can become important.

The Perfect Evasion position holds that independent of whether the U.S. can detect it, the Soviet Union may be clandestinely violating the terms of any arms control agreement, and doing so on a massive scale.

The idea behind this view is that the Soviets won't abide by their treaties and they are always cheating even if the U.S. cannot detect it. In this view, not only undetected small-scale but also large-scale Soviet Soviet cheating may be occurring. As a result, argue the proponents of this position, the possibility of ongoing massive Russian violations of arms control treaties should be a matter of vital national concern to the U.S.

An example of this point of view is given by one of its long-time proponents, Amrom H. Katz, who warns of the "covert deployment" of ICBMs by "methods not known to us, in places we do not know about, leaving target signatures that are either undetectable, or so nondescript as to catch no one's attention." He recommends a major review of the U.S. intelligence system to determine whether it could cope with the "problem of massive covert deployment."

Comments on Each Position

Critics of the strategic balance view, the position nearest to that of the authors of this book, think that its definition of acceptable verification is too abstract and imprecise, especially for deciding what constitutes strategic imbalance. Some offer in its place the definition given by Richard Perle, Assistant Secretary for International Security Policy in the Department of Defense, that a treaty is verifiable "...if behavior inconsistent with the treaty can be detected by the other party." This broad definition falls between the strict constructionist and perfect evasion points of view. In the present U.S. Administration, the latter two views dominate policy thinking.

Critics of the strict constructionist position contend that militarily and even politically not all questions or possible violations are, in fact, of equal significance. Some suggest that militarily inconsequential violations might be tolerated in order to maintain an agreement which otherwise significantly enhanced U.S. national security, if the political ramifications were small and the activity in question ceased. A strict legal interpretation may not be an appropriate or useful way to pursue questions about compliance with agreements between sovereign countries.

Critics of the perfect evasion position counter that there may always be some information that can be interpreted as suggesting a violation even when a country is in complete compliance. Others regard it as a barren tautological argument. Some, however, consider that the position has value in helping to maintain a vigilant U.S. attitude toward possible Soviet violations.

Adequate or Effective Verification

In the Nixon, Ford, and Carter Administrations, acceptable verification was called "adequate." In the Reagan Administration, the word is "effective." Both terms are subjective. The diversity of views about what constitutes adequate or effective verification is very broad, and some of the opinions may be irreconcilable.

In a certain sense, to ask whether verification is adequate, without specifying what types of weapons are being limited and in what way, is to ask an inadequate question. Some verification tasks are more difficult than others; some are more important than others. The same experts who argue that present methods are sufficient may not be so sure about the verifiability of future weapons systems, e.g., mobile intercontinental ballistic missiles.

The terms adequate and effective arise because, as indicated, no arms control agreement is totally verifiable. Any U.S. administration must acknowledge this fact as it presents the results of an arms control negotiation to the Congress and the public for approval. It is thus faced with the problem of finding a suitable modifier for the absolute word "verifiable."

On-Site Inspection

On-site inspection is sometimes promoted as the ultimate means of verifying Soviet compliance. If we could just get the Soviets to agree to on-site inspection our verification concerns would be over, goes the argument, followed by the assertion that until that day comes we can't engage in serious nuclear arms reductions agreements with the Russians.

Neither assertion is true. While the Soviets have resisted intrusive "on-site" inspections in principle, they have accepted limited on-site inspections as part of the 1976 Peaceful Nuclear Explosions Treaty. Recent history has shown the U.S.S.R. more willing to negotiate the matter of on-site inspections where such a measure may fit the verification needs. However, for many strategic arms agreements, on-site inspections, far from being a panacea, could be of little or no use.

Conviction or Compliance?

Verification is often compared with criminal investigation. According to this analogy certain types of "evidence" about the "crime" must be gathered in order for the "criminals" to be "apprehended" and "convicted." The idea that the purpose of verification is to provide the information necessary to "catch" and "convict" the other party of cheating is compatible with the strict constructionist point of view about acceptable verification.

Three distinctions can be made, however, about the context of verification of international agreements, which are quite different from the analogous situations for criminal investigations. First, arms control negotiations are not conducted between countries with comparable political systems and cultural standards. The political systems in the U.S. and U.S.S.R. are vastly different, and the two societies have dramatically different degrees of openness. Second, arms control is part of an ongoing strategic relationship between the two countries. Third, while early detection of any military activity of one nation that would threaten the security of another is crucial, the ultimate purpose of verification is to maintain the viability of negotiated agreements as long as they serve each country's interests and not principally to "catch" one country in doing something wrong.

PURPOSES OF VERIFICATION

I. To Deter Violations and Ensure Treaty Compliance

II. To Detect Any Variations From Agreed Arms Limitations

III. To Promote Public Confidence In Arms Control Agreements

Verification Is Easier for the Soviets

Whatever the standard used to measure adequate or effective verifiability, the difference between Soviet and American societies eases the task of verification for the U.S.S.R. and, unfortunately, makes it more difficult for the U.S.

The openness of American society assures that much information is available to the Soviets for the asking. Strategic military policy is debated openly in the U.S. Testimony from congressional hearings, press publications that regularly cover intelligence and defense developments, and published reports of technical agencies are all readily available. A substantial amount of militarily relevant engineering data exists in the public domain. (However, the Soviets sometimes may not know what information is accurate, particularly information "leaked" to the press.) Obviously, the U.S. does not have comparable access to information in the Soviet Union.

While there is an imbalance in the amount of information publicly available to the two countries, many parts of the U.S. are off-limits to Soviet nationals. Access to sensitive military and industrial facilities is closely controlled, and the most important militarily sensitive information is kept secret.

Recent Compliance Controversies

The U.S. has publicly charged the Soviets with numerous arms control compliance violations, and the Soviets have responded with charges of their own. For example, the United States accused the Soviet Union on several occasions of violating the Threshold Test Ban Treaty, which sets a 150 kiloton limit on the yield of underground nuclear weapons tests.

Other controversies include the reported Soviet use of chemical warfare agents, e.g., "yellow rain," in Afghanistan and southeast Asia. In

White House report are (1) the testing of a possible new missile which would be a violation of SALT II and (2) construction of a large phased array radar near Krasnoyarsk in central Siberia that appears to be a ballistic missile early warning radar of a type which is not allowed under the terms of the ABM Treaty. These charges are also included in two more recent Reagan Administration compliance reports released in October 1984 and in February 1985.

All the charges are serious. Furthermore, they illustrate the difficulty in defining exactly what constitutes an arms control violation. The strength of the charges in the Administration's report varies from "...the evidence is somewhat ambiguous and we cannot reach a definitive conclusion...(but it is) a probable violation...;" to "...almost certainly constitutes a violation of legal obligations under the Anti-Ballistic Missile Treaty of 1972..." (referring to the radar under construction in Siberia).

Among other points, the Soviets have charged the U.S. with "direct violations" of the 1979 SALT II Treaty, violating the SALT I agreements (by, for example, introducing "the practice of using shelters over" Minuteman and Titan intercontinental ballistic missile launchers — an old charge), and "systematically violating" the agreed principle of confidentiality in bilateral talks on compliance.

At this time, most of the charges — U.S. or Soviet — are not proved conclusively to be intentional violations. The Krasnoyarsk radar, however, appears to be such a violation. Chapter six discusses the U.S. and Soviet charges and their possible consequences.

Summary and Reflections from Experience

Over the past decade many senior U.S. officials have commented on Soviet compliance with nuclear arms agreements. Those who thought that the U.S. verification capabilities were adequate for the task of determining Soviet compliance have included three Presidents, two Secretaries of Defense, two Secretaries of State, a Director of the Central Intelligence Agency, and a Chairman of the Joint Chiefs of Staff. The sum of their testimony supports the assertion that, at least prior to 1983, the Soviet Union has been in compliance with the terms of the SALT agreements.

Discussing Questionable Activities

In 1972, the United States and the Soviet Union established the Standing Consultative Commission (SCC) to discuss verification problems.

It is an ongoing forum that meets in Geneva to discuss questionable incidents that might violate the terms of the SALT agreements. The SCC is a special instrument to facilitate compliance with strategic nuclear arms agreements.

Of the 13 incidents raised by the two countries (8 by the U.S. and 5 by the U.S.S.R.) in the Standing Consultative Commission as of July 1979, each was eventually resolved. In some cases, merely raising the issue was sufficient to halt the questionable activity. These cases are discussed in detail in chapter five.

On Verification and Negotiating With the Soviets

Few people have more direct experience with the problems of negotiating and maintaining verifiable treaties than Sidney Graybeal, U.S. Commissioner to the SCC from 1973-77. Reflecting on his experience, he makes the following observations:

> Verification is only one of the criteria which should be used in evaluating an arms control agreement. However, it is becoming the criterion.
>
> One cannot negotiate the perfect, comprehensive arms control agreement. There will be ambiguities, differing interpretations of some provisions, and questions concerning compliance. Verification will not be black and white.
>
> 100 percent verification of any agreement is probably not possible and probably not needed for U.S. security interests for any agreement short of general and complete disarmament—an unlikely eventuality.
>
> Verification is becoming a shield for those not interested in arms control to hide behind.
>
> One should expect that the Soviets will press up to the limits of the agreement and take advantage of loopholes in the language therein. But I do not believe that the Soviets will enter into any arms control agreement on which they must cheat to protect their national security interests.

Future Arms Control

Arms control agreements are negotiated because they are militarily, politically, and to some extent economically advantageous. In addition, they must usually be verifiable. Although verification is not the only criterion for judging the desirability of arms control treaties, it can play an essential role in maintaining the integrity of those agreements. The verifiability of future arms control agreements will depend on the nature of those agreements and on advances in weapons and monitoring technologies. New kinds of agreements may pose new problems for verification. Weapons technologies are moving in directions that may make verification more difficult, i.e., toward small size and greater mobility. However, the technology for monitoring will also improve.

New challenges for nuclear arms control include proposals for a nuclear freeze, cruise missile limitations, and elimination of anti-satellite weapons, among others. There is disagreement about whether some proposals are fully verifiable. However, examination of possible approaches to verification has been encouraging. Few, if any, can be ruled out on the grounds of being technically impossible to verify adequately.

The Task Ahead

In the future there will probably have to be more cooperation and negotiated measures taken by each side to enhance the ability of the other to verify compliance. Such measures will require careful planning, creative negotiation, clear treaty language, and a commitment to making nuclear arms agreements work.

These efforts will not be easy, but they certainly are possible. Too much is at stake for the U.S. to do other than seriously explore every avenue for reducing and eventually eliminating the possibility of nuclear war.

The issue of the adequacy or effectiveness of verification of nuclear arms treaties may always be in large measure a subjective matter. In the U.S., questions of national security are the responsibility of an elected government chosen by what must be an informed people. Thus, ultimately it is the American public who decide whether verification capability is sufficient in a particular agreement to protect U.S. national security interests. The many dimensions of this task are addressed in the following chapters.

Chapter 2

The Principles and Tasks of Verification

Verification is not something new. It is a continuation of our normal intelligence processes, because we are going to know about Soviet military forces and weapons, whatever it takes to learn of them, whether there is a treaty or not. We have to protect our country.

William Colby, Director of the
Central Intelligence Agency, 1973-1976

The strategic nuclear arms control and verification process has developed significantly over the past twenty years. The U.S. has created a strong foundation resting on (1) impressive technological capabilities for detecting and monitoring Soviet strategic activities; (2) an intricate network of operational practices, agreed provisions and procedures; and (3) the extensive experience of the U.S. intelligence community in observing and interpreting Soviet strategic activity.

The technical systems, the information processing capabilities, and the human resources needed for verification are all part of the intelligence process. By some estimates, ninety percent of the information needed to monitor compliance with current arms control agreements would be collected in any case as a part of ongoing intelligence gathering.

This chapter covers the process of verification, its connection with the larger intelligence collection and evaluation system, and the nature of specific monitoring tasks. It examines approaches to maximizing verifiability, the elements in arms control treaties which assist or impede verification, inherent limitations in monitoring and evaluation, and, in the face of an adversary who might seek to gain advantage by cheating, the risks associated with possible noncompliance and their strategic significance.

Verification: The Intelligence and Negotiating Processes

Technical systems originally developed to improve a nation's intelligence capabilities are often used at a later time to verify its arms control treaties. Most of the systems now referred to as national technical means, whether they are for reconnaissance, radar observation, nuclear explosion detection, or electronic signal interception, were originally developed for intelligence purposes.

For example, the Atomic Energy Detection System (AEDS) is now a worldwide network of seismographic, acoustic, electromagnetic, and radioactivity monitoring sensors deployed at 23 stations around the world and ringing the U.S.S.R. The System was first used by the U.S. for intelligence purposes after World War II to monitor for possible Soviet atmospheric nuclear explosions, and thus determine whether the U.S.S.R. was developing nuclear weapons. It detected the first Soviet nuclear test in 1949. AEDS, supplemented by other sources, made it possible for President Kennedy to sign the Limited Test Ban Treaty (LTBT) in 1963 and have confidence that any violations could be detected. Today, 21 years later, the Treaty is still in force and the System, since upgraded, is still the principal means for monitoring compliance with the LTBT.

What is Verification? Verification is a process of ascertaining the truth of a situation. In the language of arms control, verification refers to both the process and the means by which the parties to an agreement are able to ascertain with confidence that the other party or parties are abiding by the terms of the agreement.

The Verification Process

In the United States, the evaluation of whether certain weapons limitations can be verified actually begins early in the preparation for the negotiation of an arms agreement. Intelligence capabilities influence formulations of possible arms limitations proposals. As a proposal takes shape, it may include provisions which would assist the verification process. No specific proposal is likely to be tabled for discussion unless it seems that ways can be worked out by the negotiating powers to verify compliance. This evaluation plays a key role during the negotiation when the specific rules, collateral constraints, cooperative measures, and procedures are being discussed. The terms of a treaty often specify the verification needs as well as the means. Many of the restrictions in the provisions of a strategic arms limitation treaty will be determined by verification capabilities. In other words, the weapons limitations embodied in the treaty proposals are developed such that they can be monitored by U.S. NTM capabilities. No proposal goes forward as a formal negotiating position without thorough analysis by the representatives of the intelligence agencies, the military services, the Joint Chiefs of Staff and the negotiators.

Monitoring and Evaluation. Once the treaty is in place, the process has two components: monitoring and evaluation. Monitoring is the collection of data and its analysis by the intelligence agencies of the government. It requires (1) having various reliable and sensitive means of collecting information (e.g., satellite photography); (2) knowing where to look; and (3) knowing what to look for. If there is a question or concern about compliance, some initiative or response may be required. Evaluation is the decisionmaking component of the verification process. Largely judgmental in nature, it focuses on assessing the significance of a suspected violation (i.e., whether it is a false alarm, an ambiguous event, or a clear violation) and what actions, such as diplomatic inquiries, may need to be initiated.

Response. Any actual response is a considered political choice and is not part of the verification process. Many political and technical factors must be considered in a response. In raising the question of a possible violation or seeking clarification of an ambiguous event, information supporting an inquiry to the Soviets must avoid revealing intelligence sources, i.e., those methods or capabilities about which the U.S. does not want the U.S.S.R. to know. Response to an ambiguous situation or probable violation requires all the elements of the process of verification, including the Standing Consultative Commission (SCC), specifically created to address such situations, and political decisionmaking at the Presidential level.

U.S. Organization

In describing the verification process, some analysts draw a neat line from monitoring and evaluation on the one hand to response on the other. In practice the connection is complex. Parts of the bureaucracy are involved in all three areas at once. Any brief description is bound to be an oversimplification. Key participants in the process include officials from the Department of State, the Office of the Secretary of Defense (OSD) and the Department of Defense (DOD), the National Security Advisors office, the Joint Chiefs of Staff (JCS), the office of the Director of Central Intelligence (DCI) and the Central Intelligence

Agency (CIA), and the Arms Control and Disarmament Agency (ACDA), among others. Final decisions are made by the National Security Council (NSC) which is comprised of the President, Vice President, and the Secretaries of State and Defense. In practice, others such as the DCI often participate as well.

SECURITY AND RECONNAISSANCE

Two relatively little-known agencies handle most of the technical, remote sensing information collected for intelligence purposes. The National Security Agency (NSA) operates the network of U.S. listening posts worldwide. It is resposible for the collection of Signal Intelligence (SIGINT) and Communication Security (COMSEC), which includes, for example, data processing security. The NSA, in its SIGINT role, collects Communication Intelligence (COMINT) and Electronics Intelligence (ELINT) from all over the world,including from satellites. A separate agency, also part of the Department of Defense (DOD), manages the satellite and aircraft reconnaissance program for the entire intelligence community. It collects photographic and other military satellite reconnaissance information from around the globe. All of this data is put together with intelligence from other sources to inform the U.S. government about the actions of foreign governments and the capabilities of their military forces. It provides, for example, information about new Soviet nuclear weapons systems, the number of Russian ballistic missile-carrying submarines, and Soviet compliance with arms control agreements.

The chief agencies making up the "verification community" are (1) parts of the national security and foreign policy apparatus of the executive branch including the NSC, ACDA, the State Department, OSD and DOD, and JCS; and (2) the "intelligence community" including the DCI, the CIA, Defense Intelligence Agency (DIA), National Security Agency (NSA), and the Bureau of Intelligence and Research (INR) in the U.S. Department of State. Several other agencies are also involved, for example, the Department of Energy has a FY 1986 budget of over $31 million to support such areas as treaty verification, and intelligence collection as they relate to nuclear weapons issues. In Congress, the principal committees are the Senate Foreign Relations Committee, the

House Foreign Affairs Committee, the Senate and House Armed Services Committees, and the two intelligence committees: the Senate Select Committee on Intelligence and the House Permanent Select Committee on Intelligence.

The functions performed by Executive Branch agencies during the process include: (1) the development and implementation of options and requests for analysis; (2) the day-to-day evaluation, communication, and support (known as "backstopping") for the U.S. delegations and the U.S. team at the Standing Consultative Commission; (3) the development of verification and monitoring requirements and determination of how the monitoring systems will be utilized to fulfill these requirements; (4) the management of NTM collection resources and of analysis and dissemination of the product, which is performed by the Intelligence Community.

Interagency intelligence groups overseen by the staff of the National Security Council study particular questions. The four parts of the executive branch intelligence community, CIA, DIA, State, and NSA, each do their own analysis of intelligence information. This separation fosters consideration of different interpretations and possible responses. The DCI as head of the intelligence community, makes recommendations to the President concerning Soviet compliance with arms control agreements. Ultimately, the President, after review with the NSC, decides whether a particular issue will be raised with the U.S.S.R.

In Geneva, two bodies address verification capabilities and concerns and are backstopped by interagency groups in Washington. The delegation negotiating an agreement receives instructions from Washington on positions to take during talks including verification and monitoring concerns. The Standing Consultative Commission which addresses a range of compliance and strategic nuclear arms issues also is supported and directed by Washington.

The Means of Verification

The principal means of monitoring used are remote sensors located outside the territory of the country being monitored, i.e., NTM. The techniques of remote sensing such as close look satellite photoreconnaissance are both powerful and non-intrusive. Thus, they have the advantages of both effectiveness and acceptability to sovereign nations. As discussed briefly in chapter one and fully in chapter three, each superpower's remote sensing capabilities include a sophisticated network of satellites that monitor each country, as well as radars, electronic signal collection antennae, and seismic detectors. Unmanned sensors located inside the country being monitored (e.g., such as the seismic networks proposed during the Comprehensive Test Ban negotiations) are possible additions to NTM if agreements can be reached for deploying such systems.

On-Site Inspection. Sovereign countries are more politically sensitive to on-site inspection as a means of verification than to remote sensing. The Soviets have always rejected on-site inspection in its broadest and most intrusive form. One of the reasons the U.S.S.R. gave for rejecting the 1946 Baruch Plan, an American proposal to place all nuclear materials under the control of an international authority, was that the plan's verification inspectors would be U.S. spies.

The Soviets have relaxed some of their objections to on-site inspection in recent years, although they still oppose to the idea generally. For example, they have proposed to accept teams of inspectors at some civilian nuclear plants to verify the Nonproliferation Treaty. In addition, they have signed the Peaceful Nuclear Explosions Treaty, which, if ratified by the U.S., would allow inspectors to visit the sites of designated peaceful nuclear explosions to verify their purposes. Furthermore, they were willing to accept the placement of unmanned tamper-proof seismic stations inside their boundaries in the now suspended negotiations for a comprehensive test ban. This latter use of unmanned instrumentation is sometimes called "in-country verification."

None of these on-site provisions has been implemented, however, and none provides for "on demand" inspections whereby the U.S. is free to pick the site and time of visit or the investigators are free to inspect installations of their choice. Although that kind of on-site inspection has often been proposed, most recently in a U.S. draft treaty for a comprehensive ban on chemical weapons, many experienced observers think that neither the United States nor the Soviet Union would accept such an arrangement. The April 1984 chemical weapons proposal, presented in Geneva to the forty-nation Conference on Disarmament by Vice President George Bush, contained sweeping on-site inspection verification procedures. In announcing the initiative, President Reagan said,

> [V]erification of a chemical weapons ban won't be easy. Only an effective monitoring and enforcement package can ensure international confidence in such an agreement.

The draft treaty calls for "systematic on-site inspections" including "continuous inspection and in-place sensors;" "special on-site inspection by an international panel within twenty-four hours notice;" and "ad hoc inspections...to clarify suspicious activity" also to be accomplished on short notice. The Soviets reject such intrusive measures. It seems likely that they would, in fact, be unacceptable in practice to the United States as well. Many sections of both the U.S. and the U.S.S.R. are off-limits to nationals of the other country.

The value of inspections whereby the host country picks the time and the location would probably be minimal. For many strategic arms agreements, on-site inspections may be of little or no additional value.

ON-SITE INSPECTION – "A KEY TO VERIFICATION" OR "A STUMBLING BLOCK OF LITTLE VALUE"?

To verify that another country is keeping the terms of its agreements, there would seem to be nothing as definitive as information gained from first-hand inspection. For example, it would seem to answer whether a missile test is being conducted as claimed, whether obsolete systems are really being destroyed, whether prohibited materials or devices are being manufactured, and whether nuclear explosions detonated as so-called "Peaceful Nuclear Explosions" are covertly being used to develop new nuclear weapons.

On-site inspection might also be expected to tell whether a certain missile was "MIRVed" or not (that is, equipped with multiple warheads or a single warhead), and whether certain types of bombers were or were not being equipped to carry the new and hard-to-detect cruise missiles.

Our experience tells us that there is no substitute for first-hand information. This idea has been one of the means considered for how best to verify arms control for as long as such agreements have been discussed. Historically, this has meant human inspection of test ranges, manufacturing facilities, etc. (The term on-site inspection has sometimes been loosely used to include the placement of technical sensors in another country, such as seismometers located near a nuclear test area and the accompanying electronic equipment to code the sensors' data and beam it to satellites overhead. Such placement of sensors is usually called in-country monitoring.)

Appealing as the notion of first-hand verification might be, it has less than general applicability when examined more closely. It is not likely, for example, that a nation would agree to any time, any place, and round-the-clock inspection of suspicious activity. Such an approach would be regarded as too intrusive and viewed as a license for gathering all manner of intelligence information. If on-site inspection in practice means visits by designated individuals agreed upon in advance to specified locations at scheduled times, it would be possible in some situations to disguise operations that are not in accord with the rules of an agreement to appear legitimate for the inspectors' arrival and to restore them after the visitors have left. Proponents of this view would say: "it is easier to be fooled up close than from afar."

Some proponents of on-site inspection promote its utility in the extreme arguing, for example, that it is the only way to effectively corroborate information gathered by NTM. The opposite view is that little or no additional valuable information can be provided by on-site inspection and it is not worth incorporating into arms control agreements. For some verification tasks, the latter point of view does apply. For example, land-based ICBM launchers and submarine ballistic missile launch tubes are readily monitored by national technical means and no additional accuracy in counting launchers or launch tubes would be gained from on-site inspections. However, the truth lies between the two extremes: on-site inspection could be an important part of some kinds of agreements and it may be quite unnecessary and/or ineffective in others.

The effectiveness of on-site inspection depends on the particular verification task for which it might be used. Physicist W.K.H. Panofsky thinks that on-site inspection could be useful for selected verification problems. Even then, however, it would be useful primarily as a deterrent, i.e., in some cases the potential of an on-site inspection "challenge" or a scheduled visit would increase further the level of deceptive effort required to cheat and the risk of detection. In those cases where difficult technical questions might be most amenable to on-site resolution such as determining whether a certain missile was MIRVed or not, or whether a suspicious radar was a prohibited form of ABM radar (e.g. mobile ABM radar), Panofsky finds it implausible that either the U.S. or the U.S.S.R. would permit an inspector (or a TV camera in lieu of a human being) into the heart of sensitive, highly secret military installations. Other means including cooperative measures or type rules are now used to facilitate MIRV counting and mobile ABM monitoring (see text).

Some proponents of on-site inspection insist on the broad inclusion of on-site inspection in agreements. Such insistence is not alway in the U.S. interest. One of the political and security costs, for example, could be the total intransigence of the Soviet Union to discuss a particular arms limitation agreement which might be important to both countries' national security, because of the U.S. insistence on on-site inspection for a provision for which visits would provide little additional information. A different example of a security cost to the U.S. of a mutually agreed, broad, on-site inspection plan could be its inadvertently providing valuable technical or military information to Soviet inspectors viewing American plants under the agreement.

During the last thirty-five years of arms control proposals and discussions, the Soviets have usually been very resistant to intrusive on-site verification proposals made by U.S. negotiators. This Soviet attitude has frequently been viewed as indicative that they intend to cheat on their agreements. Yet one could also cite the Russians' historically based and deep-seated protectiveness of their homeland and extreme sensitivity about their privacy. Resistance to foreign intrusion predates the Soviet revolution. Nonetheless, the Soviets have accepted scheduled on-site inspection in the Peaceful Nuclear Explosions Treaty. They have also accepted the "on-site" presence of U.S. technicians to verify that certain dual-use high technology items, such as computers, would in fact be used for their stated purposes.

On-site inspections appear to be useful in conjunction with seismic monitoring of nuclear weapons tests. They were, in fact, discussed during the now suspended Comprehensive Test Ban negotiations. Furthermore, they have been suggested for monitoring well-known localized military production facilities.

On-site inspections may have little or no additional usefulness for verifying many aspects of weapons systems strategic nuclear arms agreements. Furthermore, some argue that such "up-close" attention, in the absence of a full and detailed overview might provide an illusory sense of being informed.

In any event, a key question in the debate over its utility is whether for a particular case on-site inspection provides enough of an increase in verification confidence to justify its political and security costs.

Monitoring Tasks

Monitoring tasks vary in kind and difficulty. Low-orbit photoreconnaissance satellites are an excellent means of monitoring ballistic missile systems because ICBM silos and submarines are relatively large, easily observed objects. On the other hand, even high-resolution cameras in such satellites, without cooperative measures to facilitate verification, may be insufficient to monitor deployment of cruise missiles. Seismic monitors external to a country can readily detect and distinguish earthquakes from underground nuclear explosions of about 10 kilotons and higher, a capability which is quite sufficient for the 150 kiloton limit of the Threshold Test Ban Treaty. Low-yield underground nuclear tests, however, require considerable precision to detect and discriminate from the signals generated by earthquakes. These issues are discussed further in chapter four.

TABLE 1. Ground Resolution Required for Treaty Verification (in metres)

Object	Detection	Recognition	Identification	Description
Radar	3	0.9	0.3	0.15
Radio-communications	3	1.5	0.3	0.15
Artillary-Rockets	0.9	0.6	0.15	0.05
Aircraft	4.5	1.5	0.9	0.15
Ground-ground missiles & anti-aircraft sites	3	1.5	0.6	0.30
Vehicles	1.5	0.6	0.3	0.05
Roads	9	6	1.8	0.6
Military Airfields	-	90	4.5	1.5
Submarines on the surface	30	6	1.5	0.9

Adapted from IEEE Spectrum

Three Approaches

Monitoring tasks also vary with the type of approach used in specific arms control treaties. There are several approaches used in different treaties.

"Weapon Systems" or "Limiting Numbers" Approach. The SALT agreements are examples of arms control measures that limit numbers or place restrictions on a given type of weapon, such as ICBMs. Arms control is accomplished by numerical limits on deployments, or restrictions on the number and types of testing programs. Monitoring tasks are focused on counting specific weapons systems. The degree of difficulty in monitoring depends on the complexity of the system and the ease of detecting (or concealing) the items in question. For example, while large missiles in silos are easy to count, small anti-satellite missiles carried under a fighter plane would be more difficult to monitor. Some suggested measures such as the Build-Down and Deep Cuts proposals, while focused on weapons systems, would use a formula or process to phase down or eliminate nuclear arms. Such suggestions have been called "process" proposals.

"Comprehensive" Approach. The term "comprehensive" may be applied to those measures which seek to eliminate a basic element underlying an entire class of weapons, i.e, biological or nuclear. Examples include the Biological Weapons Convention which banned the use of such weapons, the suspended negotiations toward a Comprehensive Test Ban Treaty which would have halted all nuclear weapons explosion testing, and the "freeze"-related proposal to cut off the production of fissile material needed for constructing new nuclear weapons. The key feature of this approach is the across-the-board prohibitory nature of the measure. In principle, monitoring such a comprehensive arms control agreement should be easier. If one event or condition that should not exist is detected, then a serious breach of the agreement is proved. In practice, however, this approach may be as demanding of monitoring capability and as complex a verification problem as the weapons system approach.

"Geographic" Approach. A third approach is to prohibit the introduction of nuclear weapons into specifically delimited geographic areas. The Outer Space Treaty, the Antarctic Treaty, the Seabed Arms Control Treaty, and the Latin American Nuclear-Free Zone (the Treaty of Tlateloco), are examples of existing arms control treaties based on this approach.

The SALT II Treaty is an example of a "weapons systems" approach in which a number of specific categories of weapons systems are limited according to numbers of deployed systems (e.g., ICBMs, ballistic missile submarines, heavy bombers) and some systems are also limited with performance restrictions (e.g. launch-weight and throw-weight of certain missiles). This combination can result in a complex web of monitoring tasks that specify the type and quality of information needed. Table 1 gives examples of the monitoring tasks created by the provisions of various treaties.

An example of an arms control agreement that combines elements of the "weapons system" and "comprehensive" approaches is the Anti-Ballistic Missile Treaty of 1972 and its Protocol of 1974. It is a "weapons systems" approach because it limits deployment of ABM systems to one site each and prohibits development of mobile "futuristic" ABM systems. Furthermore, it is also "comprehensive" because the effect for a decade has been to halt the deployment of new ABM systems altogether. (For more detail on what the ABM Treaty allows and prohibits, see the text of the Treaty in Appendix I. See Appendix II for some strategic nuclear arms control treaties and negotiations, 1963-1985.)

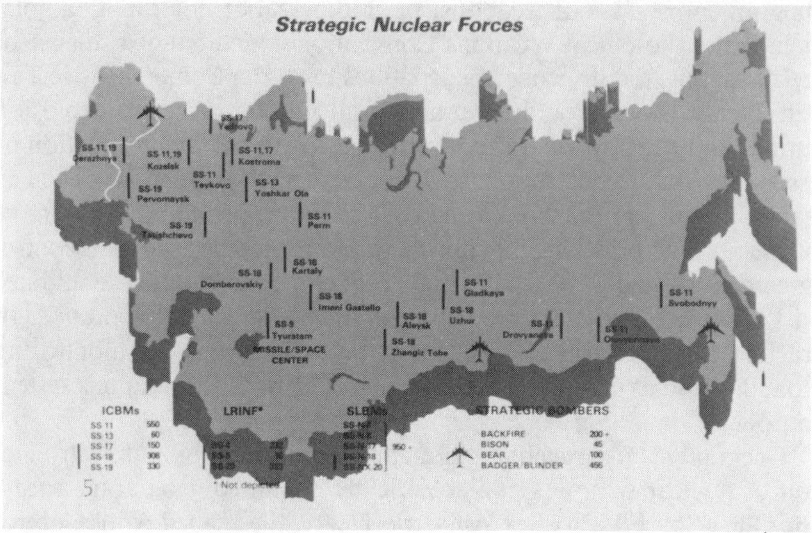

FIGURE 1. **Soviet strategic forces,** like those of the U.S., consist of land-, sea- and air-based nuclear weapons, although not in the same proportions as those of the U.S. About three-quarters of Soviet missiles are land-based. This illustration depicts the various launch areas and bases where these weapons are deployed. National technical means of verification are used to monitor these sites to ensure Soviet compliance with strategic nuclear arms control agreements. (Department of Defense)

Maximizing Verifiability of Complex Weapons Systems

Complex modern weapons systems require many phases to develop and test, and a number of components to deploy. Verifiability of a particular nuclear weapons limitation agreement can be maximized by concentrating the burden of limitations on those phases of the development process that are easiest for the national technical means to observe and those components of the deployed weapon system that are easiest to detect.

Counting Launchers. Following this principle, the SALT Treaties placed limitations on strategic missile launchers rather than missiles themselves. The term "launchers" in this context means silos for ICBMs (with a few exceptions) and submarine launch-tubes for submarine-launched ballistic missiles (SLBMs). Silos are large fixed installations which are easy to observe by satellite. Similarly, the total number of submarines and their launch tubes can be easily counted in shipyards (as they are constructed) and while entering or leaving port even though their precise location on patrol cannot be monitored.

FIGURE 2. **An aerial view of a U.S. Minuteman ICBM test launch site.** The contour of this site is very similar to other ICBM ranges. Reconnaissance satellites keep constant watch on missile bases to verify compliance with arms control agreements. (Department of Defense)

SALT I developed the "launcher counting rule," one missile for one silo, to set limits on numbers of ICBMs. To strengthen this principle, two collateral constraints were adopted for land-based ICBMs. One prohibited the "rapid reload" of ICBM silos and another delineated an area around a silo, a "launcher deployment area," where only one missile could be deployed and no extra missiles could be stored. The second constraint was designed specifically to assist the monitoring by national technical means needed to verify that there was only one missile for one launcher. Submarines at sea, of course, cannot be reloaded quickly.

Missile Testing Limitations. Limitations on development of new systems have focused on missile testing. The launch sites, test ranges, and impact areas used by both the U.S. and U.S.S.R. are well-known, and tests in progress are observable by a number of types of sensors available to each nation's national technical means. Testing limitations have previously enabled both parties to the SALT treaties to verify a number of quantitative performance restrictions (e.g. missile throw-weight) for strategic weapons systems.

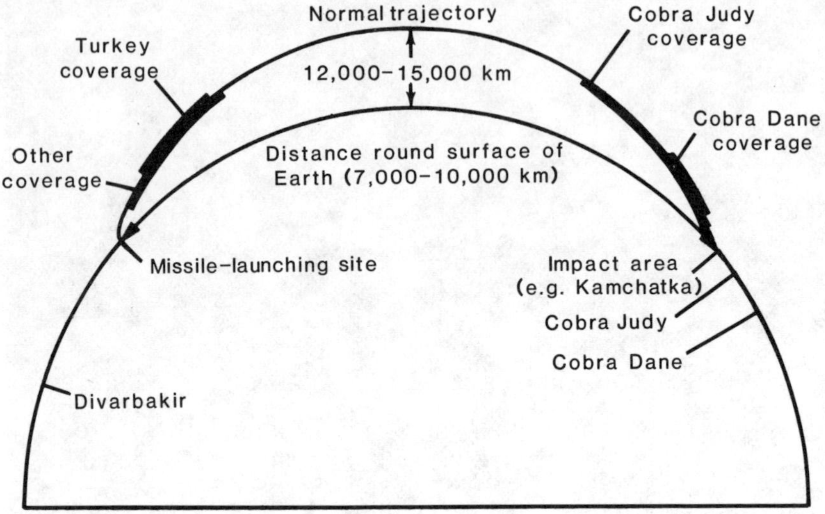

Figure 3. **The radar coverage the U.S. employs to track Soviet ballistic missile tests.** While the Iranian coverage is no longer available to the U.S., new radar stations reportedly have made up for the loss. The U.S. monitoring station in Turkey is at Divarbakir. (AAAS; adapted from SIPRI)

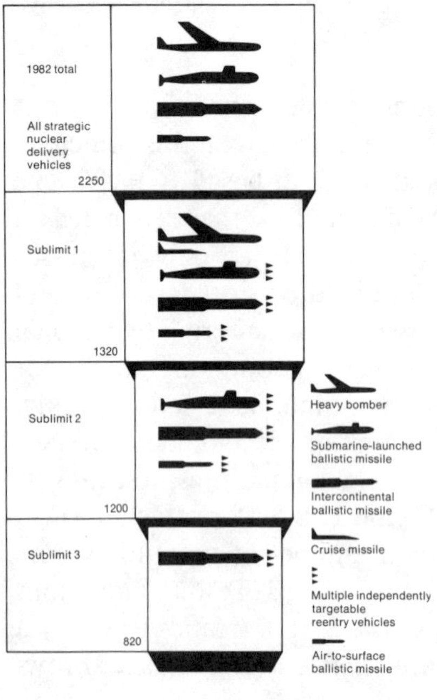

FIGURE 4. **An illustration of the limits that the SALT II Treaty placed on various weapons systems.** It limited all strategic weapons launchers to 2,250. Further sublimits were place on heavy bombers carrying air-launched cruise missiles, and also MIRVed SLBMs, ICBMs, and ASBMs. The SALT II Treaty has not been ratified, but both the U.S. and the Soviet Union have agreed to abide by its terms. (IEEE Spectrum)

Cooperative Measures

Cooperative measures are steps taken by one party to an agreement in order to enhance the ability of the other to verify compliance. The increased use of these measures over the past twelve years to assist monitoring has facilitated arms control. Such measures can be voluntary or negotiated. Examples include data exchanges and unilateral dismantling and destruction of older weapons.

Cooperative measures adopted under SALT II include the use of "counting rules" and "type rules" to ease certain verification tasks. One example of a counting rule is the agreement that once a missile has been tested with multiple independently-targetable reentry vehicles (MIRVs), all missiles of that type are considered to have been equipped with MIRVs. The effect of this rule has been to eliminate the need to distinguish between deployed MIRVed and non-MIRVed missiles as a task of verification. (Chapter seven discusses the MIRV verification question further.)

Facilitating Verification

Prohibiting Deliberate Concealment. The first strategic nuclear arms cooperative measure was the agreement in the SALT I Anti-Ballistic Missile Treaty, "not to interfere with the national technical means of verification" or to engage in "deliberate concealment measures" to "impede verification."

SALT I prohibited deliberate concealment. This was further elaborated in SALT II to include activities that would conceal, camouflage, or encrypt information needed to verify provisions of the treaty.

Other cooperative measures that have been implemented include: prior announcements of test flights of weapons systems covered by the agreement; "declarations" of the numbers and locations of launchers dismantled and destroyed to meet an agreement; "declarations" of the locations of test ranges and production facilities, and the composition and levels of strategic forces; and use of observable features, called Functionally Related Observable Differences (FRODs) and Observable Differences (ODs), which make the function of certain weapons easier to verify.

Incorporating Observable Differences. The technique of utilizing Functionally Related Observable Differences and Observable Differences is primarily associated with cruise missiles as well as with the planes and ships that carry them. For example, "strakelets" (rounded farings where the wings meet the fuselage) are the FROD chosen by the U.S. to distinguish cruise missile-carrying B-52s from others, as required by the

SALT II Treaty. They are observable by national technical means. (See figures 5a, b.) While some experts think FRODs are valuable cooperative measures, others think that while they may work in some cases they are, in general, of limited value. Cruise missiles and the use of observable differences to identify the vehicles carrying them are discussed and evaluated in more detail in chapter eight.

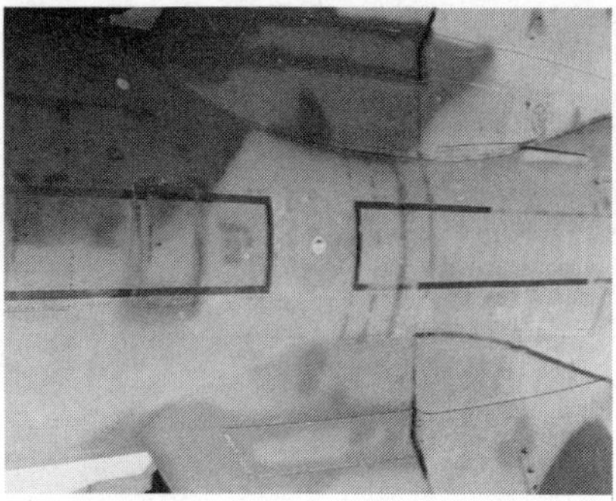

a

b

FIGURE 5a. **A top view of a B-52 without strakelets.**

5b. **A top view of a B-52 with strakelets.**

For verification U.S. B-52 heavy bombers that carry Air-Launched Cruise Missiles (ALCMs) must have a functionally related observable difference from those B-52s that do not carry such missiles. The U.S. incorporates strakelets (rounded farings on the wing of the plane where it meets the fuselage) onto the aircraft. This satisfies the SALT II requirement that ALCM-carrying bombers be differentiated from other heavy bombers. (Boeing Military Aircraft)

Declared Facilities. Declaring that specific weapons development or testing functions will take place only at certain facilities eases the task of verification. If both countries agree that a certain activity, such as aircraft production or missile testing, can only take place at declared locations, then such an activity occurring outside the declared area would violate the agreement. The result, known as the "localization effect," eases the task of monitoring because the means of verification can be more efficiently and effectively directed toward a smaller number of locations.

Standing Consultative Commission

Under SALT I, the U.S. and the U.S.S.R. agreed to establish the Standing Consultative Commission (SCC), described briefly in chapter one. The SCC and its deliberations are discussed in detail in the next chapter. Many observers view the SCC as the most valuable cooperative measure of all, because of its continuing role in facilitating the implementation of agreements and clarifying compliance questions.

Cooperative measures ease what would otherwise be difficult monitoring tasks. However, perhaps the most important aspect of these measures is the commitment they represent. Each country demonstrates its willingness to facilitate verification of treaty compliance because it considers the treaties in question to be in its own best interests.

Treaty Language

Negotiators try to balance specificity and flexibility in treaty language. The exact wording of a treaty, as well as the way the parties agree to interpret it, are crucial to verifiability. It is the language of the treaty, after all, to which each country must return in order to assess the other's compliance.

Specificity

Specificity of language eases the task of verification. The advantage of specificity is, of course, that ambiguity is reduced, thereby improving the chances that compliance issues will be clear-cut. In some cases, however, specificity is not achieved because some other goals have priority for one or all negotiating nations.

Agreed Statements and Common Understandings. SALT II uses Agreed Statements and Common Understandings to clarify the meaning of certain provisions. They are distinct from the Treaty itself, but are just as binding as the main provisions. (The Common Understandings of SALT I were not signed and are therefore not binding, while those of SALT II were specifically negotiated as part of the Treaty.) These Statements and Understandings introduce a higher level of precision into provisions which might otherwise have contained loopholes. Usually, these statements refine and specify the reciprocal commitments and monitoring tasks thereby facilitating verification.

One example of greater specificity resulting in improved verifiability is the following Agreed Statement in SALT II defining Multiple Independently-targetable Reentry Vehicles (MIRVs):

> Third Agreed Statement. Reentry vehicles are independently targetable:
>
> (a) if, after separation from the booster, maneuvering and targeting of the reentry vehicles to separate aim points along trajectories which are installed in a self-contained dispensing mechanism or on the reentry vehicles, and which are based on the use of electronic or other computers

in combination with devices using jet engines, including rocket engines, or aerodynamic systems;

(b) if maneuvering and targeting of the reentry vehicles to separate aim points along trajectories which are unrelated to each other are accomplished by means of other devices which may be developed in the future.

The effect of this Agreed Statement is to define MIRVs in terms of the most readily verifiable parameters, i.e., maneuvers, separate aim points, unrelated trajectories, self-contained dispensing mechanisms (or other future devices), and computer guidance.

The SALT Treaties also contain unilateral statements which are entered into the record but are not formally binding.

Avoiding Specificity and Preserving Flexibility. On occasion, one or both countries may wish to preserve their flexibility in weapons development and/or deployment. One reason a country might seek flexibility in treaty language is to keep open the option of deploying a weapons system to which it is already committed, e.g., for the Soviets, SS-19s in SALT I; and for the Americans, cruise missiles in SALT II. Another reason is to protect intelligence practices. A third is the desire on both sides for leeway in dealing with future developments.

Protection of Intelligence

In pressing for clarification of a compliance question through diplomatic channels it is often important to phrase the inquiry in such a way that the request itself does not reveal either the source or the precision of the supporting information. Furthermore, because collecting information for verification purposes is such an integral part of intelligence gathering, it is prudent to formulate compliance monitoring tasks in ways that protect intelligence sources. The tasks associated with a particular provision, for example, can be formulated to depend on two or more sources. In drafting a treaty, negotiators can make sure that verification can be accomplished with acknowledged and/or less sensitive means rather than the newest, most sensitive and secret intelligence systems so that the exact capabilities of these systems are protected. (See, for example, the observations on encoding missile test data in chapter six.)

Limitations

Limitations of Monitoring

It is usually not possible to collect complete information about a compliance activity. Reasons for this include both the technological/design limitations of the monitoring systems and simple practical considerations, such as limited time, that apply to any information collection effort. Technical sensing instruments can malfunction. However, in order to avoid a complete monitoring failure, they are normally deployed with sufficient depth and back-up to assure that at least one source of information is available at any one time. Several different highly effective systems monitoring the same area or weapons limitation rule, even if each is less than perfect, means a very low probability that some significant event would go undetected. It is possible, nonetheless, that the best source of information may not be available at a crucial moment.

Despite the large amount of information provided by the national technical means, verification of compliance is often like putting together a puzzle with some of the pieces missing. As discussed in chapter one, however, the overriding concern should be not whether information is complete and verification perfect, but whether possible significant violations could be promptly detected and appropriate clarification, negotiation, and, if necessary, countermeasures could be implemented. (An adherent of the strict constructionist viewpoint might not agree with that statement. Certainly, a proponent of the perfect evasion position would not.)

Limitations of Evaluation

Two different situations may arise in evaluating incomplete information. The most obvious is that preparations for or actual violations may be overlooked, a situation which greatly worries proponents of the perfect evasion viewpoint. The second is the erroneous assessment that a violation has occurred.

"False alarms" have penalties. First, they can exacerbate international tensions. Second, they can degrade the effectiveness of the verification process either by increasing the likelihood of swamping the analysis-decision making process with numerous false alarms so that intensive analysis of suspected violations cannot be properly managed, or by building in a predisposition not to believe the alarms.

Risk Assessment

Since perfect verification is not a feasible goal, it is important to examine the risk associated with uncertainties that will occur despite the best possible monitoring procedures. A basic principle guiding this task is that the risk should be primarily determined by the military value of an undetected violation by the other party. (Certainly, in the U.S. there are political risks and possible costs in any real or apparent noncompliance even if the military significance is small. One of the costs could be loss of a treaty. Another could be reduced public support for future arms agreements. U.S. administrations must manage such costs, if they occur, as particular circumstances require.)

a

FIGURE 6. **Multiple Independently-Targetable Reentry Vehicle (MIRVed) Missiles.** MIRVed missiles present a serious problem for arms control because one missile can launch many warheads to different targets as the missile's post-boost vehicle, or bus, travels through space. Photo (a) shows multiple warheads being placed on top of a U.S. MX ICBM. The metal structure in the center is part of the bus. The size of the warhead can be measured against the man at right. (Department of Defense)

b
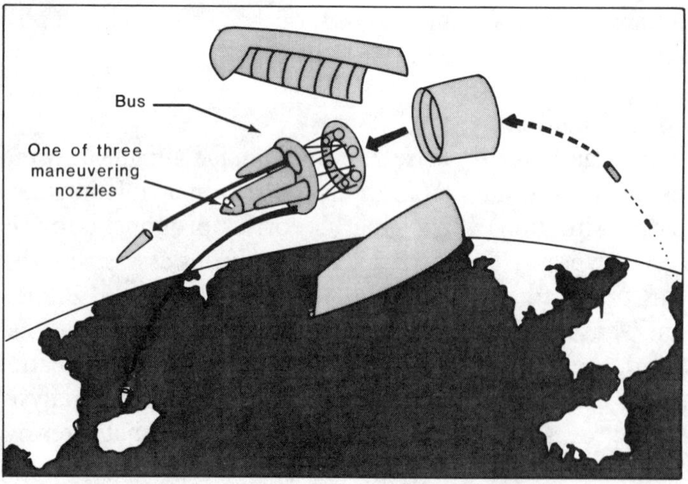

The artist's conception (b) portrays the MIRVs in action. As the bus travels through space it releases warheads to different and varied targets by rotating and repositioning itself. (AAAS; adapted from Department of Defense)

Different types and components of strategic systems have different military value, depending upon their (1) specific offensive or defensive capabilities, (2) vulnerability to attack or survivability, i.e., "hard" or "soft" target, and (3) ease of replacement with other existing systems. An anti-ballistic missile system, for example, has basically four visible components: the missile, the launcher, an "acquisition" radar that picks up the trajectory of the target, and an "engagement" radar that guides the missile to its interception point. Each of these components has a different military value.

For example, there may be a small risk associated with one additional suspected "early warning" radar perhaps positioned to be part of an ABM target acquisition network, as in the case of the Krasnoyarsk construction (described in chapter one and in more detail in chapter six). However, if there are also suspicious interceptor and other radar activities which are not violations but "at the margins of an agreement," the risk associated with the radar construction could be judged large. Such a situation would suggest to some that the Soviets could be laying the groundwork for "breakout," an apparent sudden advance in strategic weapons capability, should either country abrogate the ABM Treaty. If one believes or has evidence to support that scenario, the military and political value of even one radar could be very great.

Covert Deployment of ICBMs

The military value of covert deployment of a large force of modern ICBMs could be quite high, especially if those missiles had sufficient targeting accuracy to pose a "first strike" threat, i.e., the potential to mount an accurate ballistic missile attack which could destroy the other country's ICBMs (and command and control centers) before they could be launched.

However, it is highly unlikely that covert deployment of substantial numbers of ICBMs would go undetected. The launchers are easily countable by national technical means, their earthworks are distinctively recognizable (the distinctive pattern in the vicinity of Soviet launchers as seen from the air confirmed to the U.S. in 1962 that Soviet Premier Khrushchev was attempting to put missiles in Cuba), and ICBM silos take years to construct. In the future, smaller mobile ICBMs could pose more formidable monitoring problems.

In contrast, the military value of a few hidden, older, and less accurate missiles would be lower, especially if each contained a single warhead, since each would have a low probability of destroying a single missile on the other side. Of course, disclosure that either country had attempted to hide even a few missiles would have enormous political consequences.

If a country is considering covert deployment of a military system restricted by an arms limitation agreement in order to gain a strategic advantage, it must weigh the value of that advantage against the cost of detection and exposure. On the other hand, as a country weighs the potential benefits and costs of a proposed agreement to which it might commit itself, it must attempt to specify the likelihood of an undetected covert deployment by the other country, as well as the military significance and overall national security risk of such a deployment.

Confidence Levels

It is important, therefore, that the U.S. determine the amount of risk it will tolerate if the Soviet Union covertly deploys a weapons system (or part thereof), contrary to an agreement. The risk is sometimes estimated in quantitative terms giving the degree of confidence, called confidence level, as a percentage. Confidence levels are intelligence judgements about monitoring expressed in terms of high, moderate and low confidence. While percentage probabilities are commonly attached to these confidence levels, they usually represent an optimistic or pessimistic consensus among experienced professionals rather than hard quantitative calculations. High confidence would mean that, having weighed potential assets and problems, monitoring experts are very optimistic that the particular monitoring task can be performed, moderate would mean fairly optimistic, and low would mean pessimistic.

In practice, intelligence experts usually forecast monitoring confidence by hypothesizing plausible, representative cheating programs that would add to military power in some substantial way. Because the U.S. wants to minimize the risk that the Soviets could gain advantages through noncompliance, intelligence forecasts about monitoring confidence are intentionally conservative in at least two respects. First, if the chances of noncompliance are thought to be no better than 50-50, then monitoring confidence would be judged to be low. Second, they are based solely on surveillance by programmable U.S. collection systems. Monitoring judgments anticipate no bonus such as a breach in Soviet security or access to a knowledgeable defector.

In recent years, the agencies responsible for intelligence and defense have frequently used quantitative calculations of risk assessment. However detailed, these do not form a basis for determining how much risk is acceptable. The answer to that question comes from comparing those risks with an assessment of potential benefits.

Risk and Strategic Significance

As explained in the introduction, there are sharply differing political views as to what constitutes adequate verification. Some of the sharpest differences occur over the question of how much risk is strategically significant.

For example, in the case of a prohibition on construction of more intercontinental ballistic missile silos, the question of strategic signficance might be, how many covertly constructed silos (and ICBMs) would represent a significant increase in destructive military capability? Given that the SALT Treaties allow each side to have over 1,000 ICBM silos, the covert deployment of 10 hidden silos might not be militarily significant. If a future treaty limited each side to 100, the significance of 10 successfully hidden ICBMs would be much greater.

Those who hold the "strategic balance" position might accept a verification uncertainty of ten (or even more) hidden ICBMs for the sake of an otherwise strong and balanced treaty judged to be in the U.S. national interest. Those who hold the "perfect evasion" point of view might find this verification uncertainty unacceptable. They might reject any treaty for which the limit for reliable verification is ten undetected ICBM's.

Summary and Observations

Each superpower's NTM is a unilateral means of verification, and part of its overall intelligence capability. Monitoring tasks are specific and tailored to individual treaties. Cooperative measures can enhance the verification capabilities of the national technical means.

While in certain cases on-site inspection can provide useful information not available to national technical means, it is not generally the answer to the verification needs of strategic nuclear arms agreements.

Verification capabilities are considered before a treaty is negotiated to assure that compliance can be monitored. Treaties are generally designed to maximize verifiability. Furthermore, careful drafting of the treaty language at the time of negotiation can enhance verifiability at a later time.

Perfect verification is impossible, so the risk of some noncompliance must be considered. As a factor weighing against the signing of an agreement, the risk of noncompliance must be judged not only in the light of the military and political significance of the possible violation, but also compared to the risk to national security of not having the agreement at all. All treaties carry risks, but comparable, or even greater, risks may occur without a treaty. In other words, the risk of undetected noncompliance, due to possible failures of verification, should be weighed against the risk of unconstrained arms competition without a treaty. More than once in the past decade defense analysts have determined that the destabilizing effects of competition between the superpowers without arms control was more dangerous than the risk of noncompliance with imperfect treaties.

In deciding what constitutes adequate or effective verification the following factors should be considered: the capabilities and confidence a country has in its NTM; the ease of monitoring of the weapons systems restricted by a treaty; the degree of enhanced verifiability as a result of cooperative measures in a treaty; the value of the treaty itself; and the estimates of noncompliance risk as well as the military advantage that one country's analysts judge that the other could achieve through covert deployment. These questions should be considered in the political, military, and intelligence capability contexts of each treaty negotiation.

Chapter 3

National Technical Means

We have spent billions of dollars on these systems, and it has been money well spent. I find our intelligence capabilities truly astonishing in their technological capacity—especially to a soldier who began his career in World War II, when we seldom knew what was happening six hundred yards away, let alone six thousand miles away.

General George M. Seignious II
Director, U.S. Arms Control and
Disarmament Agency (1979-81)

Each of the superpowers has its own national technical means of verification. For the United States, this consists of an extensive network of technological capabilities, collection systems, and other intelligence and analytical resources. The technology includes photoreconnaissance satellites, radars of various kinds, sensitive electronic communication interception and collection equipment, and seismic and acoustic sensors. For strategic nuclear arms agreements such as SALT I and SALT II, the single most important of these are reconnaissance satellites. However, full compliance could not be assured without additional and complementary information from other systems. Indeed, were those systems not also available for monitoring and cross-checking, many provisions of the agreements would never have been negotiated. For monitoring compliance with nuclear explosion limitation agreements, seismic sensors are the most important, and several other systems also play crucial roles.

This chapter examines each of the major technological components of NTM.

Reconnaissance Satellites

The multi-purpose array of reconnaissance satellites deployed both by the U.S. and the U.S.S.R. is the backbone of each nation's verification system. The general idea that the superpowers use such means to monitor each other's activities was publicly discussed at the time of the SALT I negotiations in the late 1960s. The use of photoreconnaissance satellites was first officially declassified by President Johnson in 1965 during a press conference and later by President Carter during a speech at Cape Kennedy, Florida in 1978.

The observing powers of these satellites have improved since they were first deployed in 1960, and they can now "see" in remarkable detail from orbits of 100 miles and higher. Some are built for wide-area surveillance, while others are designed to take a close look at new and suspicious activities.

The satellite systems have many types of sensors besides the imaging sensors mentioned in chapter one. These include infrared (heat) and other radiation sensors, radar, and electronic listening devices for collecting signals from the other party's radars and communications. Such sensors are located not only on satellites, but also on aircraft and ships and at ground stations.

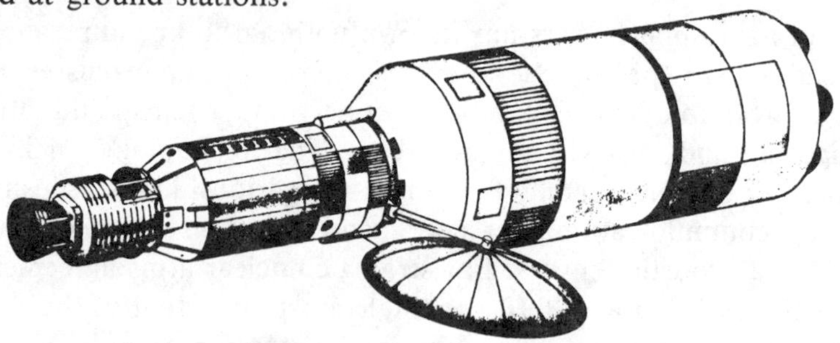

FIGURE 1. **An artist's conception of a U.S. search and find satellite.** (The Balance of Military Power)

The term "national technical means of verification" comes from the 1972 Anti-Ballistic Missile Treaty. The systems that constitute the NTM have not been specifically defined either in the texts of the agreements or in the negotiating record. They were deliberately left undefined for several reasons: first, to protect intelligence sources and methods; second, to permit maximum flexibility in the use of a broad variety of means at the disposal of each country; third, to ensure that each party maintains unilateral control over its own means and the information they provide; and fourth, to continue the uncertainty about the capabilities of each party's NTM, in the belief that such uncertainty further deters cheating by the other side.

Limits of Aircraft Photoreconnaissance

Aerial photographic reconnaissance has been practiced since before World War I. High-altitude photoreconnaissance aircraft include the U-2 as well as the newer and more sophisticated SR-71. As admitted by President Eisenhower in 1960 at the time a U-2, piloted by Francis Gary Powers, was shot down over Soviet territory, photographing Russian military installations was among the missions of the high-altitude aircraft.

Experience using the U-2 for photoreconnaissance over the Soviet Union revealed three important deficiencies: the aircraft's limited range, limited coverage, and vulnerability to the surface-to-air missiles which downed Powers' plane. The limited range of the aircraft meant that only selected, small portions of the Russian land mass could be covered on a given mission. To cover a large amount of territory, it would have been necessary to provide either a large number of aircraft flying staggered missions or develop means to conduct reconnaissance on multiple overlapping passes. (See figure 2, chapter 5.)

By the late 1950s, satellite technology provided the answer to these range, coverage, and vulnerability deficiencies. As noted in the introduction, satellite technology and other remote sensing detectors provide the least intrusive ways of gathering information needed for verification.

Surveillance Orbits

Two types of orbits, low and high, are employed for surveillance satellites. Low-altitude orbits are preferable for observing features with fine resolution. U.S. photoreconnaissance satellites are generally in orbits 100 to 500 miles high. A trade-off is made between proximity and surveillance mission duration. When the altitude becomes too low, atmospheric drag limits the time the satellite maintains its orbit. Satellites in low altitude orbits circle the earth approximately every 90 minutes. An imaging satellite in a low orbit of 100 miles altitude, tilted at the optimum inclination, can cover the Soviet Union in approximately six passes during an average eight-hour period.

Satellites in high-altitude geosynchronous orbits are in the best position for stationary monitoring. Such satellites can continually monitor the Soviet land mass. For example, this type of satellite equipped with an infrared sensor which detects the heat of an operating rocket engine gives an early warning of any ICBM launch.

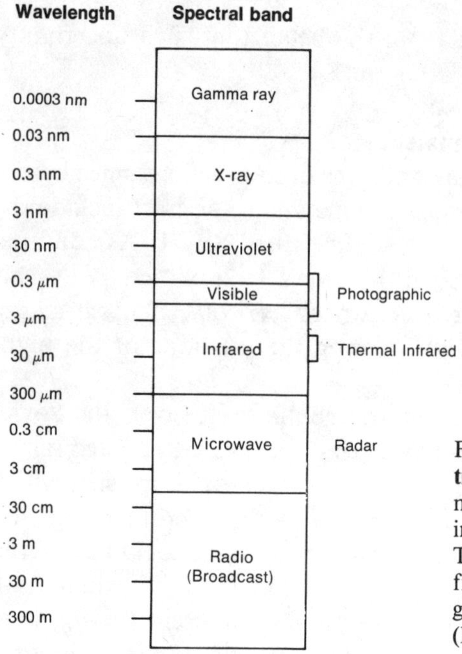

FIGURE 2. **The electromagnetic spectrum.** This depiction of the electromagnetic spectrum illustrates the range in which NTM equipment operates. The entire electromagnetic spectrum, from long radio waves to very short gamma waves, is used to verify treaties. (IEEE Spectrum)

U.S. Reconnaissance Satellites

The U.S. has at least three kinds of reconnaissance satellites used for imaging. Some are "search and find" satellites for surveillance, while others are designed to take a "close look" at suspicious activities.

First, some satellites take television pictures and photographs from an altitude of 100 miles and higher. These are "search and find" satellites designed to observe large areas of land and ocean. In addition, film taken by such satellites can be jettisoned in pods and retrieved by planes able to catch the package as its parachute floats to earth (see chapter four). When developed, such film permits more detailed examination of chosen targets.

Second, some satellites take enhanced color and infrared television pictures. They are also "search and find" satellites operating at altitudes over 100 miles. These satellites provide "real time" information to the ground after passing over the Soviet Union. Because of their multispectral capability to form images in several bands of visible and infrared light, they can distinguish certain types of features, such as camouflage, not apparent in normal light. (See the next chapter for a fuller discussion of this area.)

Third, high-resolution satellites operate at altitudes as low as 80 miles

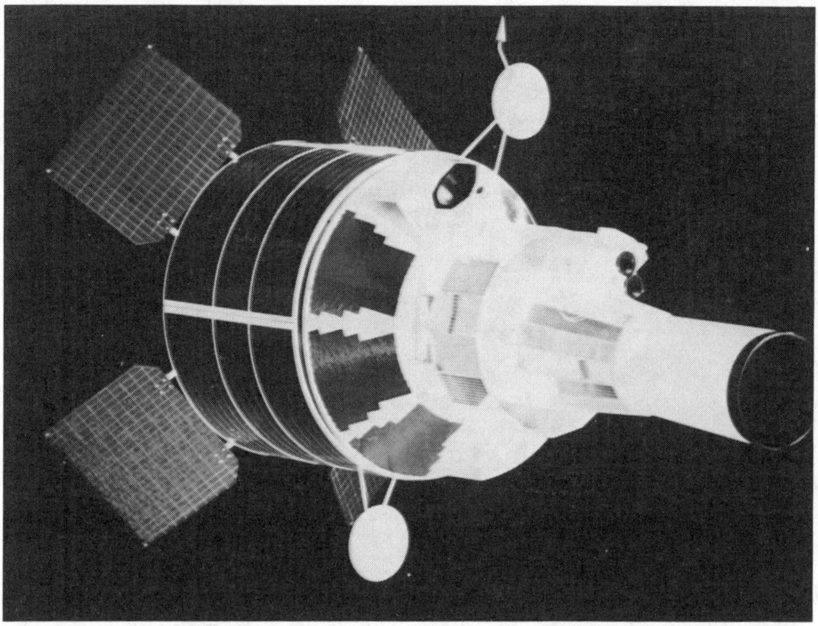

FIGURE 3. **An artist's conception of a U.S. early warning satellite.** Early warning satellites, such as the one depicted here, use infrared telescopes to detect the hot plume from a ballistic missile almost immediately after launch. (U.S. Air Force)

and take detailed pictures which, for example, clearly show objects as small or smaller than windows and doors on buildings. These close look satellites stay in orbit a shorter time than others because they run out of fuel and film more quickly. (See figure 2, chapter 4.)

Other U.S. satellites operate in high-altitude orbits. These special purpose satellites monitor and provide early warning. Some are positioned in geosynchronous orbits 22,300 miles above the Soviet land mass. Others, such as nuclear test detection satellites, orbit at still higher altitudes. These include early warning satellites that use infrared sensors to detect the hot exhaust plumes from missiles launched on land or at sea. The warning is delivered within one or two minutes (and perhaps in much less time) after launch. (They extend the warning time provided by ground-based early warning radar from about 15 minutes to almost 30 minutes, the flight time of a land-based ICBM.) These satellites remain at fixed positions in geosynchronous orbit. Another group consists of relatively old nuclear explosion detection satellites that register the flash and radiation from nuclear explosions occurring above the

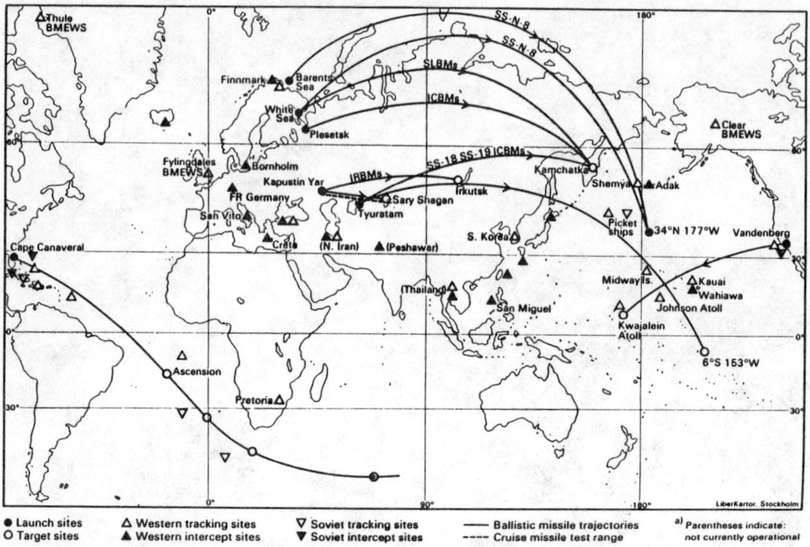

FIGURE 4. **Ballistic missile test ranges and important monitoring sites.** This drawing illustrates the earth-based equipment that the superpowers use to monitor strategic weapons tests. This equipment includes both radar and listening posts. (SIPRI)

ground and in space. One of their functions is to monitor land, sea, and space in support of the provisions of the Limited Test Ban Treaty of 1963 that prohibit nuclear explosions in space. A third group includes satellites in geosynchronous orbit collecting electronic signals emitted by Soviet weapons.

Both the U.S. and the U.S.S.R. have the satellite reconnaissance capability to monitor each other's activities on the oceans. One method is passive electronic surveillance, i.e., merely listening for what can be picked up. Another is active surveillance with radar systems on board the satellites.

Soviet Reconnaissance Satellites

Soviet spacecraft include: military reconnaissance, electronic intercept, missile warning, navigation, ocean surveillance, and imaging reconnaissance satellites. The Soviet's reconnaissance satellites have several distinguishing features, including the launch site (which in the past has generally been at the Plesetsk site north of Moscow) and the unique characteristics of the launch vehicle. Their time in orbit is typically much shorter than that of American satellites, reportedly because of Soviet space technology deficiencies. Furthermore, their photoreconnaissance satellites generally rely on film recovery systems. Other types of Soviet satellites include navigation, communication, meteorological, and early warning spacecraft.

As indicated, while their surveillance capability may be comparable to the U.S.'s, Soviet space technology may lag behind in some ways. Reportedly, the Soviets lag behind in optics, electronics, and resolution. They may rely less on photoreconnaissance than the U.S. because they get much of their information from open sources, their own gathering of intelligence data by human sources (HUMINT), and telemetry intercepting trawlers, as well as because of deficiencies in their space intelligence capability. For example, in 1979, the U.S.S.R., in order to maintain the surveillance it desired, had to launch 84 military-related satellites, including photoreconnaissance ones, while the U.S. needed to launch only 10. (This may, however, be partially due to a different and cautious Soviet approach to satellite use and recovery. The principal driving force behind this kind of discrepancy in launch rates then may well be the well-known Soviet philosophy of simplicity and proliferation.) Their program, however, is improving and, in 1982, one low-orbit reconnaissance satellite mission stayed up for 50 days, setting a Soviet record. As of August 25, 1984, the Soviet satellite Cosmos 1552 had been operating for 103 days. In one two-month period from September 25, 1984 to November 21, 1984, the U.S.S.R. launched 13 reconnaissance satellites, Cosmos 1599 to Cosmos 1611.

In their latest satellites, the Soviets may now be using electronic digital imagery transmission, backed up by film return, as well as other improved space technology. If so, the Soviets have made dramatic improvements in satellite surveillance technology in the last five years.

Limitations of Satellite Surveillance

Satellite surveillance does have limitations. For example, technical systems sometimes fail, the best means of observation may not always be available at a critical time, and the country being monitored usually knows the time and general capabilities of the surveillance systems. Some types of satellite surveillance will be obscured by cloud cover. Most strategic verification problems that could arise, however, would take much longer to develop than the few-weeks maximum time period during which the area in question might be covered by clouds. Sometimes fragments of information need to be built up over a period of time before some activity or construction is understood. For example, it apparently took the U.S. about 18 months to determine that certain initial construction markings meant that a new Soviet radar was being built at Krasnoyarsk in central Siberia. (However, it will be four or five more years before the project is complete.)

Electronic Intelligence: Radar and Telemetry

The process of collecting, intercepting and analyzing electronic intelligence is politically sensitive, very technical and highly classified. Diverse types of radio signals provide information useful in verification. These signals arise from many sources broadcast at different frequencies. Some are returns from radar signals from monitoring stations actively seeking information. Others broadcast by the country being monitored as part of some ongoing operations are merely collected or "listened to." Some of these are encoded, and some are not. Direction finding techniques can aid in locating and identifying a broad range of emitters. Radar returns, particularly with phased array radars, provide information which analysts can use to determine many missile and aircraft parameters including size, weight, payload, speed, and maneuvers.

Radar

The capabilities of radar complement those of photographic reconnaissance in important ways. Radar systems send out microwave signals which bounce off a target and return. The return signals give information about the size, speed, and direction of the target. An important advantage of radar, of course, is that it can operate effectively through cloud cover or in darkness. Three types of radar are "line-of-sight," "phased array," and "over-the-horizon."

Line-Of-Sight Radar. Simple radar is line-of-sight radar, which operates only when there are no obstructions between the radar antenna and the target. Its effectiveness for observing events at low altitudes is limited by the curvature of the earth, i.e., it cannot look over the horizon. Line-of-sight radar is used for observing missile tests. For example, according to the Senate Foreign Relations Committee hearings of 1976 on U.S.-Turkish Defense Cooperation, the U.S. has ground-based radars in Turkey and other areas on the periphery of the Soviet Union, for observing Soviet missile tests.

Phased Array Radar. A powerful improvement on simple radar is phased array radar, which is a large system composed of many individual

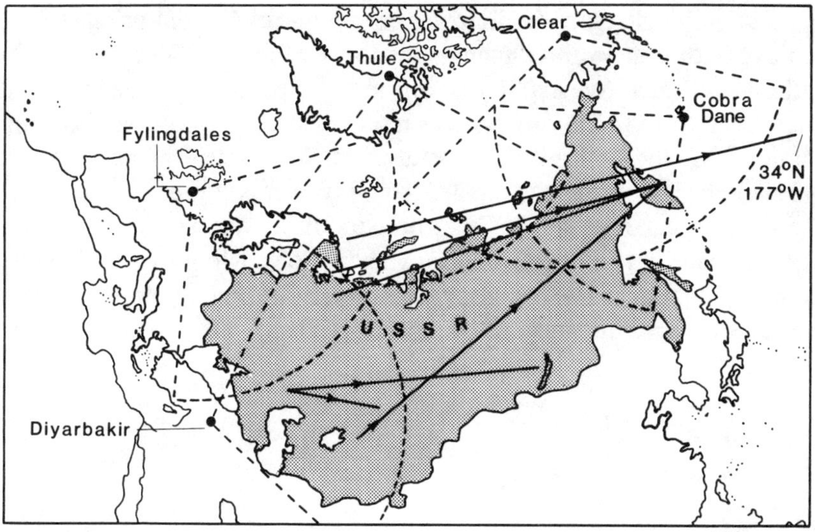

FIGURE 5. **Coverage of Soviet missile tests by U.S. long-range radars.** Soviet ICBM and SLBM tests are tracked by U.S. long-range radars as shown in this drawing. These radars include both line-of-sight and over-the-horizon types. (AAAS; adapted from SIPRI)

small radars. Their electronically combined signals can provide an image of very fine details of a target, even at a great distance. Phased array radar operates on a line-of-sight principle, and produces a high-quality radar picture.

There is a large phased array radar, Cobra Dane, at Shemya Island, Alaska at the western end of the Aleutian Island chain. The radar itself is a six-story high monolith facing the Soviet Union 450 miles away. It is in an ideal position to observe Soviet missiles and warheads, under test, as they "break the horizon" over the heart of the U.S.S.R. and proceed on their trajectories to the Kamchatka Peninsula impact site. This radar gives information from which the U.S. can infer missile size and weight, as well as number and type of reentry vehicles.

Over-The-Horizon. There are other types of radar including over-the-horizon which, as its name implies, is not limited to line-of-sight detection. Over-the-horizon radar is primarily for air defense and would be used to locate air-breathing missiles, such as cruise missiles, and bombers. It is also used to augment missile trajectory information provided by line-of-sight radar monitoring Soviet tests. This system makes use of atmospheric reflection and refraction phenomena to extend its range of detection beyond that of horizon-limited line-of-sight radar.

Electronic Communication Monitoring

There are many types of electronic communication monitoring sensors deployed for general intelligence purposes which can also be used as national technical means. These are most applicable to collecting information during weapons systems tests which are monitored for compliance with the limitations of strategic arms control agreements.

Telemetry. Telemetry is the electronic transmission of performance and other data from sensing instruments on a country's missiles, aircraft or spacecraft to its missile tracking stations. Monitoring telemetry from missile tests is one of ways the U.S. verifies that a Soviet weapon's capabilities are, in fact, those prescribed by an arms limitation agreement.

FIGURE 6. **The RC-135 reconnaissance plane** (shown here) is filled with electronic equipment that is used to monitor the Soviet Union. When Soviet pilots shot down the Korean commercial airliner (KAL 007, in September 1983), an RC-135 may have been in the area shortly before the passenger plane entered that vicinity. Some observers have speculated that Soviet air defense may have mistaken the passenger plane for the intelligence-reconnaissance plane. (See inset on Monitoring Soviet Missile Tests on the Pacific Rim, p. 58.)(Department of Defense)

Telemetry is produced by transducers, instruments that measure the physical characteristics of the flight. Transducers are strain gauges, thermocouples, vibration pickups, gyros, accelerometers, etc. Thus, telemetry is the method by which missile engineers determine in "real time" how well the test vehicle is working. They want as much information as possible from each test flight. Telemetry is limited by the large number of data channels required, the competition for the frequency ranges required, and the loss of radio communications at reentry due to nose cone heating and attendant plasma, i.e., ionized air, effects. Transmission paths for telemetry may be air-to-ground, space-to-ground, air-to-air (in the case of airborne receiving stations), and ground-to-ground depending on the type of system being tested and the stage in the test program. Received telemetry is analyzed by test engineers according to an overall "performance model," a complex series of calculations which define the optimal performance requirements for the system.

The U.S. and the U.S.S.R. intercept, collect and "read" this telemetry from the other country's missile tests as a valuable means of verifying compliance with performance-related restrictions specified in an agreement between the two nations. These data can be interpreted to get weapons information and missile characteristics such as payload, range and numbers of warheads. Since each new missile may require 10 or 20 tests (some of them failures) before it is ready for deployment as a strategic weapon, collecting the telemetry can provide extensive information.

The ability of one country to collect and interpret telemetry from another's test programs can, in principle, provide its analysts with the same performance data as the nation doing the testing. Neither the U.S. nor the Soviets want to give that technical information away. Both the U.S. and the U.S.S.R. use various techniques including encryption to deny the other access to that part of the telemetry not required for verification.

Encryption. Soviet encoding of a large part of their missile telemetry is a compliance issue for the U.S. The Americans charge that it is a violation of the SALT II Treaty in that it impedes verification. The Soviets say they are not encrypting the data required for verification.

The practice of encrypting signals from test flights of weapons systems can at least complicate and at worst impede efforts to gain information needed to assure treaty compliance. Encryption intended to block verification violates treaty provisions against such interference. Encoded data is, of course, readily detected. Furthermore, introducing false data or patterns of signals can often be detected because they are inconsistent with data from other sources. Telemetry, however, is only one source of information about missile test characteristics. (The issue of encryption of telemetry by the Soviet Union is discussed further in chapters five and six.)

MONITORING SOVIET MISSILE TESTS ON THE PACIFIC RIM

The following exerpt from "The Last Flight of KAL-007 (How the U.S. knew so much about what happened)" by James Bamford (author of **The Puzzle Palace**), appeared in **The Washington Post Magazine,** January 8, 1984. It provides a colorful and detailed impression of how data collection on Soviet missile tests might occur.

> For more than 30 years the United States has been locked in an unseen war of high-tech espionage with the Soviet Union and the Communist Orient. The object is not the capture of mighty cities but of telltale signals.
>
> From snatched voice transmissions come current plans and future intentions; radar signals betray limitations and allow for countermeasures; telemetry provides insight into nuclear capabilities; and high-altitude imagery reveals new missile and submarine bases. Sensors are the weapons of this quiet war and they stretch from the muddy floor of the ocean to the emptiness of deep space.
>
> In late August of 1983 the American intelligence community was becoming increasingly nervous about Soviet compliance with the Strategic Arms Limitation Treaty. U.S. government sources say there was evidence that the Soviets were testing two new solid-fuel long-range missiles in violation of treaties. One missile was called the SSX24, believed similar to the proposed U.S. MX missile, the other a smaller, perhaps mobile-based missile called the PL5. (The SALT II Treaty permits the United States and the Soviet Union to develop only one new missile each.) Most Soviet long-range missiles tested over land are launched from centers such as the one at Plesetsk, near Archangel in Russia's bleak Northwest, on a trajectory that brings them down in a missile impact zone on the Kamchatka Peninsula in the Soviet Far East.
>
> By the end of August, indications had been received that the Soviets would conduct another missile test. Typically, such information flows into the secret Defense Special Missile and Astronautics Center located at the National Security Agency headquarters at Fort Meade outside Washington. Manned by satellite and missile watchers from the NSA and the Defense Intelligence Agency, DEFSMAC is the focal point for warning indicators received from the intelligence community's worldwide array of sensors.
>
> This is how DEFSMAC would operate in that situation: Confirming that a test would likely take place about September 1, the alert would have

gone out to all listening posts. The first indication of a test would come from intercepts of a countdown picked up by a secret American listening post tucked away near Qitai in China's remote Xinjiang Uighur Autonomous Region. Then, within one minute of liftoff, an early warning satellite would spot the rocket plume and signal back to DEFSMAC that a launch had occurred. Several minutes later the rocket would be picked up by a lonely listening post on Shemya, a tiny Alaskan island near the end of the Aleutians.

The centerpiece of that island is a six-story-high, missile-tracking radar system called "Cobra Dane" by the Air Force. Facing northwestward toward the Kamchatka Peninsula, a brief 450 miles away, the electronic wonder can spot an object the size of a baseball 2,000 miles out in space. In its tracking mode, it can follow as many as 200 objects simultaneously.

As a missile being tracked goes off the screens at Shemya, several other surveillance platforms can pick it up and follow it to impact on the Kamachatka Peninsula. By far the most sophisticated of these platforms is a recently commissioned U.S. Navy ship, the Observation Island. Resting alone on what looks like a carrier deck on the aft section of the 563-foot vessel is an enormous radar system shaped like a 3½ story sugar cube. Called "Cobra Judy," the 250-ton rotating box is a complex phased array radar system used to monitor the final near-earth paths of Soviet ICBM tests. (See figures 7 and 8.)

The key to the system rests in the gray, octagon-shaped face on one side of the cube. Made up of 34,768 separate elements, the computer-controlled radar can follow single or multiple warheads as they speed through the atmosphere. From information supplied by Cobra Judy, intelligence experts could determine characteristics such as a missile's size, shape, probable point of impact, and its radar "signature," which might aid in designing anti-ballistic missile systems.

Adding to the ship's strange appearance are two giant geodesic domes, each 32 feet in diameter. Inside these huge golf-ball-like spheres are secret microwave antennas used to intercept telemetry from the missiles and, possibly, ground communications.

Often cruising high above Cobra Judy are several airborne platforms aboard a variety of RC135 electronic surveillance aircraft, the military's version of the Boeing 707. Among the different types of the aircraft are the RC135B and RC135C, fitted with special side-looking radar "cheeks" that bulge out from the forward fuselage. Other models include the RC135D, which has an extended, "thimble" nose packed with special sensors in pods that hang from the wings. The RC135U is so crammed with sophisticated eavesdropping equipment that special sensors and antennas cover almost its entire airframe.

One RC135 mission, called "Cobra Ball," involves the use of infrared and other optical sensors for the tracking, measuring and filming of an ICBM test up until impact or near impact. Other sensors are used to intercept telemetry from the missile. RC135 aircraft contain a wide variety of sophisticated tracking devices as well as communications and radar interception equipment.

Operated by the 6920th Electronic Security Squadron, Misawa (on Japan's main island of Honshu) is NSA's largest base in Japan, employing about 1,600 Air Force and Navy personnel.

Finally, slicing through the heavens over the Soviet Union are a Star Wars assortment of odd-shaped photo and eavesdropping satellites that supply the United States with more than half of all its usable intelligence. Some cross over the Soviet Union about every 90 minutes in a north to south orbit at altitudes between 90 and 300 miles. Others are permanently parked over the equator at a distance of 22,330 miles out in space where they can constantly monitor much of the Soviet land mass.

Electronic and Communications Intelligence

Collected emissions from a range of different electronic systems, such as radars, radio transmitters, beacons, and transponders are known as "electronic intelligence" (ELINT) and "communications intelligence" (COMINT). Electronic satellites, called ferrets, listen in on military radio communications and signals from missile tests.

Often the systems with electronic sensing capabilities have radar capabilities as well. For example, there are ground-based monitoring posts in Turkey and other countries peripheral to the Soviet Union. (See figure 1 in chapter one.) These posts are well placed to monitor Soviet ICBM tests. A post in northeast Iran was lost in 1979. According to U.S. officials, the lost capability has been made up by other resources and systems. Reportedly the U.S. has the capability to track tests from both the Soviet test bases at Leninsk (where ICBM tests are launched over Siberia with impact on the Kamchatka Penninsula or in the western Pacific Ocean) and at Sary-Shagan (where anti-ballistic missile systems are tested).

Another type of post is the ship U.S. Observation Island which also carries a rotatable phased array radar, Cobra Judy, on its afterdeck for ICBM test monitoring. (See figure 7.) In addition, there are reconnaissance aircraft and other ships with electronic sensors and listening devices that can be deployed around the perimeter of the Soviet Union.

FIGURE 7. **The U.S. surveillance ship Observation Island.** It uses "Cobra Judy" phased array radar and other listening devices to track Soviet missiles and gather information on them. (U.S. Navy)

FIGURE 8. **A Soviet intelligence gathering ship.** It uses radar and other electronic means to gather information about U.S. strategic forces. (Department of Defense)

Nuclear Test Detection Sensors

A variety of sensors are used to verify compliance with nuclear test bans. These include underwater acoustic sensors to detect forbidden underwater nuclear explosion tests, x-ray sensors aboard satellites to monitor for nuclear tests in space, and sensors that would indicate disturbances of the ionosphere from space tests.

Even more important are electromagnetic, acoustic and seismic sensors located world-wide at 23 stations around the Soviet Union which comprise the Atomic Energy Detection System (see chapter two). During the 1950s, the system was supplemented with airborne instrumentation for radiochemical sampling of the debris from above-ground nuclear tests. Radiological sampling is still used to monitor for Limited Test Ban Treaty (1963) violations and the radioactive levels produced by atmospheric tests by other countries, e.g., France. However, since the LTBT forced all Soviet nuclear testing underground, the radiochemical component of AEDS is less active.

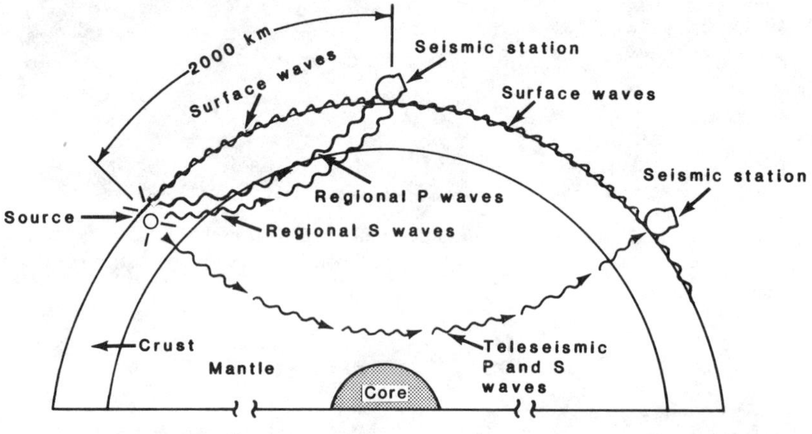

FIGURE 9. **An illustration of how seismic waves are detected.** The source of the underground disturbance sends out waves that travel on the surface and through the body of the earth. These types of seismic waves provide different information about the event when they reach the stations that monitor seismic phenomena. The seismic stations then analyze and evaluate the information and determine the source of the disturbance. (See text here and in chapter 4 for further explanation.)(AAAS)

Seismic Detectors

For detecting underground tests the heart of the System is its world-wide network of high-quality seismometers. Usually, such sensors, which detect seismic signals from underground nuclear tests, are instrument packages inserted about 100 meters into bore holes. They pick up the band of low-frequency vibrations, e.g., 0.02-20 Hz (a hertz or Hz is a vibration per second), from underground disturbances. They could be deployed over a country as a number of single instruments, as an array of instruments in a localized area, or as a country-wide network of arrays. Arrays of seismometers are more sensitive than individual seismic stations at the same site, and arrays can be electronically "steered" to focus on a nuclear test site (or anywhere else) in order to maximize their sensitivity to nuclear tests. On the other hand, for a given number of seismometers, deploying them as single instrument sites maximizes their capability, e.g., 25 single instrument stations dispersed over a continent would give more capability than a single localized array of 25 instruments. If only one or a few sites are available, arrays at each site could be used to improve on the results of single instruments.

The signals from underground nuclear tests and earthquakes usually have different characteristics. One function of seismic detectors is to record the several types of data used in the discrimination process. It is also necessary to discriminate nuclear tests from the background of microseismic activity, i.e., to distinguish the vibrations of an underground explosion from the continuous noise of earth vibrations and those induced by a variety of mechanisms in the atmosphere.

AEDS has functioned effectively for over 30 years, and can, under certain circumstances, detect the existence of Soviet underground nuclear tests down to a level at least as small as one kiloton. More discussion of the seismic discrimination of nuclear tests from earthquakes and the controversy over exactly how small a test can be detected appears in chapter four.

Supplements to National Technical Means

Supplements to NTM include information from human sources and bilateral arrangements such as in-country monitoring devices, on-site inspection, and cooperative agreements (see chapter two).

Human Sources

Information provided by human sources (e.g. spies, recent emigres, visitors, etc.) can provide clues about activities which merit closer examination by NTM. Such information can provide advance warning of activity, but it is often fragmentary and sometimes misleading or unreliable. Human sources sometimes reveal new areas for examination, but more often corroborate or supplement other sources. In fact, HUMINT, as it is often called in the intelligence community, must usually be background rather than primary information supporting, say, a compliance question since "sources" can't be revealed without compromising them and their future usefulness. However, the existence of human sources, even if their identity is not known to the host country, can often be a useful deterrent to cheating.

In-Country and On-Site

In-country verification by technical means has also been discussed extensively, but not implemented. Detailed procedures for in-country seismic monitoring stations were worked out in the suspended Comprehensive Test Ban negotiations. These stations would have been unmanned, tamper-proof systems, about the size of a small house trailer, and connected to seismometers deep in nearby holes. They would have their own power sources, and transmit both "real time" and stored seismic data to satellites.

The concept of on-site inspection by human investigating teams is as old as arms control. Some observers believe that NTM have come so far that any on-site verification which could improve upon them would be so intrusive that neither the U.S. nor U.S.S.R. would accept it. They also believe that such inspectors can be fooled, while others believe that it is the only foolproof method of verification. Limited on-site inspection was agreed to by the U.S. and U.S.S.R. as part of the Peaceful Nuclear Explosions Treaty, signed in 1976 but not yet ratified by the U.S., and thus those provisions have never been implemented. The Antarctic Treaty, which has been ratified, provides for on-site inspection of other countries' bases on the Antarctic continent. Such inspections have been carried out by parties to the agreement. On-site inspection as a verification approach is discussed further in chapter two.

Summary of Capabilities of National Technical Means

The United States and the Soviet Union have extensive networks of sensors, including radar, electronic communication collection, seismic, acoustic, and imaging capabilities. Their sensor capabilities have progressively improved over the years. The most important of these, imaging sensors in satellites, made possible major advances in photoreconnaissance monitoring over the past two decades.

Soviet satellite sensing capabilities are similar to U.S. systems, although less extensive and possessing somewhat lower resolution. Soviet satellite space technology has generally not been as good as that of the

U.S., however, recent information indicates it is rapidly catching up.

New weapons developments are intensively monitored. Secretary of Defense Harold Brown testifying before the Senate Committee on Foreign Relations in July of 1979 clearly and forcefully described the extent of the U.S. monitoring and evaluation capabilities applied to Soviet development of ICBMs. He said:

> Our intelligence system has enabled us to build a comprehensive understanding of the Soviet ICBM system from design through deployment. We know that the Soviets have four design bureaus for the development of their ICBMs. We monitor the nature of the projects and the technologies pursued at these bureaus. We know which bureau is working on each of the new or significantly modified ICBMs known to be under development. We have a reasonably good idea of when they will begin flight-testing of these missiles...We monitor the Soviet ICBM deployment areas on a regular basis, observing construction activity, movement of people and materials, and training exercises. We have a good understanding of the organizational and support structure for deployed ICBM units.
>
> We regularly monitor key areas at the Soviet ICBM test ranges. We monitor missile test firings with a wide variety of sensors: cameras taking pictures of launch and impact areas; infrared detectors measuring heat from the engine; radars tracking ICBMs in flight; and radios receiving Soviet telemetry signals (the Soviets use telemetry signals to measure the performance of their test missiles in flight, and we use them to deduce technical characteristics of their missiles). The use of multiple sources complicates any effort to disguise or conceal a violation. In the course of 20 to 30 tests of a new ICBM, we collect thousands of reels of magnetic tape and spend tens of thousands of hours processing, analyzing and correlating this vast array of data to determine the characteristics of the new missile.
>
> It is inconceivable to me that the Soviets could develop, produce, test, and deploy a new ICBM in a way that would evade this monitoring network. We have missed some data on some firings—and will in the future. But we have not erred significantly in our assessment of any Soviet ICBM.

The capabilities of the U.S. national technical means are extensive and produce a great deal of detailed information. Its very volume, however, can be a limitation. High-resolution imaging systems could produce so many detailed images that the monitoring system would be inundated with data. Such a possibility makes it all the more important to have priorities for directing the surveillance systems. Information from human sources and cooperative agreements, e.g., to localize weapons functions (see chapter two), assist in directing the powerful NTM monitoring and data collection technologies.

Remote sensors for imaging surveillance have excellent coverage and the ability to monitor many detailed activities. In addition, they are deployed in a complementary and redundant fashion. They do have limitations, however.

The national technical means, while not perfect, continue to improve and provide each superpower with the ability to collect detailed information about the other's strategic military capability and testing program.

Chapter 4

Image & Seismic Information Processing

The only difference between the normal flow of high quality intelligence and verification of a particular treaty is – I suspect – in the footnotes. You can't really step up to the negotiating table without considerable confidence in the intelligence apparatus.

Leslie C. Dirks, Deputy Director for Science and Technology, Central Intelligence Agency, 1976-1982

Collection of data, much of the technology for which was described in chapter three, is only part of the task of monitoring arms control agreements. The next phase of the verification process, analysis of the data sent back by the national technical means, is also crucial.

Analyzing and interpreting the data, in fact, consists of several steps. The first is transformation of raw data into a more readily analyzable format. The second is organizing and processing the data to extract useful pieces of information. The third step is integration of these pieces of information with others from different sources. The final step is to decide, as well as possible, what it all means. These three steps sketch the process more neatly than it actually occurs.

The two types of information processing discussed extensively in this chapter are image interpretation, including enhancement techniques and the use of "signatures," and seismic signals from nuclear tests. The monitoring of seismic signals from underground nuclear explosions is examined in detail because it is a good example of detection capabilities, problems and complexities, and the verification process.

Analysis of Image Information

Image Interpretation

Once images have been collected, either from photographs or television pictures, they are analyzed for the information they contain. Techniques for doing this were developed initially during World War II, and many of the standard techniques persist, often enhanced by the power of the computer. (See box on p. 69.)

The magnitude of the task can be illustrated by noting that one 9″x9″ aerial photograph, taken with a scale typical of photoreconnaissance (1/10,000) could theoretically contain the images of 56 million objects one foot in diameter. Obviously, not all one-foot diameter objects will be significant. The task of image interpretation, however, is to find the significant ones.

While elaborate discussion on photographic interpretation is not appropriate in this primer, a few general descriptive comments are.

Large structures or facilities (for example, a Minuteman ICBM base in which the "flights" of missile silos are spread over an area measuring several hundred square miles) are often more readily understood from a distance than up close.

Contrast between objects and background can provide important information inferred from the differences in their reflectivities.

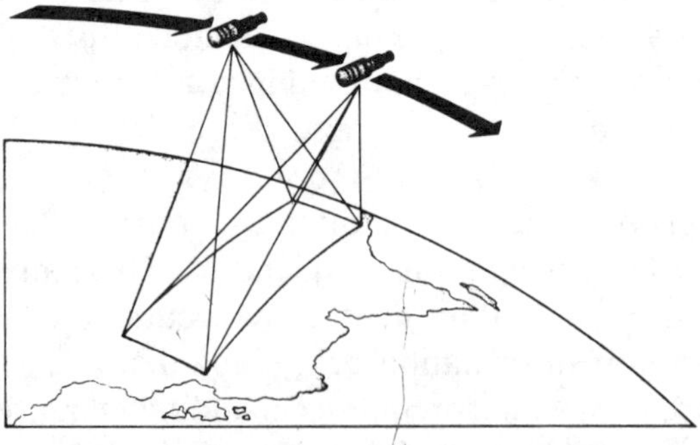

FIGURE 1. **An artist's conception of a U.S. reconnaissance satellites' stereoscopic method of photographing the earth.** (Salamander, London)

Imagery studied by analysts is three-dimensional. In most instances imagery obtained for monitoring arms control agreements is stereoscopic, that is, at least two images are obtained from two angles. Stereoscopy makes it possible to construct a minutely detailed three-dimensional terrain model. More information can be extracted from three-dimensional images than from the usual two-dimensional photographs through photogrammetry, scale measurements of objects in photographs. The sun's angle, ground conditions, or an object's sheer physical size assist in the three-dimensional description of weapons or facilities observed from above. Small but significant objects as well as changes to those objects can often be readily identified. This capability makes it possible, for example, to monitor changes in missile silo volume as required by both SALT I and SALT II, in order to verify that silo modernization limits specified by those two agreements are being observed.

Image Interpretation

The following description of image interpretation is drawn from an article in the Federation of Atomic Scientists' **Public Interest Report** of September 1982.

> Techniques for interpreting pictures taken from the air were already highly developed by the end of World War II and probably did not change much during the early 1960s when the first spy satellites became available. Now, however, the advent of high-speed, high-capacity computers has given the image interpreters a whole new set of tools.
>
> Traditionally, photo-interpreters have analyzed the pictures collected for them by examining the size and shape of objects, the shadows they cast, the patterns that objects and their surroundings form, the tone or shade of the light coming from the objects or their background, and the texture of the surfaces. The interpreters could then draw both on their own experience and knowledge and on specially designed "keys" to draw conclusions about the pictures. The key would probably consist of both verbal descriptions and actual pictorial examples of the different kinds of installations of military interest.
>
> For example, the interpreter might see a picture with excavations, mine headframes, derricks, piles of waste, conveyor belts, bulldozers and power shovels, but with just a few buildings. His key would suggest that this is a mine. Special kinds of equipment, the tone or color of the waste piles and the ore piles, as well as knowledge of the local geology, might further indicate that this was a uranium mine.
>
> Another picture from a different location might show facilities for storing

and handling large quantities of the same kind of ore observed coming out of the mine. Provisions for large sources of heat and mechanical energy and particular types of processing equipment identify the plant as a uranium mill. (The shadows cast by the equipment might help to determine its shape and measure its size.)
Still another plant, elsewhere, might show characteristics of being highly enriched uranium fuel fabrication plant. Besides a few characteristic buildings, it would probably have extraordinary security arrangements (fences and watchtowers) and special facilities for handling radioactive materials. (A plutonium reprocessing plant for extracting fissionable plutonium from spent nuclear fuel would have those features and particular patterns of chemical processing equipment and waste storage facilities as well.) From the science of "cratology" – the study of special-purpose containers – the interpreters might get a very good idea of where the nuclear fuel was being shipped and why.

Modern image gathering and processing have greatly refined the traditional art of the photo-interpreter. For example, the interpreter doesn't just form a general impression of the tone of the light reflected from the surfaces in the picture. With digital images, he gets an exact measure of the amount of light which registered to form each pixel, or dot, making up the whole picture. Through "multi-spectral" imaging, the analyst has a record of how much light of different kinds was reflected, absorbed, scattered or emmitted by the same surface. With that information, the analyst can deduce more information about the surfaces in the picture. Camouflaging and the surrounding foliage, for example, would have different spectral reflectance properties.

Computers can take the image information gathered by the satellite and futher enhance it in a variety of ways. Some of the techniques of image processing include:

- Building multi-colored single images out of several pictures taken in different bands of the spectrum, making the patterns more obvious;
- Restoring the shapes of objects by adjusting for the angle of view and lens distortions;
- Changing the amount of contrast between objects and backgrounds;
- Sharpening out-of-focus images;
- Extracting particular features while removing the background;
- Enhancing shadows;
- Supressing glint.

With two or more images of the same scene, the computers can build three-dimentional "stereo" pictures, fit other pictures taken at different angles onto the same grid, and detect how the scene has changed from one picture to the next. The change detection is useful, for example, in spotting new weapons deployments, such as mobile nuclear missile sites. The image interpreters can use all of these techniques to extract more information from the pictures they examine. But the computers can also use the techniques to help the interpreters decide which of the many thousands of pictures gathered every year to pay more attention to. The computers are learning themselves to recognize patterns. For example, the computer might be fed all the pictures of Soviet ICBM fields and told to display only those which show some difference with previous pictures; the differnce might indicate construction of new launch silos.

Processing large amounts of information can be a formidable and time-consuming task. It could limit the effectiveness of the national technical means. Therefore, knowing where to look and what to look for is critical. This task is made easier by cooperative agreements localizing facilities, which reduce the number of areas for detailed monitoring; HUMINT and SIGINT which can give clues about where to look for what; and new, faster methods of data processing.

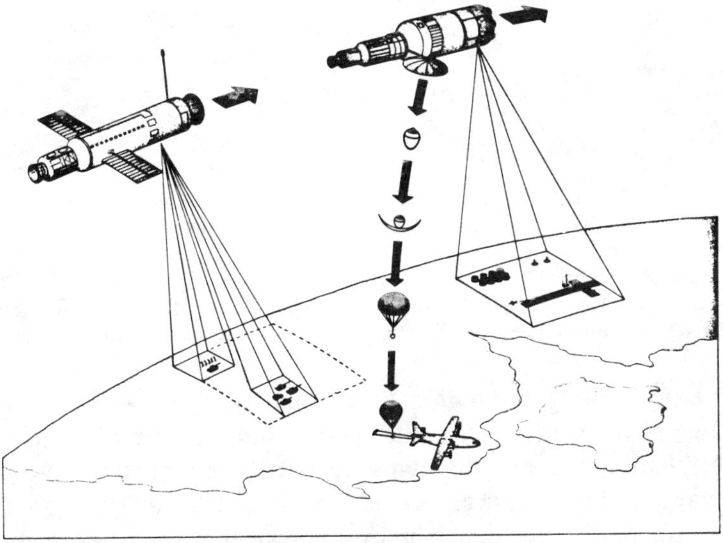

FIGURE 2. **The sequence that U.S. reconnaissance satellites follow.** The search and find satellite scans the earth and returns its data for analysis, then the close look satellite photographs areas of importance with higher resolution. (Salamander, London)

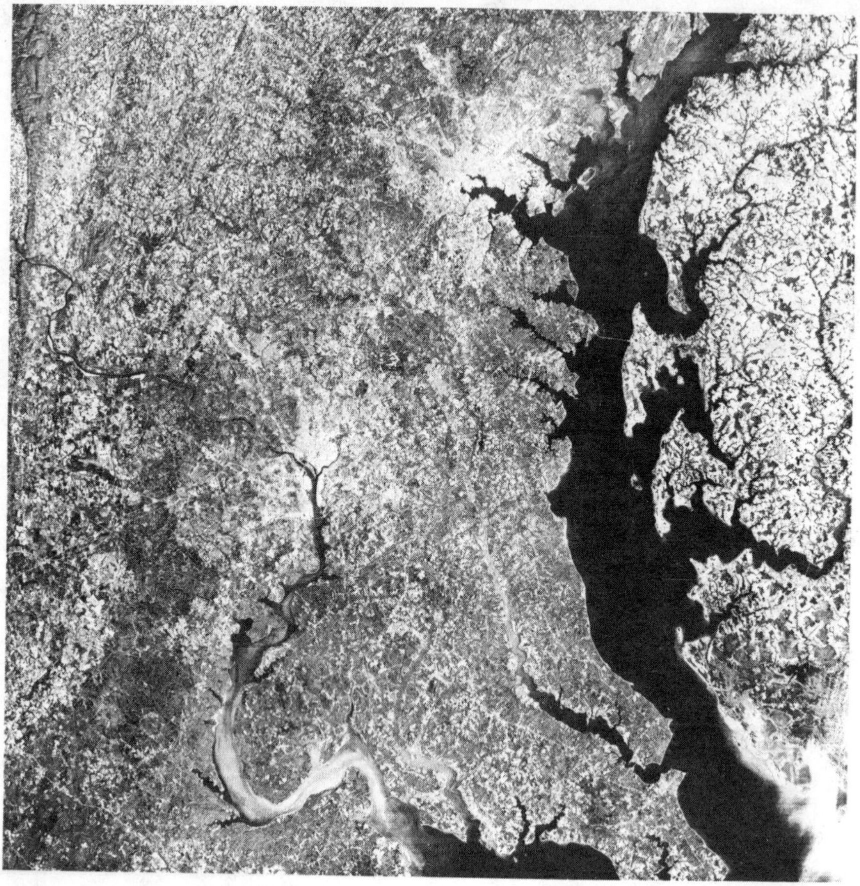

a

FIGURE 3. **Image enhancement.** The satellite image of the Washington, D.C. area (a) was taken by a Landsat satellite at an altitude of approximately 438 miles. The predominant feature on this image is the Chesapeake Bay, extending from north to south near the eastern edge of the photograph. Washington, D.C., is just left of center, on the Potomac River. Dulles International Airport, west of the city, and Andrews Air Force Base south and east of Washington, are clearly visible. (cont. to next page)

Recovering More Information From Images

Image enhancement techniques permit more information to be extracted than appears to the human eye or is in a single photograph. One way to enhance images is to add information from the non-visible part of the light spectrum. It is well known that the amount of light available in the entire photosensitive spectrum is substantially broader than that part which is visible to the human eye. Other ways include digital imaging technologies and computer assisted image enhancement techniques which produce even more additional information.

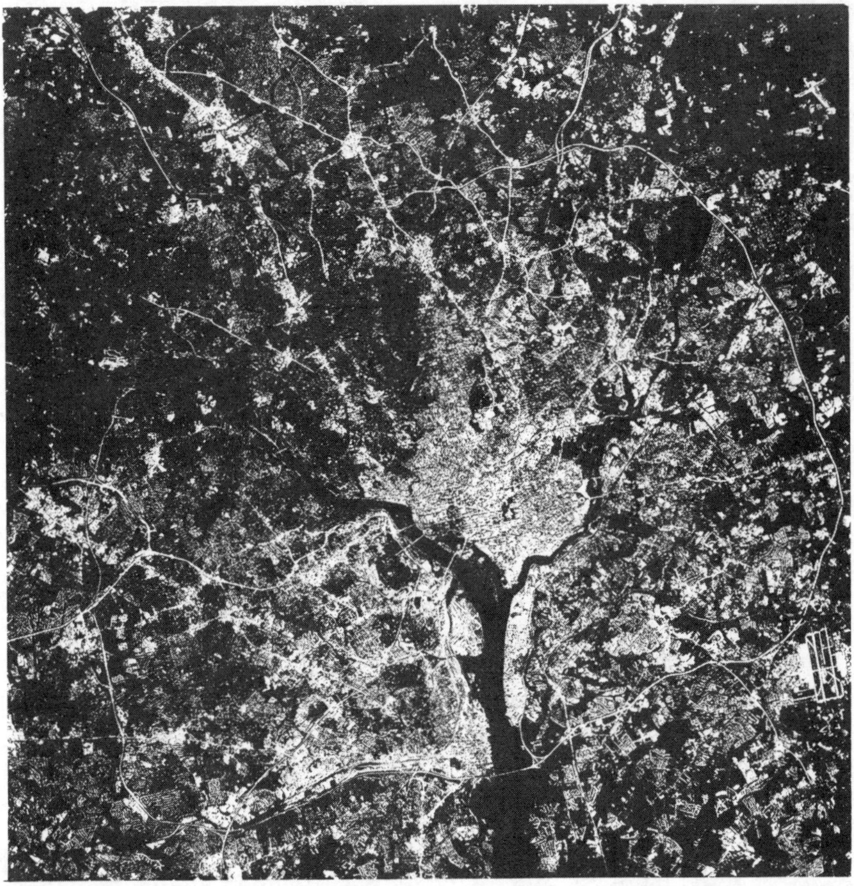

b

(Cont.) The enhancement of this image (b) shows the Washington area enlarged about 14 times. In an 8½ x 12 size photo, Washington landmarks such as the Capitol building and the Lincoln Memorial are clearly visible; Andrews Air Force Base is located on the eastern border of the picture. The information in the original Landsat photograph has been enhanced until individual houses are detectable. The resolution of military intelligence photoreconnaissance is reportedly more than one hundred times better, and objects smaller than a suitcase detectable. (NOAA)

Some satellites carry specially tailored TV cameras, called multi-spectral scanners, which record images from light outside the visible spectrum, e.g., in the infrared region. These devices record separate pictures in each of several spectral color bands. Objects that are effectively camouflaged when observed in visible light may stand out sharply when they are viewed in extended spectral bands.

Digital image processing (DIP) is a technique used to recover more information from an image than appears in an unenhanced photograph.

For example, ground details apparently largely obscured by clouds in a satellite photograph can be brought out quite sharply by this technique. The image's shadings on the film are converted, small region by small region, into corresponding numbers. The DIP technique, performed by a digital computer, restores apparently lost or blurred lines and edges.

Another innovation which advances information recovery from images is the charge-coupled device (CCD). This light-sensitive semiconductor device stores electrical charges in its individual small regions, called pixels, in proportion to the amount of light falling on them. CCDs are read directly by computers, eliminating film retrieval, developing, and digital conversion of images. They are more efficient and sensitive to a broader spectral range of light than film and do not saturate or overexpose.

Signatures

A signature is the set of characteristics (shape, radar image, electronic "noise" emitted, type of wake or trace remaining, sequence or periodicity, etc.) which are specific to a particular weapon or system. It may not stand out particularly in close observation. It is often not defined by a single aspect or characteristic. The signature of a particular bomber, submarine, missile type, launcher, or production facility may not be predictable, since remote sensing may not be sensitive to some features and enhance others. After a number of observations of the same object over a period of time, a signature emerges.

Signatures usually consist of permanent aspects of a particular object. For example, a characteristic signature of a certain type of missile-launching submarine might be the shape of the bow, missile bay, stern assembly, and wake. Putting such information together as a signature data base for various weapons systems is an analysis tool which allows not only recognition of new weapons and their associated equipment when they are tested and/or introduced, but also detection of any changes or modifications in them.

Signatures also play an important role in the analysis of electronic intelligence. Specific electronic systems may have unique signatures. Generally speaking, signatures are essential tools for identifying and counting weapon systems and facilities.

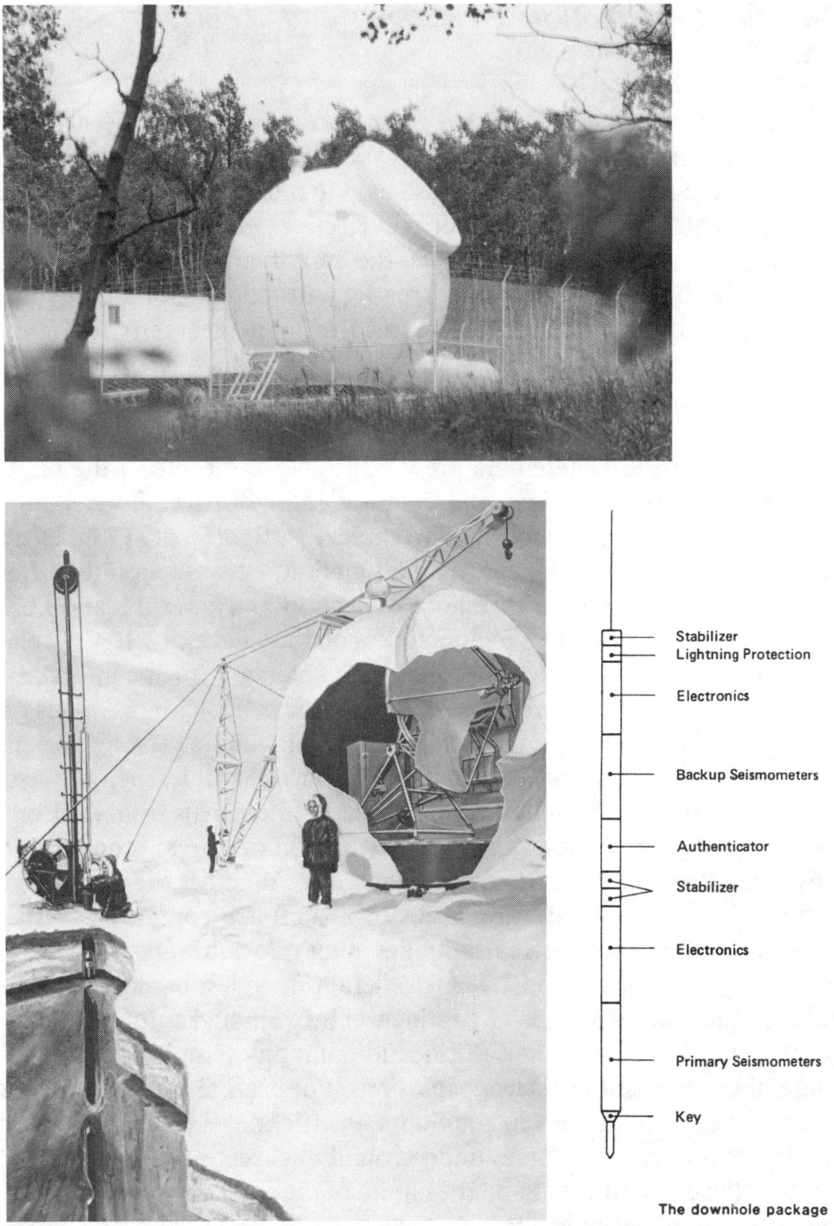

FIGURE 4. **The seismic monitoring of a comprehensive test ban** would be done by the seismic monitor shown here. The surface station (a), which is visible above the ground, would provide electrical power and data storage, and serve transmission (bearing to satellites overhead) and control functions. It is the downhole package (b and c), which is inserted into the earth, that contains the seismometers. (Department of Energy)

Seismic Information Processing and Analysis

Nuclear Weapons Tests

Seismic monitoring was used to gather information on nuclear testing even before the Limited Test Ban Treaty (1963) that prohibited all but underground tests. Currently it is also used to monitor Soviet compliance with the pair of treaties that put an effective ceiling of 150 kilotons on the yield of all underground tests, the unratified Threshold Test Ban and Peaceful Nuclear Explosion Treaties. Although neither treaty has been ratified, both nations have agreed to limit their tests to 150 kt or less.

Seismic monitoring data give the amplitude, timing, and spectral composition of the various seismic waves produced by an underground nuclear explosion. These data are used to locate the site of the blast, identify it as an explosion, and determine its approximate yield.

The monitoring tasks for the Threshold Test Ban Treaty (TTBT) are detection, discrimination, and yield estimation. Because the Treaty imposes a moderately high threshold, detection and discrimination are readily made and the focus of attention is on the yield estimates, calculations for which have been in contention. The tasks for a comprehensive test ban (CTB) type of agreement are the same with the focus on detection and identification. If a low threshold nuclear test agreement prohibited nuclear tests above a one kiloton yield limit, then the seismological challenge would be to readily detect the signals from relatively small underground explosions, e.g., a fraction of one kiloton, and to discriminate them from those of earthquakes. Whether the technology exists to meet the monitoring needs of a CTB is a contentious issue.

Distinguishing between earthquakes and explosions. Over the years, seismologists have arrived at some general principles, based on a great deal of quantitative analysis, to distinguish between underground nuclear tests and earthquakes. First, the location of many seismic events eliminates them as possible nuclear explosions. For example, a seismic event located below open seas in the South Pacific may be safely counted as an earthquake and not an underground nuclear test. Other criteria, such as the depth of focus and the nature of the spectrum of earth vibrations, can then be applied to those events occurring in the "right" areas. For example, since underground nuclear test explosions will not be as deep as earthquakes, the depth of focus of the event may be an important distinguishing characteristic. An event occurring below about thirty kilometers (and perhaps below twenty kilometers) can be confidently classified as an earthquake.

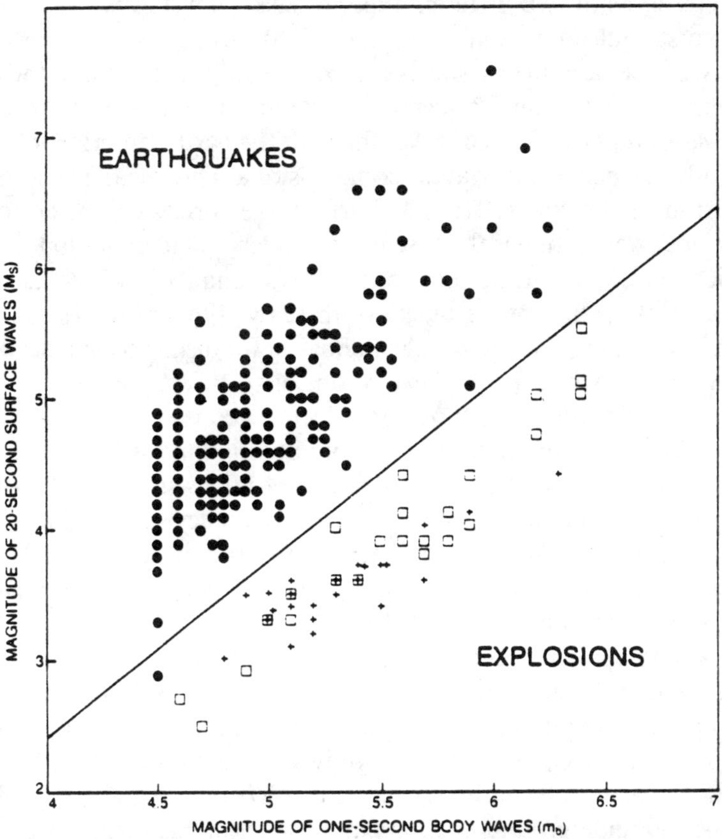

FIGURE 5. **Clear distinction between earthquakes and explosions** is evident in this plot of the magnitude of long-period surface waves (Ms) against the short-period body waves (mb). The 383 earthquakes represented by the black dots were compiled from a set of all the earthquakes recorded worldwide in a six-month period that had an mb value of 4.5 or more and a focal depth of less than 30 kilometers. (There are fewer dots than earthquakes because the magnitudes of some of them coincided.) The squares designate underground explosions in the U.S. and the crosses underground explosions in the U.S.S.R. Only one earthquake falls within the explosion population, as defined by the straight line separating the two groups of events. This single event, which had the smallest magnitude of any of the earthquakes in the survey, took place in the southwest Pacific Ocean, a region where the sensitivity of the network of seismic sensors is poorer than in most of the northern hemisphere. The mb values were adjusted to take into account regional variations in the amplitudes of short-period waves. (Scientific American)

Comparing the relative amplitudes of different types of waves from the earthquakes and explosions provides the basis for distinguishing one source from the other. For shallow-focus seismic events, the ratio of the strengths of two different types of seismic waves has long been used to distinguish between the signals of earthquakes and explosions. These two types are surface waves of about twenty-second period which propagate along the earth's surface, and compressional "body" waves of one-second period which travel through the earth's interior. (There are two kinds of "body" waves, compressional and shear.) A greater proportion of the energy from an earthquake is released in the form of "surface" waves than is the case for an underground explosion, more of which is released in the form of compressional "body" waves. For this reason, the ratio of the strength of these two types of waves, usually written Ms:mb, provides an excellent criterion for distinguishing between shallow-focus earthquakes and explosions of sufficiently large size, i.e., under specific conditions, those of a few kilotons.

Other spectral criteria, applicable both at long- and short-range, are also of great use in distinguishing the source of the seismic disturbance. All of them depend on the dominant high-frequency signals characteristic of explosions. At short distances the seismogram (seismic wave picture) is more complicated. It contains several other types of seismic waves which provide other useful discrimination criteria.

The ability to detect nuclear tests with yields of about one or two kilotons and distinguish them from earthquakes is well documented for tamped, i.e., contained and well-coupled underground explosions with normal microseismic noise and known test-site geological information. In the past, problems have occurred with detecting and distinguishing low-yield underground nuclear explosion tests, e.g., below one kiloton. As the seismic signals from explosions become smaller, ambient levels of microseismic noise makes both detection and identification more difficult, and the referent data base is smaller. If a number of single instrument sites over a large area is unavailable, processing of the data from an array of seismometers spread over a few kilometers and associated with one station can greatly enhance the signal-to-noise factor recorded at that location. (Of course, with any seismic network, the seismic waves from a tiny explosion or earthquake can be so small that it may be impossible to determine whether a disturbance occurred or not.) Recent seismological research work indicates that a low-yield detection and identification threshold of a small fraction of an underground kiloton blast is possible with an in-country network of 25 single or non-array seismic stations whose sensors operate at frequencies of about 30 Hz, which is higher than current monitoring practice.

Explosion yields. Yield estimates of large events can be made with equal accuracy using either body or surface waves. The former wave type is more useful in calculating smaller yields. The principal problems in estimating yields from underground nuclear explosions have resulted from different approaches to quantitative evaluations of the several factors which cause variations in the magnitude and character of recorded seismic signals for underground explosions of a given yield at different sites. Such factors include (1) variations in the geological structure and properties of the surrounding rock which determine the coupling at the source; (2) variation of earth properties at depths up to 150 km which determine the degree of attenuation of signals by the earth's mantle; (3) geologic structure beneath the monitoring station; (4) tectonic strain; and (5) microseismic activity at the station which creates a seismic background noise that may make the detection of small explosions more difficult. Of course, the proximity, nature, and number of monitoring seismic sensors also affect the quality of the data.

Monitoring the 150 Kt Threshold Test Ban Treaty Limit

How accurate are U.S. calculations of Soviet nuclear test yields? American scientists know the geological information about the Nevada Test Site (NTS) and they have calibrated the seismic signals that U.S. nuclear tests produce in a monitoring network to the known yields of those underground tests. Most Soviet nuclear testing has occurred near Semipalatinsk in south-central Siberia. To estimate the yields of tests occurring at Semipalatinsk, Novaya Zemlya, Azgir and other places in the U.S.S.R. requires that the NTS calibration be extrapolated to the Soviet sites. The U.S. is presented with a problem of how to do that extrapolation in the absence of verified field calibration data taken in the Soviet Union. (The U.S. does have access to data published by the Soviets, and use of this data is one of the ways the U.S. calculates calibrations for U.S.S.R. sites.)

In fact, there is disagreement regarding the best method for determining the yield of Soviet weapons tests. To calculate the yields of individual Soviet tests, seismographs located in various places around the world (and considerable distances from the U.S.S.R. tests) record the seismic waves that are generated by the underground explosions.

Extrapolating the Calibration. The extrapolation of the calibration basically depends on information of two kinds: (1) the geologic properties of the rock material immediately surrounding the explosion and (2) the characteristics of the earth's crust and upper mantle to depths of about 150 kilometers. The first can be well determined from available geologic data since empirically there is little or no detectable sensitivity of signal amplitude to variations of rock character. That is, tuff, rhyolite, granite, and salt sites within the U.S. generate nearly the same amplitudes of radiated waves for explosions of the same yield.

The second is important when estimating yields using "body" waves. It can be determined by analysis of several types of available geophysical data. While obtaining these data for Semipalatinsk would provide valuable confirmation of the accuracy of U.S. calculations, such information is not essential to determine yields of Soviet explosions at that site to within a factor of about one-and-one-quarter, i.e., to within about 40 kt or less at the 150 kt level.

The validity of present procedures for estimating yields of underground explosions around 150 kt would appear to be established by (1) the agreement of estimates obtained by two independent seisomological procedures and by (2) agreement of those results with yield estimates obtained from observed cavity dimensions for craters produced by Soviet peaceful nuclear explosions. Even with these agreements, some assert that, without on-site calibration of the Soviet test site, calculated yields could be in error by as much as a factor of two. If that is true, then a calculated yield of 300 kt or less is not necessarily evidence of Soviet cheating.

Conclusions About Yield Estimates. These uncertainties mean that seismologists, in calculating yield estimates for Soviet tests, usually qualify such values with a degree of possible error. Some Defense Department seismologists concluded that some Soviet tests probably have been well over the 150 kt limit of the Threshold Test Ban Treaty. Others, both within and outside the U.S. government, using data from more stations and taking into account the crustal properties mentioned above, conclude that probably none of the Soviet tests have exceeded the limit.

The Threshold Test Ban Treaty provides for the exchange of geological information about the characteristics of nuclear test sites and unverified calibration information for two nuclear tests, i.e., yield, date, time, depth, and coordinates, for each geophysically distinct area. Since the Treaty has not been ratified, however, the geological and calibration information has not been exchanged. Ratification of the Treaty by the U.S. would result in Washington's obtaining the information which some think is required to ascertain whether any Soviet tests at Semipalatinsk have exceeded the threshold. Exchange of this information

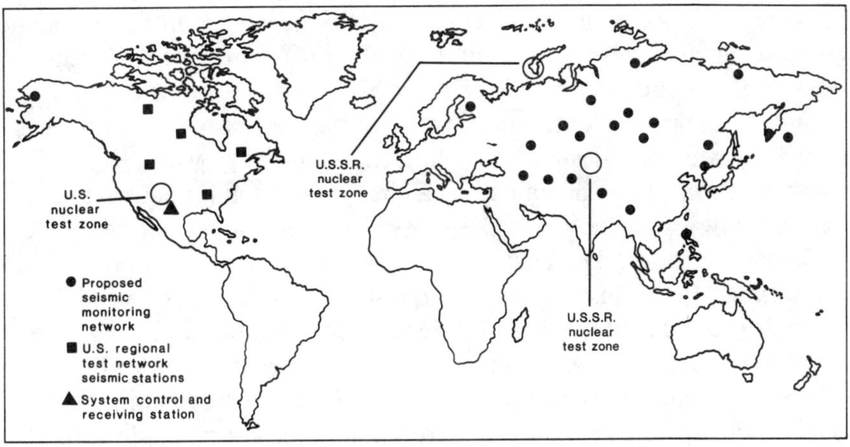

FIGURE 6. **Monitoring a comprehensive test ban.** This illustration shows the possible locations at which seismic stations could be placed in the U.S.S.R. to monitor a CTB. Also shown are seismological test stations in the U.S. In a CTB, each country would probably have a comparable number of seismic sensors. (AAAS)

would certainly help in refining the calculations. The unverified nature of the calibration information and questions about the degree to which it was completely representative of the area would still lead some to uncertainties.

Monitoring a Comprehensive Test Ban: Evasion Schemes and Other Problems

To determine whether a CTB could be readily verified, signal-to-noise ratios required for detection, location, discrimination, and possible evasion schemes must be examined.

The present threshold for detection of seismic events in the Soviet Union, based on a network of first quality stations external to the U.S.S.R. and on the use of proven conventional procedure, corresponds to a yield of about one kiloton for tamped explosions in hard rock. This limit corresponds to a nuclear weapon of very low yield (much smaller than any strategic weapon). If it could be assumed that no measures would be taken to muffle the seismic signals, such a low threshold could be the basis for an agreement providing for a drastic reduction in the yield level of test explosions and be a major step in the direction of a CTB treaty.

Some nuclear weapon experts say that even such small tests could nonetheless be significant. We do not know whether tests below a kiloton would provide information useful in the design of strategic weapons or to check weapons stockpile reliability. They could allow some maintenance of design capability. Dealing with questions of weapons design is beyond the scope of this book. Some questions to consider, however, include: Would nuclear tests of, say, a few hundred tons yield advance weapons design in a militarily significant way? Would the amount of information gained by a country in attempting secret testing at very low yields be worth the risk of detection and the possible loss of treaty benefits? The answers to these questions have important implications. If the answer to either question is no, it must be widely accepted if a CTB treaty is to be negotiated, ratified, and maintained.

Evasion Schemes. Assuming no changes in detection procedures, the detectable limit changes, however, if the Soviets were to employ measures to reduce the seismic signal from an underground explosion. One suggested method is putting the test in a geologic medium with a high porosity, such as dry alluvium, which could reduce the seismic signal to as much as one-tenth of its unmuffled size. However, there are only two such sites in the Soviet Union and while this method might achieve that reduction, it works only for yields below about two kilotons.

Another method, that has been known for 15 to 20 years, is to conduct the test in a sufficiently large cavity. The space must be large enough that the blast does not cause inelastic deformation of the cavity walls, e.g., does not fracture the walls in a hard rock cavity. This technique, called decoupling, can substantially muffle the blast and reduce the peak amplitude of the seismic signal to as little as 1/200th of that of a tamped blast of the same yield. A geological medium usually considered for decoupling is salt, although granite and other materials are also quite possible. Two U.S. tests in salt deposits in Mississippi in 1963 demonstrated the reality of the decoupling phenomenon, though at less than optimum conditions and with less than maximum effect. However, a test of a weapon whose yield would be greater than about ten kilotons would require such a huge cavity to fully decouple the blast that, in reality, it is not possible to use decoupling in order to substantially reduce the seismic signal from large explosions.

Department of Energy scientists at the Lawrence Livermore National Laboratory (LLNL) are investigating other geometries, including long tunnels, to determine whether they have useful decoupling properties. Results of ten years ago indicated no useful additional decoupling by such techniques. These results, however, have been questioned. Reportedly, construction of such cavities is easier than the spherical ones and the shape may have some effect on the ease with which the test signals are recognized.

Another possible evasion technique which has been suggested would be to conduct small nuclear tests in an active seismic region, timing them so that the signal from the test is masked by that of an earthquake. The timing and other circumstances of having an earthquake actually mask an explosion would appear to be a formidable and unpredictable undertaking. (According to seismologist Jack F. Evernden, if a monitoring network were detecting in the 5 to 40 Hz band, the explosion would be detected even if the timing of such an attempted evasion were possible.) If a Comprehensive Test Ban Treaty existed and a country was considering violating it, would it risk detection on the basis of an earthquake which might (and more likely would not) mask the explosion? At the present time, given current seismological knowledge and capabilities, such masking does not appear to be feasible.

False Alarms. The general problem of occasional unidentified events may persist in a sensitive detection system. Reportedly, earthquakes can occur which have some of the characteristics of underground nuclear explosions. Would such events, if they existed, cause false alarms in a system monitoring CTB compliance? For events of mb about 4.0 or greater, at least, extensive analysis of data shows no examples of earthquakes which have seismic wave characteristics of explosions. Thus, the contention that earthquakes could mimic underground explosions is not supported. Most seismologists state that such earthquakes have not been shown to exist, although some point out that to extend the conclusion to small earthquakes depends on an extrapolation. The "no-example" case is more difficult to prove for small events due to lower signal-to-noise and fewer detections.

Some express concern that high explosive chemical blasts, such as those used in large construction or mining projects, could be possible sources of false alarms or confusion in a seismic detection system capable of monitoring very low yield tests. The largest chemical explosions would be about 200 tons yield and most would be just a few tons. While such explosions could be a problem, permitting such confusion would not seem to be in any treaty party's interest. To eliminate the problem of chemical explosion false alarms, a CTB could include provisions for calibration tests for such blasts, prior notification procedures, and perhaps even on-site visits to the construction projects.

Detection Thresholds. The sensitivity of seismic monitoring improves substantially if each party to a test restriction treaty could deploy seismic stations inside the others' boundaries. There is some disagreement among seismologists about how elaborate the in-country seismic network would have to be for monitoring a CTB. However, seismological detection is changing. It appears that at frequencies of 20 Hz or higher, a test of a fully-decoupled 1 kiloton weapon could be detected with an in-country network of 25 single-station sensors. Monitoring at this frequency, however, is not yet a proven method. In detection sensitivity, this is equivalent to reliably distinguishing an unmuffled nuclear explosion of about 100 tons' yield. To achieve the same level of detectability with the more conventional and proven detection system operating at a frequency of 1 Hz requires 30 or more arrays or stations each one of which consists of a number of seismic detectors (see description below). For contrast, an external network could not reliably detect a fully decoupled ten-kiloton test.

Despite important areas of general agreement, there is still disagreement about precisely what type of seismic detection capability is necessary, as well as the extent of the possible evasion threat and the degree of confidence necessary to support comprehensive test ban negotiations.

Willard J. Hannon and other scientists at the Lawrence Livermore Laboratory believe that reliable detection of a Soviet one-kiloton decoupled nuclear test, with detection at 1 Hz, requires a network of seismic detectors at 30 stations in the U.S.S.R. According to their scheme, the detecting apparatus at each station would not be a single sensor. Rather, each would include an array of about 25 seismometers distributed over an area with radius of 5 km, i.e., an area of about 30 square miles. Such a network presents somewhat bigger problems with maintenance and especially acceptability to the Soviets than one consisting of single stations. The suspended negotiations for a comprehensive test ban included provisions for a network of single stations, not arrays. However, arrays were discussed in earlier negotiations and the Soviets have asked for more information about them.

Other scientists, including Charles B. Archambeau of the University of Colorado, Jack F. Evernden of the U.S. Geological Survey and Lynn R. Sykes of Columbia University's Lamont-Doherty Geological Laboratory, think that a network of 25 single non-array stations inside the Soviet Union would be quite sufficient to reliably monitor a comprehensive test ban against the possibility of covert testing using decoupling. Their conclusion is based on a markedly different mode of conducting seismological surveillance than the traditional approach used by Livermore Laboratory researchers. Both the LLNL and the non-array schemes would be secure against tampering.

The research of Archambeau, Evernden, and Sykes indicates that even the possibility of test blast decoupling may no longer be a barrier to verification. Detection of signals from Soviet explosions is now routinely done by measuring seismic waves with a frequency of 1 Hz. If seismic monitoring by a network inside the U.S.S.R. is done at higher frequencies, e.g., 20 Hz or higher, smaller signals are readily detected and the effectiveness of decoupling, as a possible concealment measure, is drastically reduced. This result is confirmed by U.S. tests. The technical question not yet fully resolved is whether the 20 Hz to 30 Hz signals will be fully detectable at the necessary distances. Scientists generally concur that this higher frequency approach may offer a technical solution to the problem. If either approach works as well as they promise to, cavity decoupling as a possible means of evading a comprehensive test ban treaty would become much less of a concern.

Conclusion. As with other verification technologies, there is no perfect system. Any seismic network, no matter how extensive and sensitive, has a detection threshold below which tests could be clandestinely conducted. However, the seismic networks discussed above would detect quite small tests, i.e., from less than one kiloton to possibly a few tens of tons nuclear explosion yield depending on the circumstances of the tests and the monitoring system used.

Once again, the questions to ask concern the possible costs and benefits for a country contemplating cheating and for one worried that the other might cheat. If the Soviets would cheat at these low levels, would they gain an edge? Would that edge be significant? Would the cost to the Soviet Union of being exposed as cheating on a test ban be worth the benefits of clandestine tests at these low levels? Would the benefits to the U.S. of a comprehensive test ban which may be verifiable to below one kiloton outweigh any costs of possible Soviet covert testing at very small yields? Comprehensive test ban verification and other related issues are discussed further in chapter seven.

Summary and Observations

Satellite and other imagery can produce vast amounts of detailed information. Computer processing and image enhancement technologies can dramatically recover even more information from the images.

Particular weapons or weapon systems have distinctive signatures which not only aid in their identification, but also in revealing modifications to those systems.

Given a sufficient number of in-country seismic stations, verification of (a) the Threshold Test Ban Treaty and (b) a comprehensive test ban to thresholds below one kiloton appears to be quite manageable. Possible evasion scenarios, such as masking with earthquakes, do not appear to be very likely methods of deception. They will become even less so as seismic detection methods improve. Masking explosions with earthquakes, if it would work at all, requires knowledge and technologies beyond what currently exists. At the present time, cavity decoupling as a way of muffling blasts is not feasible for yields larger than about ten kilotons. If proposed high frequency monitoring systems work, as we have every reason to think that they would, decoupled explosions smaller than one kiloton would be readily detectable.

Chapter 5

Twenty Years of Practical Experience

Soviet and American Officials sat across from each other at long tables, sipped mineral water and discussed military matters that used to be the stuff that spies were paid and shot for...The process was the product...(and) The process acquired the institutional mass...that served as a kind of deep-water anchor in Soviet-American relations.

Strobe Talbot
Endgame: The Inside Story of SALT II
(Harper and Row, 1980)

The United States has had more than two decades of experience in verifying arms control agreements, beginning with the Limited Test Ban Treaty (1963), continuing through the SALT agreements, including the unratified but mutually observed SALT II Treaty (1979), to the present.

This chapter recounts the negotiating, verification, and compliance history of the LTBT, examines the compliance record of the U.S. and the U.S.S.R. under the SALT I accords from 1972 to 1980, and reviews the role of verification and compliance issues in the debate over SALT II in the U.S. Congress.

Limited Test Ban Treaty

The Limited Test Ban Treaty of 1963 bans nuclear weapons tests or any other nuclear explosions in the atmosphere, in outer space, and under water. While not barring underground nuclear explosions, the treaty prohibits venting of "radioactive debris" from such tests if fallout is detected "outside the territorial limits" of the country conducting them.

History of the Negotiations

The Limited Test Ban Treaty has its origins in extensive efforts in the 1950s to stop all nuclear testing and eliminate nuclear weapons. Indeed, the early negotiations included possible prohibitions on underground explosions as well as eliminating them in the atmosphere, oceans, and space. Strong disagreements between the U.S. and the U.K. on the one side and the U.S.S.R. on the other about verification stalled attempts to work out a comprehensive agreement. No arms control measure since World War II had so intensely sustained the interest of the international community. Study of the technical and political verification issues that came up during those negotiations helps to understand many of the issues which continue even to this day.

Efforts which culminated in this limited agreement extended over eight years. They involved dealing with complex verification problems and reconciling strongly-held opposing approaches of the U.S. and the U.S.S.R. The ups and downs of the East-West political relationship also contributed to slow progress. Furthermore, in the mid- to late-1950s the treaty proposal was linked with more ambitious arms control and nuclear disarmament initiatives.

The central issue, however, was that of adequate verification. Could the two superpowers and the other two nations possessing nuclear weapons at that time, the U.K. and France (which eventually dropped out of the negotiations) agree to establish a system of monitoring, controls, and even inspection that would eliminate the possibility of secret testing?

From the outset, the Soviet position was that existing technology was sufficient to detect violations and the force of world opinion would ensure compliance. In a letter to President Eisenhower in 1956, Soviet Premier Nikolai A. Bulganin urged that there be immediate agreement to prohibit all tests without any further verification provisions or means of international control since the state of scientific knowledge then was adequate for verification. He wrote:

> Would not the best guarantee against the violation of such an agreement be the mere fact that secret testing of nuclear weapons is impossible and that consequently a government undertaking the solemn obligation to stop making tests could not violate it without exposing itself to the entire world as the violator of an international agreement?

Western governments were not convinced. President Eisenhower responded that verification means must "be effective, and not...a mirage." He stated that:

> A simple agreement to stop the H-bomb tests cannot be regarded as automatically self-enforcing on the unverified assumption that such tests can instantly and surely be detected.

Proposals and counterproposals see-sawed back and forth between East and West. At the suggestion of the western nations a group of experts from eight countries including the U.S. and the U.S.S.R. was set up in 1958 to work out the details of a control system. Their report laid out the technical characteristics of a system to monitor a ban on tests in the atmosphere, under water, and underground. It proposed a network of 180 land control posts, 10 shipborne posts, various aircraft flights, and, under certain conditions, on-site inspections.

The U.S. and the U.K. welcomed the report and declared their willingness to negotiate. However, they had continued testing during a period when the Soviets had discontinued theirs and had called upon America and Britain to end tests. Soviet Premier Nikita S. Khrushchev attacked the U.S. and U.K. for continuing and the U.S.S.R. promptly resumed its testing. A few months later the three negotiating powers began a moratorium on testing which lasted for three years and which was dramatically broken first by the Soviets in September of 1961.

The U.S. Arms Control and Disarmament Agency in its 1982 edition of the texts and histories of negotiations, **Arms Control and Disarmament Agreements**, notes that:

> Throughout the various conferences and exchanges on a test ban, the complexity of the central problem brought successive deadlocks, breakoffs, and renewals of discussion, shifts in position, searches for compromise and new approaches, and for new techniques of verification, and successive suspensions and resumptions of tests.
>
> The effort to achieve a test ban, and to resolve the stubborn issues involved, had been pursued in a wide variety of channels. Successive U.N. General Assembly sessions had debated the issue. It had been a major item on the agenda of the U.N. Disarmament Commission and its Subcommittee of Five (later ten). The United States, the United Kingdom, and the Soviet Union had engaged in a long tripartite effort -- the Conference on the Discontinuance of Nuclear Weapons Tests -- in almost continuous session in Geneva from October 31, 1958, to January 19, 1962.
>
> After the three-power conference adjourned in January 1962, unable to

complete the drafting of a treaty because of the Soviet Union's claim that national means of detection were adequate for all environments, the principal forum for negotiations became the newly formed Eighteen-Nation Disarmament Committee (ENDC), which began its meetings in Geneva under the aegis of the General Assembly in March 1962.

Among the points of contentious disagreement were the following: (1) the U.S.S.R. sought to have a veto over operations of any system; (2) the Soviets refused to allow more than three on-site inspections per year; (3) the U.S. continued to press for on-site inspections; (4) the two powers disagreed as to whether control posts should be nationally or internationally owned; and (5) differences over the number and location of these posts and seismic stations.

When the ENDC talks came to an impasse, as had several previous initiatives, over Soviet insistence that the West accept Khrushchev's quota of three inspections per year, the three countries arranged yet another channel. On June 10, 1963, President Kennedy announced that the three nations would hold meetings on the test ban in Moscow. This announcement coincided with a shift of Soviet interest toward a treaty that did not deal with underground tests. (The U.S.S.R. had earlier rejected a similar U.S.-U.K. proposal.) An agreement prohibiting tests in the atmosphere, in outer space, and under water, but not underground, could be readily verified by each nation with its own systems.

FIGURE 1. **A Vela Satellite** used for the detection of nuclear detonations in the atmosphere. Six pairs of these satellites were launched from 1963 to 1970. The Vela's are placed on opposite sides of the earth at altitudes reportedly between 60,000 and 70,000 miles. Each Vela satellite is equipped with different kinds of sensors. (TRW Inc.)

The long years of often difficult negotiation had clarified areas of agreement and disagreement and laid a foundation for speedy action. A treaty was negotiated in ten days. It was formally signed in Moscow on August 5, 1963 and on the U.S. side, ratified by President Kennedy on October 7, 1963, entering into force shortly thereafter. The treaty is of unlimited duration.

Experience With the LTBT

The Soviet Union, the United States, and the United Kingdom have not conducted atmospheric tests since the Treaty went into force. The U.S. NTM has confirmed Soviet compliance with the principal purposes of the Treaty. It is widely known, however, that both the U.S. and the U.S.S.R. have, over the years since the signing of the LTBT, apparently inadvertently vented some radioactive materials beyond their borders from underground nuclear tests. Such venting usually occurred when the detonations were near the surface for excavation and other peaceful purposes. France, China, and India, nonsignatories to the Treaty, have conducted atmospheric tests during this period and there has been measurable fallout from them.

Glenn T. Seaborg, former chairman of the U.S. Atomic Energy Commission, in his book **Kennedy, Khrushchev, and the Test Ban** (1981) wrote:

> While a few U.S. and Soviet tests have vented into the atmosphere, the resultant releases of radioactivity have been very small. While these apparently inadvertant infractions of the treaty have led to exchanges of notes and requests for explanations, neither side has chosen to make major incidents of them.

These ventings of small amounts of radioactive material have not defeated the purpose of the Limited Test Ban Treaty and no Soviet leader or U.S. President has declared that they are either a breach of the Treaty or a threat to their country's security. They have been described as technical violations of the LTBT. Surprisingly, the General Advisory Committee of the U.S. Arms Control and Disarmament Agency issued the "GAC Report" in October 1984 accusing the U.S.S.R. of "numerous violations (since 1965) of the prohibition on conducting nuclear tests that cause...(venting) beyond the borders of the Soviet Union." Earlier, on January 30, 1984, the Soviets publicly released an Aide Memoire which chided the United States about "instances of the ejection of radioactive substances"beyond its borders. As a current compliance issue, this charge is discussed further in chapter six.

As described in chapter three, monitoring for the LTBT is accomplished by a network of electromagnetic, acoustic, seismic and radiochemical stations. These sensors and especially the world-wide network of seismometers detected nuclear tests. Airborne and other radiochemical sampling detected the Soviet ventings. Overall, verification monitoring for the LTBT has worked superbly.

a b

FIGURE 2. **U.S. high-flying reconnaissance planes.** The U-2 (a) and SR-71 (b) reconnaissance aircraft are both used to monitor Soviet activity. The SR-71, the more modern of the two, flies faster and higher. While satellites now provide reconnaissance photographs of sensitive military installations in the Soviet Union, these planes are still used for a variety of intelligence missions. (Department of Defense)

History of SALT I Compliance: 1972 - 1980

Resolving Compliance Issues

Prior to 1972, demarches, statements of position or procedure from one country to another, and requests for explanations about arms control compliance matters were handled through diplomatic channels, in some special discussion body, or during ongoing negotiations.

In 1972, a special U.S.-U.S.S.R. strategic arms negotiating body called the the Standing Consultative Commission (SCC) was established to resolve ambiguous questions concerning strategic arms treaties. Created by Article XIII of the 1972 Anti-Ballistic Missile Treaty, the SCC meets in Geneva on an ongoing basis and is mandated to (1) consider questions concerning compliance and related ambiguous situations; (2) provide information on a voluntary basis to assure confidence in compliance; (3) consider questions involving unintended interference with national technical means; (4) consider possible changes in the strategic situation bearing on the provisions of the Treaty; (5) agree on procedures and dates for dismantling weapons systems in excess of those allowed by treaties, e.g., anti-ballistic missile systems disallowed by the Treaty; (6) consider proposals for further increasing the viability of the Treaty; and, (7) consider proposals for further measures aimed at limiting strategic arms.

This bilateral forum has two ambassadorial-level commissioners, one each from the United States and the U.S.S.R. The U.S. Commissioner is supported by senior professional staff from the Defense Department, the CIA, the State Department, and the ACDA.

What are the circumstances of the SCC discussion? First, there will always be some events that can be perceived as possible treaty violations. Second, it is not as easy to prove a violation as it is to allege one. Innocent actions can sometimes look suspicious. Third, as a consequence of this ambiguity, raising questions in the SCC is not the same thing as charging that a violation has taken place. The Commission is not a court in which a final judgment is rendered, but a formal body authorized to raise and clarify ambiguities about suspicious actions.

Issues Raised by the U.S. and the U.S.S.R.

During the period 1972-1980, the United States raised the following eight issues with the Soviet Union which required clarification under the SALT I agreements:

1. Construction by the U.S.S.R. of special purpose silos which appeared to be possible additional fixed land-based intercontinental ballistic missile (ICBM) launchers;

2. An expanding pattern of substantial Soviet concealment practices tending toward possible future impeding of verification;

3. The SS-19 issue, i.e., the U.S. questioned the Soviet definition of new heavy ICBMs;

4. The possible testing of the Soviet SA-5 air defense radar in an anti-ballistic missile mode not permitted by the ABM Treaty;

5. Inaccurate reporting of dismantlement of excess ABM test launchers pursuant to SCC agreed procedures;

6. A Soviet ABM radar at a non-declared test range on Kamchatka Peninsula;

7. Failure of the Soviet Union to dismantle or destroy replaced ICBM launchers pursuant to SCC agreed procedures; and

8. The placement of a net over an ICBM test launcher at a Soviet test range which could be deliberate concealment.

During the same period, the Soviet Union has raised the following five issues with the United States:

1. The concealment of Minuteman silos undergoing conversion as a possible violation of the Interim Agreement;

2. Partially dismantled Atlas and Titan I launchers in possible violation of SCC dismantlement Protocol;

3. Construction of a new, large phased array radar on Shemya Island, Alaska, as an unpermitted ABM radar;

4. Failure of the U.S. to adhere to SCC regulations regarding privacy of SCC proceedings; and

5. Incomplete dismantlement of partially constructed ABM radar at Malmstrom Air Force base.

The issue of compliance with the SALT I agreements has affected domestic U.S. politics as well as the political relationship between the two countries. It has been the subject of protracted and heated controversy.

In each case the facts and circumstances have differred. The purpose here is to lay out the record of the various allegations in an objective way and to offer lessons for future verification.

Lessons From the Issues Raised by the United States

In this section, five of the eight issues raised by the U.S. are examined to draw out negotiation and verification lessons. All eight are discussed thoroughly in the U.S. Department of State Documents **Compliance with SALT I Agreements** (1979) and **Verification of the Proposed SALT II Agreement** (1978).

Special Purpose Silos. In 1973, the United States determined that additional silos appeared to be under construction at a number of ICBM sites in the Soviet Union. The new silos were similar to those of existing ICBM launchers. Article I of the SALT I Interim Agreement states that "The Parties undertake not to start construction of additional fixed land-based intercontinental ballistic missiles (ICBM) launchers after July 1, 1972." The U.S. questioned the Soviet Union about whether these constructions were intended to be new ICBM launchers. The Soviets responded that the structures would be hardened facilities built for "launch control purposes," not ICBM launchers.

The key verification question for the U.S. was whether the silos in question were dual-purpose systems, i.e., able to function either as launch control facilities or as ICBM launchers. In 1977, following further discussions and additional intelligence and monitoring by national technical means, the United States concluded that they were, in fact, built to serve a launch control function.

Expanding Pattern of Concealment. The United States monitored Soviet strategic weapons concealment practices in the early 1970s and concluded that the extent of those concealment activities increased substantially during 1974. The Soviets increased the use of covering or camouflage to hamper photoreconnaissance. Article V of the Interim Agreement states that neither party shall "...interfere with the national technical means of verification of the other Party..." nor use concealment measures which impede verification by national technical means. It also states that this obligation "...shall not require changes in current construction, assembly, conversion, or overhaul practices." Although none of the Soviet concealment activities prevented verification of the provisions of the SALT I agreements, the United States was concerned that if the expanding pattern of concealment practices continued, it could impede verification of future agreements. The United States raised this concern in the SCC and discussed it with the Soviets. In early 1975 after careful analysis of intelligence information, the U.S. concluded that there no longer appeared to be such a pattern in Soviet activities.

This case illustrates that determining what constitutes impeding verification by national technical means can be difficult and that the Soviets can be persuaded sometimes to moderate their penchant for secrecy.

There are two opposing schools of thought on what constitutes an impediment to verification. One holds that the denial of any data about a weapon covered by a treaty constitutes impeding verification. The other holds that the scope of the verification requirements includes only data specifically required by the treaty.

Furthermore, interpretations vary over whether impeding means (a) to prevent verification, (b) to make it more difficult, or (c) to hinder it. The differences in these three interpretations are matters of both degree and attitude. "To prevent" means that only the loss of virtually all data constitutes impeding verification. "To make more difficult" refers to the loss of particular classes of data, the absence of which reduces analytical confidence. "To hinder" means that the loss of any data degrades the overall ability to understand the complete weapon system and therefore impedes verification.

Soviet Radar Tested in ABM Mode? During 1973 and 1974, U.S. intelligence monitoring of several Soviet ballistic missile tests led American officials to believe that a radar which is part of the U.S.S.R.'s SA-5 surface-to-air missile system was being used to track strategic ballistic missiles during flight. The ABM Treaty says that "to enhance assurance of the effectiveness of the limitations on ABM systems and their components provided by this Treaty, each Party undertakes: (a) not to give missiles, launchers, or radars, other than ABM interceptor missiles, ABM launchers, or ABM radars, capabilities to counter strategic ballistic missiles or their elements in flight trajectory and not to test them in an ABM mode..." Article VI of the ABM Treaty prohibits testing non-ABM systems or their components in an ABM mode.

In the case of a radar, the United States had unilaterally interpreted "tested in an ABM mode" to mean "to make measurements on a cooperative target vehicle during the reentry portion of its trajectory." Radar activity for range safety or instrumentation, for which the nature of the radar activity is substantially different, was exempted. Radars are crucial components of ABM systems. An ABM radar is typically a large phased array radar tailored for tracking a number of reentry vehicles at once. Early warning radars are similar but they are restricted by the ABM Treaty to a country's periphery and required to be oriented outward.

The Soviet action raised the specter that, contrary to the ABM Treaty, they were upgrading their widely-deployed air-defense system to an anti--ballistic missile system. Since the Soviets have thousands of SA-5 systems, the U.S. was particularly eager to determine the radar's use and, if it had been used to track missiles as suspected, prevent any further such activity.

The United States raised this issue in the SCC substantially as described above. The Soviet Union denied the activity, noting that the use of non-ABM radars for range safety or instrumentation was not limited by the ABM Treaty. A short time later U.S. intelligence observed that the radar activity of concern had ceased.

Several important points are raised by this example. First, a unilateral statement by one country is not a binding obligation to another. It is unrealistic to expect the Soviet Union to abide by unilateral statements made by the United States. Second, the monitoring capabilities of the U.S. remote sensing network worked quite satisfactorily to pick up the Soviet radar activity. Third, while the exchange in the SCC led to results the U.S. wanted, ambiguities remained. Did the radar activity cease because the U.S. raised the issue or because the Soviet test plans were completed? Whatever the answer, more testing of a substantially different character, as well as extensive modifications, would have been necessary in order for the SA-5 system to achieve an effective ABM capability. Neither the necessary testing nor the modifications have occurred.

Dismantling Reporting. Two cases raised by the United States in the SCC involved procedural questions. In both cases, treaties called for the dismantling of certain weapons systems to meet agreed limits. In one case, the Soviets inaccurately reported the dismantling of excess ABM launchers at an ABM test range in 1974. In the second, the Soviets did not complete the required dismantling of land-based (ICBM) launchers within the prescribed time period. However, they agreed not to have anymore sea trials of new submarine-based launchers (which were to replace the dismantled ICBMs) until they were back on schedule. Subsequently, they did get back on schedule.

One of the Commission's first tasks was to negotiate detailed procedures for dismantling of the excess ABM launchers and ICBM launchers to be replaced by SLBM launchers. The agreed procedures entered into force on July 3, 1974. The Soviet ABM test launchers were deactivated before the procedures went into effect. The U.S.S.R. notified the SCC that the excess launchers had been dismantled in accordance with the procedures. U.S. information was that several launchers had not, in fact, been dismantled in complete accordance with those detailed procedures.

The U.S. raised the matter in the SCC as a case of inaccurate reporting or notification, even though the launchers were deactivated and reactivation would be of no strategic significance. It wished to make clear its expectation that future notification should be in strict accordance with agreed procedures.

In the case of the ICBM launchers, the Soviets were to replace old land-based launchers with new submarine-based launchers according to a formula. One question was, "If the Soviets are behind schedule in dismantling of the old launchers, should they be allowed to continue producing the submarine-based replacements?"

Under the SALT I Interim Agreement, the Soviet Union was permitted 950 submarine-based launchers, the first 740 of which were "free." After that, for every new submarine launcher, it had to dismantle an ICBM launcher. Observing the progress of this activity by its NTM, the United States concluded that the Soviets would not complete the required dismantling on time. The U.S. decided to raise the issue with the Soviets at the March 1976 SCC session. Before it could do so, however, the Soviets announced that they would not complete the dismantling of 41 older launchers within the required time period. The Soviets explained the situation and promised that all the dismantling activity would be complete by June 1 of that year. They also agreed to the U.S. demand that no new missile-carrying submarines begin sea trials before the dismantling was complete. Both conditions were met, although minor technical discrepancies remained at a few ICBM sites.

For the U.S., the principal point of raising these two cases was to set a record on the importance of strict adherance to the detailed requirements of agreed procedures.

Carefully framed procedures, closely followed, can enhance the verifiability of an agreement. The SCC dismantlement procedures were developed with an eye toward completeness and verifiability. Dismantling and destroying actions must be conducted in such a manner that they are absolutely transparent to the national technical means, and the dismantling proceed such that the systems cannot be reconstituted more quickly than if they were built anew.

A Net Over Soviet ICBM Launcher. In early 1977, the United States observed that the Soviets were using a large net to cover an ICBM test launcher undergoing conversion at a test range. The net interfered with the U.S. ability to monitor the launcher. As noted earlier, the SALT I Interim Agreement prohibits deliberate concealment measures that would impede verification. It also states that "construction or conversion of ICBM launchers at test ranges shall be undertaken only for purposes of testing and training."

The United States raised the issue in the SCC. It took the position that, according to the Interim Agreement, concealing activities at an ICBM silo from national technical means could impede verification.

Furthermore, such an action could reduce the confidence and trust needed to establish and maintain strategic arms limitations. The U.S.S.R. took the position that the provisions of the Interim Agreement were not applicable to the activity in question. Subsequent to this exchange, the U.S.S.R. removed the net covering.

Lessons From the Issues Raised by the U.S.S.R.

The Soviet Union raised five questions in the SCC related either to U.S. compliance with the Interim Agreement or the ABM Treaty. In this section, the five issues are briefly examined. They are discussed more fully in the State Department Document **Compliance with SALT I Agreements.**

Concealment of Minuteman Silos. Beginning in 1973, the Soviet Union observed that the United States had placed structures covering some 2,700 square feet over its Minuteman II silos. The U.S. had built these structures in connection with modernization and hardening of the silos. These prefabricated shelters were made of wood and corrugated aluminum and completely covered the area under construction. The size and materials differed from other shelters used for environmental protection during initial construction, as well as modernization, from 1962 through 1972.

The U.S.S.R. first raised this subject in 1973 bringing it formally to the SCC in 1975. This activity, it claimed, was inconsistent with Article V of the Interim Agreement, particularly paragraph three which prohibits deliberate concealment measures that impede verification by NTM. It is possible that the Soviet Union had difficulty verifying that the modernization activities claimed by the U.S. were consistent with those permitted by the Interim Agreement, since virtually the entire above and below ground components of the silo area were covered. The United States took the position that this activity was consistent with Article V because the shelters were temporary and used strictly for environmental protection (much of the construction work took place during winter at ICBM bases in the Midwest).

In 1977 the U.S. decided to modify these shelters by reducing their size by roughly half. This decision was made as a result of a mutual understanding that neither side should use shelters that impede verification over ICBM silos. Reducing the structures' size by half indicated that the job could be successfully done in a more verifiable way, since the reduced shelters allowed the Soviets visible inspection of shipments into the silo area. Dealing with this issue reinforced the interest of both parties in the non-concealment paragraphs of Article V.

Dismantling Atlas and Titan I Launchers. Beginning in 1973, the U.S.S.R. raised questions regarding the status and condition of supposedly deactivated U.S. Atlas and Titan I launchers. The Soviets questioned the amount of dismantling which had been done and its effect on the possible reactivation of the launchers. As mentioned, SCC dismantlement protocol requires that reactivation of dismantled launchers take substantially more time than construction of new ones.

At one time, the U.S. had 177 former launchers for obsolete Atlas and Titan I ICBM systems at various locations around the U.S. These launchers were deactivated by 1966 prior to the Interim Agreement. The U.S. stated that these launchers were not subject to that Agreement because they had been deactivated prior to it. The U.S. did, however, provide information to the Soviet Union illustrating that the launchers could not be reactivated quickly or easily. Discussion of this issue ceased in 1975.

a b

FIGURE 3. **Cobra Dane phased array radar**. This is one of the primary radars used to track Soviet ballistic missile tests. The completed structure in photo (a) has a wood face that allows the signals from the radar transmitters within to pass through without interference. Photo (b) shows a scientist examining the phased array radars' elements. This radar is located on Shemya Island, Alaska. (a. Department of Defense; b. Raytheon Corporation)

U.S. ABM Radar on Shemya Island? In 1973, the U.S. began construction of a large phased array radar on Shemya Island at the western end of the Aleutian Islands. The U.S.S.R. raised a question in the SCC suggesting that this was an ABM radar which was not permitted at that location. The U.S. responded that the radar in question was to be used for NTM of verification, tracking space vehicles, and early warning. The matter was discussed further with the Soviets. After the radar became operational in 1977, the Soviets did not raise the issue again. Apparently they accepted the U.S. explanation. The issue was re-tabled in 1984, however, in response to U.S. charges of Soviet noncompliance also issued that year.

Privacy of SCC Proceedings. In early 1975, prior to a special SCC session called by the U.S. to consider some compliance issues, several articles appeared in the U.S. press indicating that the actions to be discussed were "violations" of the SALT agreements. These articles cited what was purported to be accurate intelligence information from unnamed U.S. government officials. Paragraph eight of the SCC Regulations requires that SCC proceedings be conducted in private, and that only with the express consent of both Commissioners can they be made public.

After the articles appeared, the U.S.S.R. raised the issue in the Commission that the U.S. had violated the SCC Regulations. The Soviets were particularly concerned about what appeared to be the sanctioned use of the press by the U.S. to predispose SCC discussions. The U.S. reconfirmed its belief in the usefulness of maintaining the privacy of SCC deliberations. However, it also explained that the U.S. government had a requirement to keep the American public adequately informed.

The requirement of privacy falls upon both parties and whether it is observed or not can affect the substance and tone of SCC discussions. As long as privacy was observed, the tone of the SCC deliberations

a b

FIGURE 4. **U.S. ABM system known as Safeguard**. The ABM site (a) consisted of exoatmospheric and endoatmospheric interceptor missiles and a phased array radar (b). The U.S. activated one Safeguard site in Grand Forks, North Dakota, in 1975, but deactivated it after just a few months. The Soviets monitored the dismantling process by NTM. (Department of Defense) were productive and the Soviets were willing to make at least indirect concessions. When privacy was not observed, the Soviets were less willing to cooperate.

Dismantlement of the ABM Radar Malmstrom. The U.S. had two Safeguard ABM sites under construction at the time of the signing of the ABM Treaty. Under the terms of the Treaty and its 1974 Protocol each side was allowed only one site. Therefore, the U.S. was required to dismantle one site. The July 3, 1974 SCC dismantlement protocol mentioned earlier applied in this case.

At the time of the signing of the ABM Treaty in 1972 the U.S. stopped construction of the ABM site at Malmstrom AFB, Montana, and began dismantling it. This activity was completed in May 1974 and at the fall 1974 meeting of the SCC the U.S. reported that the dismantling of the Malmstrom site was complete. Later, the U.S.S.R. questioned one aspect of the dismantling which they said had not been carried out in full accord with SCC procedures. The U.S. reviewed the dismantling actions with the Soviets and showed them before and after photographs. The U.S.S.R. has not raised the issue again. (See fig. 4)

One lesson from this example is that if either nation is concerned about the other's adherence to agreed procedures for, say, dismantling weapons, then it can get the information it needs to be assured in the SCC. Some suspect, however, that the Soviets raised the question of the Malmstrom ABM site only because the U.S. questioned their reporting of ABM test launcher dismantlement. According to strategic arms negotiations veterans, this tit-for-tat approach has been standard Soviet practice. Whatever the case, SCC procedures worked as they should in this example and probably increased each country's respect for the usefulness of the forum.

ABM INSTALLATIONS

Under the terms of the 1972 Anti-Ballistic Missile Treaty and its 1974 Protocol, the U.S. and U.S.S.R. are each limited to one ABM site. The Soviet Union's site includes approximately 100 missiles in the area around Moscow. U.S. analysts consider it and its missiles to be old and of limited effectiveness and therefore of little strategic significance. Its principal purpose may be reassuring the Moscow population, though even that is uncertain. The U.S. had two installations, one at Malmstrom Air Force Base and the other at Grand

Forks, North Dakota. The partially-completed Malmstrom site was dismantled in 1974 to comply with the Treaty and Protocol. The Grand Forks site was completed, but unilaterally deactivated in 1975. The consensus of experts is that the ABM systems of the early 1970s would not have provided an effective ballistic missile defense. In deactivating the Grand Forks site, the U.S. had decided that no useful strategic military or political purpose was served by its existence.

SALT II: Congress and Verification

Concern about U.S. verification capabilities and Soviet compliance increased during the last half of the 1970s. This was reflected by the increased involvement of Congress in the process of developing strategic arms agreements. The ability of the United States to verify SALT II provisions was scrutinized by congressional committees. This section focuses on verification in the congressional SALT II debate in the U.S.

As indicated in chapter one, there is no consensus in the U.S. on what is meant by adequate verification. This lack of consensus is reflected in the U.S. Congress where opposing factions express strongly held views on the value of arms control agreements and the adequacy of verification. For example, a 1979 Senate Intelligence Committee report on the ability of the U.S. to monitor the SALT II Treaty concluded with the following:

> The Committee's examination of the U.S. monitoring capabilities shows that, under current Soviet practices, most counting provisions can be monitored with high or high-moderate confidence. Monitoring qualitative limitations on weapons systems is a far more difficult task and is dependent on the collective capability of a large number of systems. In general, these qualitative limitations present some problems but most can, on balance, be monitored with high to moderate confidence. There are some provisions of the Treaty which can be monitored with only a low level of confidence.

When the report first leaked to the press, it was interpreted by some as a congressional endorsement of the Treaty, i.e., a statement that SALT II was "adequately verifiable." The opposition on the Senate Intelligence Committee would not permit that impression to stand, however, and the ensuing debate made it clear that there was no consensus on even definitional issues involving verification.

The Role of the U.S. Congress

Prior to the signing of SALT I in 1972, Congress played a much smaller role in the strategic arms control process than it has since. Various committees and subcommittees in both houses concerned with armed services, foreign affairs, arms control, and appropriations were active in their jurisdictional areas and had considerable influence, but the Congress as a whole did not exert direct influence upon SALT policy until the first SALT negotiations were complete.

The congressional debates over the merits of the SALT I accords showed that Senate and House concerns would have to be taken into account in the formulation of future strategic arms control negotiations. By the start of the Carter Administration in early 1977, congressional interest in SALT policy not only continued to focus upon strategic equivalence, which emerged as a congressional concern in the debates of 1972, but also increasingly on matters of compliance and verification. In August 1977, Congress declared that adequate verification should be an indispensable part of any arms control agreement.

To understand the struggles that sometimes occur between the legislative and executive branches, one must recognize the importance for the U.S. of the principle of separation of powers. Often in the case of foreign policy the two branches have shared powers, in particular, the power to make and approve treaties.

Making Treaties. Under the U.S. Constitution, the President has the authority to negotiate and sign treaties. However, in the United States, the word "treaty" is reserved for an agreement that is made "by and with the Advice and Consent of the Senate" (Article II, Section 2, Clause 2 of the Constitution). Only after the Senate has provided its "advice and consent" and approved the treaty by a two-thirds vote can the President certify its ratification. The executive branch is best suited to manage negotiations. Once a treaty is concluded, however, it operates as law. Congress as the U.S. law-making body must participate. Over the last fifteen years, as Congress sought to regain powers over foreign policy lost to the executive branch, the President and Congress have fought over the ratification of arms control treaties. Congress, especially the Senate, has chosen to interpret its Constitutional mandate to provide "advice and consent" on treaties with increasing breadth.

International agreements not submitted to the Senate are known as "executive agreements," but they are considered treaties and therefore binding under international law. For many reasons, including avoiding the Senate two-thirds vote requirement, Presidents have increasingly tended toward concluding executive agreements. However, for arms control agreements, Congress requires majority approval of both houses.

This sharing of power provides fertile ground for political struggle and uneven action on arms control treaties. For example, the U.S. signed but did not ratify the 1974 Threshhold Test Ban Treaty, the 1976 Peaceful Nuclear Explosion Treaty (even though they contained long-sought provisions for on-site verification), and the 1979 SALT II Treaty. In fact, the U.S. signed but did not ratify a 1969 treaty on a Law of Treaties.

Ratification Record. With these facts in mind, the record of U.S. treatment of negotiated agreements is not so admirable. Such actions have come back to "bite" the U.S. The Soviets take many opportunities to remind the U.S. that it has not ratified these treaties. The SALT II treaty is being observed only by mutual consent. As mentioned, the geological and calibration data which the two countries agreed to exchange in the TTBT and PNE Treaties have never been exchanged. Furthermore, according to some experts, Soviet negotiators regarded the inclusion of some carefully worded "on-site inspection" provisions in the 1976 PNE Treaty as a "precedent." However, in what is perhaps an apocryphal story, when U.S. negotiators raised that point in one of the subsequent CTB discussions, the Soviet response reportedly was "Nyet, you've never ratified the PNE."

Foreign Relations Committee SALT Reports

Comparison of the Senate Foreign Relations Committee (SFRC) reports on the two SALT agreements, which came seven years apart, further illustrates the changing nature of the congressional role.

The tone, as well as the depth and intensity, of the Senate's examination of the SALT II Treaty, stands in marked contrast to its treatment of the 1972 SALT I Agreements. The SFRC report in June of 1972 on the Interim Agreement and the Anti-Ballistic Missile (ABM) Treaty contain no similar treatment of the Senate's role in the treaty process. The 1972 report does not discuss either the Resolution of Ratification and the appropriateness of Senate actions or their consequences for the agreement. In 1972, no amendments were offered to the SALT I agreements. In 1979, however, the Committee approved 23 reservations to the SALT II Treaty.

Advice and Consent: How Far Does It Extend? The SFRC report of November 1979 on the SALT II Treaty offers an extensive explanation of the Senate's role in the treaty process. It provides a detailed account of the Committee's action in proposing amendments and conditions to the submitted treaty, and their effect on the "Resolution of Ratification." The Committee asserted that it was within its powers to provide "advice and consent" and make such conditions and amendments binding on the Executive. In unmistakable language, the Committee observed in a resolution offered by Senator Henry Jackson (D-Wash) that:

> All such conditions or qualifications to advice and consent would be equally binding upon the President in accordance with their terms...But insofar as the U.S. President is concerned, he could not bring the Treaty into force without accepting the terms of each condition in the resolution regardless of category. Failure by the President to agree to, observe and implement any of these conditions would violate the basis upon which the Committee recommends that the Senate gives its advice and consent to the Treaty.

The Jackson resolution set out conditions to be met by future agreements. While it illustrates the bid by the Congress for more authority, there are doubts about its constitutionality and certainly about its practicability. The SFRC's qualifications about SALT II were extensive. If the Jackson resolution were binding on a President, would it force him to renegotiate any treaty with the U.S.S.R. which the Senate didn't wholeheartedly approve? Is it within the powers granted to Congress in the Constitution to change treaties already signed by the President? Does "advice and consent" extend that far?

Access to Information. The issue of access to information is part of this struggle. Congress points to both constitutional and statutory bases to support its contention that it should have access to all information the executive possesses pertaining to matters under legislative consideration. In the case of arms control treaties with the U.S.S.R., this information includes both classified and unclassified material on Soviet military and political matters. It includes the results of monitoring existing arms control agreements as well as analyses of future monitoring capabilities. The executive has historically taken the view that congressional access to certain categories of sensitive intelligence should be restricted or, in rare cases, denied. Over the last decade, however, congressional access to information has steadily improved. With the establishment of the Senate Select Committee on Intelligence (SSCI) in 1976 (and the House Permanent Select Committee on Intelligence in 1977), the U.S. Congress is informed of all matters related to monitoring arms control agreements and the evolution of proposals. Through its intelligence agencies budget authority, it has full access to all information on future intelligence resources including reconnaissance systems that would be used to monitor future arms control agreements. The SSCI has complete access to the same information as the Administration, and both are working from the same factual basis in making judgments on verification.

Thus, in 1979, the Senate, which was asked to ratify the SALT II Treaty, for the first time had full information to independently assess the capabilities of the U.S. to verify the agreement.

The SALT II Ratification Debate

In 1977, Congress began to exert an unprecedented influence on the conduct of negotiations by furnishing some of its members as advisors to the U.S. SALT delegation in Geneva. In addition, key Senate leaders were kept informed about the negotiations. Despite these efforts to involve and inform Congress, there was considerable question even before 1979 whether a SALT II Treaty would command the two-thirds vote of the Senate necessary for ratification.

The key role of verification in arms control agreements was evident in the debate on ratification of the SALT II Treaty. The formal debate did not commence until after the Vienna Summit in June 1979 when the SALT II Treaty was signed. In some ways, however, it was the continuation of controversies that had been going on for years. The issue of verification, whether raised in questioning Soviet compliance with SALT I agreements or the adequacy of our monitoring resources, was often at the center of the controversies which arose during the seven years between the SALT I and II treaties.

Soviet Encryption. Loss of telemetry, for example, was a major verification-related concern during the SALT II debate. The issue has two aspects: (1) concern over increasing Soviet use of encryption of telemetry from missile tests; and (2) the loss of U.S. facilities in Iran, which could look at and listen to Soviet missile tests right at liftoff. Members of Congress were asking the questions: "What is the impact of the loss of data on monitoring of key provisions of the SALT II Treaty? Was there adequate redundancy built into the monitoring system? Could the losses be made up either, in the case of encryption, through exploitation of other data, or in the case of the Iranian sites, through other means, e.g., satellite information and new sites?" Eventually, it was clear that the answer to the latter two questions was yes. (See chapters three and six for more on this issue.)

The debate on the telemetry issue centered around three views. First, there is the view that all data provided by telemetry is vital. According to this outlook, if any are lost or denied, adequate verification is seriously impaired. Second, is the view that only certain types and quality of data are required for arms control monitoring. If these data are lost or denied and cannot be replaced, then verification would be impeded (see chapter six for a discussion of "impeded"). Third, is the viewpoint that telemetry is only one of the many sources of data that constitute verification monitoring. Losses, while serious for intelligence purposes, do not seriously diminish U.S. ability to verify, since redundancy is built into the system.

Senate Intelligence Committee Study

In January 1977, the Senate Select Committee on Intelligence undertook a study of U.S. capabilities to monitor Soviet compliance with the SALT II Treaty. The Committee's study was a first-hand review of all intelligence data pertaining to Soviet strategic weapons development, both retrospectively back to 1959 and prospectively with estimates of possible future developments. In addition, it covered details of current and estimated future reconnaissance system capabilities. The study considered all points of view, with the objective of establishing a basis for common understanding in the Senate of the U.S.' ability to monitor the SALT II Treaty. While the majority of the study's results are classified, the SSCI published its "Principal Findings on the Capabilities of the United States to Monitor the SALT II Treaty" in October 1979. Perhaps the most important finding was the evaluation of monitoring capability.

> Overall, the Committee finds that the SALT II Treaty enhances the ability of the United States to monitor those components of Soviet strategic weapons forces which are subject to the limitations of the Treaty. The Treaty permits measures short of "deliberate concealment" which could impede monitoring, and does not indicate what types of collection systems are to be considered national technical means. In the absence of the SALT II Treaty, however, the Soviets would be free to take more sweeping measures, such as unrestrained concealment and deception, which could make monitoring these strategic forces still more difficult.

The Committee unanimously endorsed the "Findings". The report refrained from concluding, however, that the SALT II Treaty was verifiable. There were three reasons behind the report's approach which was aimed at securing the unanimous vote. First, since adequate or effective verifiability of SALT II is ultimately defined by an individual's subjective evaluation, the study was to provide a solid evidentiary basis on which members of the U.S. Senate could make their own evaluations. Second, an assessment of verifiability falls within the jurisdiction of the Senate Foreign Relations Committee, which had initially requested the SSCI study. Third, in the interest of effective operation of the ratification process, the SSCI sought consensus at the level it thought it was attainable.

Summary and Observations

Both the U.S. and U.S.S.R. have raised issues in the SCC in connection with the ABM and SALT II Treaties and the Interim Agreement. In most cases raised prior to 1980, the questionable activity proved to be either misinterpreted or ambiguous and was eventually resolved.

Both countries objected to the practices that impeded or tended to impede the observation of strategic weapons systems by national technical means of verification. In some cases, the practices slowed or stopped after discussion between the two countries. In others, the practices abated after the issue was raised in the SCC.

The ability to verify the required dismantling of weapons systems is indispensable to continued participation in the strategic arms treaties. The SCC agreed procedures are important in this regard. Both sides raised dismantlement questions. The responses to these questions, in addition to the information from each nation's national technical means, convinced the concerned country that systems supposed to be dismantled were, in fact, permanently disabled.

Both countries are sensitive to any indications that satellite tracking, early warning, or air-defense radars could also function as ABM radars. The deliberations of the SCC from 1972 to 1980 helped assure both that such prohibited ABM radar development was not covertly occurring.

What was the overall U.S. assessment of Soviet compliance with SALT I and SALT II up to 1982? In May of 1982, before the Senate Foreign Relations Committee, Secretary of State Alexander Haig, in response to probing questions from Senators John Glenn and Charles Mathias regarding Soviet compliance with SALT II and SALT I, answered:

> [T]he Soviets have not moved outside of the SALT II limits...(While) [t]here have been some questions of timing...they are generally complying with the provisions of existing (SALT I) agreements.

The Soviet compliance record with the SALT I accords had important implications for monitoring SALT II. What lessons had been learned about Soviet behavior? What were the best ways for the U.S. to deal with problems? What areas needed improvement?

As with almost all verification questions, there existed different views within the U.S. government on the implications of the Soviet compliance record. One view was that the SALT I record showed that the process worked. A second stressed that while there may have been no significant violations, a pattern of ambiguous activity combined with an apparent Soviet willingness to take advantage of loopholes in provisions required a more aggressive policy on pursuing compliance questions and even greater monitoring vigilance. A third held that the Soviet Union had clearly violated SALT I and the TTBT, and would continue to violate future arms control treaties. Therefore, proponents of this view argued, arms control had failed and the only way to achieve political and military security was through unilateral military build-up. (See discussion of different views in chapter one.) All of these views were represented in the congressional debate over SALT II.

The advice and consent role of the Senate and general involvement of Congress in making treaties is essential, contentious, and complex. The failure to resolve differences between the executive and legislative branches and the devisiveness caused by partisan politics, however, has led to several unratified treaties.

The SCC has proven to be a valuable forum. Sidney Graybeal, U.S. Commissioner to the Standing Consultative Commission from 1973-1977, stated:

> The SCC is a unique body. It is the first of its kind and in my opinion, it has proven an effective body for implementing the SALT agreements and for considering the questions concerning compliance and those ambiguous situations which arise in the interpretation of any agreement.

Institutionalized, privately held diplomatic discussion about matters not resolved by the national technical means is an effective process. It has broader applicability to strategic weapons control and other areas of arms control, including chemical and biological weapons protocols. The SCC works well when both sides want it to and when the privacy of discussions is observed. When the international climate for diplomacy deteriorates and privacy is not observed, the mechanism falters.

Chapter 6

Current and Ongoing Compliance Issues

Soviet noncompliance is a serious matter. It calls into question important security benefits from arms control, and could create new security risks.

U.S. Report to Congress
The President's Report on Soviet Noncompliance with Arms Control Agreements
January 23, 1984

Instances when the American side deviates from the strict fulfillment of concrete legal and political commitments---and sometimes even violates them directly are becoming ever more frequent.

Soviet Aide Memoire—
The United States Violates Its International Commitments
January 30, 1984

Since 1980, charges and countercharges by the U.S. and U.S.S.R. about arms control violations and cheating have ricocheted around the international arena. In 1983, the situation escalated. Each side officially and publicly cited several violations and cases of foot-dragging by the other. Such behavior is not conducive to ironing out differences or fostering willingness to negotiate. It reinforced the impression held by some that, rather than checking the arms race and seeking meaningful limitation and reduction measures on new systems such as cruise missiles and anti-satellite weapons, the two superpowers were more interested in exploiting loopholes or gaining advantages.

Serious matters are at the root of these charges. Have the Soviets, in fact, systematically exploited loopholes in agreements? Are some of the charges much more serious than others? How should these infractions be handled? Are some of the charges leveled at the U.S. by the Soviet Union valid? If so, how serious are they and what should be done about them? These questions are addressed in this chapter.

The U.S. and U.S.S.R. Exchange Charges

In 1981 and 1983, the U.S. questioned whether the Soviets were (1) violating the 1925 Geneva Protocol and the 1972 Biological Weapons Convention by using chemical warfare in Southeast Asia, and (2) violating the Threshold Test Ban Treaty by conducting underground nuclear tests with yields greater than the allowed limit of 150 kilotons.

U.S. Reports

On January 23, 1984, President Reagan publicly released a **Report to the Congress on Soviet Noncompliance with Arms Control Agreements.** He wrote:

> The United States Government has determined that the Soviet Union is violating the Geneva Protocol on Chemical Weapons, the Biological Weapons Convention, the Helsinki Final Act, and two provisions of SALT II: telemetry encryption and a rule concerning ICBM modernization. In addition, we have determined that the Soviet Union has almost certainly violated the ABM Treaty, probably violated the SALT II limit on new types of (ICBMs), probably violated the SS-16 deployment prohibition of SALT II, and is likely to have violated the nuclear testing yield of the Threshold Test Ban Treaty.

In addition to the possible chemical warfare and Threshold Test Ban violations, the seven specific U.S. charges in the fact sheet accompanying President Reagan's letter include:

- The Soviets are constructing a large new phased array radar at Krasnoyarsk, Siberia, that has technical capabilities "almost certainly prohibited by the Anti-Ballistic Missile Treaty.";
- The U.S.S.R.'s telemetry encryption practices deliberately impede verification of compliance "in violation of...Soviet political commitment (to SALT II).";
- The U.S.S.R. has tested a prohibited "second new type" of ICBM, the SS-X-25, which "is a probable violation of the Soviets' political commitment to observe the SALT II provision limiting each party to one...."; and
- The Soviets probably have deployed the SS-16 ICBM "in spite of the ban (in SALT II) on its deployment" and this is "a probable violation of a political commitment (to SALT II)."

The report also charged that the U.S.S.R. "violated its political commitment (under the 1975 Final Act of the Conference on Security and Cooperation in Europe) to observe the Confidence-Building Measure requiring appropriate prior notification of" a 1981 military exercise.

FIGURE 1. **An artist's conception of a silo-based MX ICBM and attendant launch equipment.** Silo-based missiles are very easy to verify because they are larger and stationary. U.S. and Soviet satellites keep constant watch over each other's missile bases to ensure compliance with arms control agreements. (Department of Defense)

On October 10, 1984, the U.S. Administration sent to Congress another report on Soviet compliance. This document, known as the GAC report, was prepared by the General Advisory Committee on Arms Control and Disarmament reportedly after three years of study. It is a review of Soviet practices under arms control obligations since World War II, and presents a long list of charges of Soviet violations including, for example, sending missiles to Cuba in the early 1960s. It reiterates the compliance charges of President Reagan's 1984 report. The GAC report concludes,

> [T]he development of means to safeguard the U.S. against Soviet noncompliance is essential if the arms control process is to avoid being further

undermined, if it is to have favorable long-term prospects, if it is to build trust among nations, and if it is to contribute to U.S. national security and the cause of peace.

On February 1, 1985, President Reagan transmitted another "Report to the Congress on Soviet Noncompliance with Arms Control Agreements" as required by the FY-1985 Defense Authorization Act. In the President's words, "This unclassified report...reaffirms the conclusions" of the January 1984 report.

Soviet Charges

On January 30, 1984, one week after President Reagan issued his report, the Soviet Union presented an "Aide Memoire" entitled **The United States Violates Its International Commitments** to the U.S. Department of State detailing seven charges of arms control violations by the Americans. The Soviet report, issued as a press release by the Soviet Embassy in Washington, contends that:

- The U.S. failed to "put into operation" (ratify), the SALT II Treaty and failed to pursue obligations included in the Protocol to the Treaty which would have the two countries negotiate mutually acceptable limitations of long-range sea- and ground-launched cruise missiles....;
- By deploying in Western Europe Pershing II missiles and ground-launched cruise missiles capable of reaching targets on the territory of the U.S.S.R., "the American side violated the provisions of the SALT II Treaty prohibiting circumvention...through any other state or states....";
- The U.S. has taken an "ambiguous, essentially negative approach...to the treaties on underground nuclear...tests...thereby blocking a number of important measures directed at raising (compliance) confidence..."; and "...there have been repeated instances of the American side exceeding" the 150 kiloton TTBT limitation according to "data in the possession of the Soviet side....";
- The U.S. has "unilaterally stopped the talks on the general and complete prohibition of nuclear weapons tests...(and) on anti-satellite systems...Thereby the United States has disorganized the process of" arms control negotiations developed over the years. By stopping the CTB negotiations, the U.S. has not followed through on its "commitments under Article 6 of the Nuclear Nonproliferation Treaty...to conduct (such) talks....";

- The U.S. may not have properly observed "at least some of the provisions of the 1972 interim agreements" and impeded verification by introducing "the practice of using shelters over ICBM launchers.";
- The U.S. has "in contradiction with the commitments under the (ABM) treaty,...deployed a big radar station on Shemya Island, the construction of which entailed the utilization of radar system elements tested for ABM purposes... etc." Furthermore, the United States is constructing new big "Pave Paws" radar stations in locations and orientations in the continental U.S. that are "contrary to the commitment not to deploy ABM systems on the territory of the country and not to create a foundation for such defense...."; and
- The U.S. "systematically violates the agreed-upon principle of observing the confidentiality of the discussion of (private diplomatic strategic arms) questions...(which is) detrimental to the normal activity of the Soviet-American Standing Consultative Commission."

In addition, the Soviet report implied that the U.S. may have failed "to honor" a SALT II commitment limiting the number of MIRVed ICBMs and raised a spectrum of other concerns including one that plans set in motion by President Reagan's "Star Wars" speech of 1983 would "lead to undermining of the (ABM) treaty"; the growth in U.S. strategic forces "is being done with the aim of achieving military superiority"; and the U.S. has fostered "a drastic growth of the military danger in Europe" some of which sound rather like familiar propaganda themes.

The following sections examine these various charges and draw out important points related to compliance, verification and treaty interpretation.

Issues Raised by the United States

New Radar at Krasnoyarsk

Is it true that the new Soviet phased array radar under construction at Krasnoyarsk, in central Siberia "almost certainly constitutes a violation of legal obligations under the Anti-Ballistic Missile Treaty of 1972" as the U.S. charges?

Background. In the late 1970s, the Soviets began construction of a large phased array radar at Krasnoyarsk in central Siberia (or actually in a less well-known village in that area called Abalakova). This location is approximately 500 miles north of the Soviet southern border with Mongolia and 2,000 miles from the Soviet Union's eastern Pacific coast. The radar has 120 degree fan-shaped coverage, oriented eastward. The Soviets could never have expected to conceal the Krasnoyarsk radar from the U.S. national technical means of verification.

FIGURE 2. **An artist's conception of what the Krasnoyarsk, Siberia phased array radar would look like when completed.** The U.S. has charged that the construction of this radar is a violation of the ABM Treaty. (AAAS; adapted from Department of Defense)

According to a January 24, 1984 Arms Control Association paper on "Compliance Issues Contained in the Reagan Administration Report" the radar appears to be similar to several other Soviet radars constructed for early warning. Phased array radars are complex structures as large as ten-story buildings. They are technically sophisticated requiring substantial time to complete and test. If work proceeds at past rates, the Krasnoyarsk radar will be completed by about 1989.

Article VI, paragraph (b) of the ABM Treaty states that: "...each Party undertakes ....not to deploy in the future radars for early warning of strategic ballistic missile attack except at locations along the periphery of its national territory oriented outward."

If the Krasnoyarsk radar were being built on the Soviet Pacific coast rather than mid-country, it would have complied with the ABM Treaty requirements. If it is an early warning radar as it appears to be, then it is a violation of the ABM Treaty. The U.S. has reportedly raised questions about the radar with the Soviets through private channels of the SCC. The Soviets have reportedly replied that the radar is for tracking satellites in space and said the U.S. will know this when the radar is turned on.

Paragraph D of the ABM Treaty Agreed Statements says that "The Parties agree not to deploy phased array radars...except for the purpose of tracking objects in outer space...." The technical characteristics of the new radar, however, do not coincide with those of other radars used exclusively for space tracking, and the U.S. has not accepted the Soviet explanation. The United States has also reportedly questioned Soviet compliance with Article I, paragraph two of the ABM Treaty, which states that "Each party undertakes not to deploy ABM systems for a defense of the territory of its country and not to provide a base for such defense...".

Not all observers are convinced that the situation is as serious as the Administration indicates. The Federation of American Scientists (FAS) on their March 1984 **Public Interest Report** concluded that the radar is "very poorly suited for the early warning role," "does not appear to be optimized for the ABM battle management function," and its "most plausible function...is as a battle management radar for their anti-satellite (ASAT) weapon." The FAS report adds that this is "consistent with the Soviet explanation of the radar, as well as with (its) observed characteristics...and with recent developments in (their) ASAT program." The interpretation of the Krasnoyarsk construction as an ASAT battle management radar does not, however, mean it is in accord with the ABM Treaty.

Observations. Certain lessons from past deliberations of the SCC apply to this issue. As mentioned, both the U.S. and the U.S.S.R. are sensitive to the possibility that phased array and other radars can have multiple purposes, e.g., verification, space-tracking, and early warning, including functioning as ABM radars. In the past, questions have been raised in the SCC by each side about the other's radars. (See discussion in chapter five.) The careful wording of the definition of an early warning radar in the ABM Treaty itself and especially in its Agreed Statements, Common Understandings, and Unilateral Statements indicates this sensitivity. (See ABM Treaty in Appendix I.)

This appears to be the most serious charge the U.S. has raised. Resolving this matter is of major importance for further progress in strategic arms control. If the U.S. remains convinced that the Krasnoyarsk radar facility is a violation of the ABM Treaty, there is time to negotiate with the Soviets to stop its deployment or arrive at some other mutually satisfactory solution of the issue before the radar becomes operational. Perhaps it would be possible to get the Soviets to halt or delay construction, although this seems unlikely. Both countries could exchange verifiable information about each other's radars (since the Soviets have expressed concern about some of the ones the U.S. is constructing) which might allay their concerns. For the future, the difficulty the U.S. has in defining precisely the function of the Krasnoyarsk radar may suggest refinements in information exchange and ABM Treaty definitional issues to be taken up in the SCC.

Encoding Missile Test Data

Does the Soviets' excessive encoding of missile test data constitute a violation of a legal obligation prior to 1981 and a subsequent political commitment to observe SALT II? The U.S. charges that "the nature and extent of (their) encryption of telemetry on new ballistic missiles is an example of deliberate impeding of verification of compliance in violation of this Soviet political commitment."

Background. Both countries can encode telemetry to protect information about a missile's performance. (See chapter four for a discussion of telemetry.) The Soviet Union regularly encodes some of its telemetry to prevent the U.S. from simply collecting general performance data and other intelligence about Soviet missiles. The U.S. has also used such encryption on occasion. Both sides use other techniques to make monitoring more difficult or impossible, e.g., the U.S. often uses on-board recorders which are ejected during flight and retrieved.

Soviet use of encryption was one of the most contentious verification issues during the SALT II negotiations. Predictably, the Soviets maintain that what the Americans really want is to gather more extensive military intelligence on Soviet weapons than is required simply for SALT II verification.

The SALT II language eventually agreed upon (Second Common Understanding of Article XV, Paragraph three) to deal with telemetry encryption states that:

> Each Party is free to use various methods of transmitting telemetric information during testing, including its encryption, except that...neither Party shall engage in deliberate denial of telemetric information, such as through the use of telemetry encryption, whenever such denial impedes verification of compliance with the provisions of the Treaty.

In other words, both countries are free to encrypt those portions of telemetry not required for verification.

The Soviets reportedly used encryption heavily in testing their new submarine-launched ballistic missile, the SS-NX-20, and their new ICBMs. Some reports have put the encryption level as high as 60 to 90 percent. The President's unclassified Report seems to imply that such a high level of encryption constitutes Soviet noncompliance with Article XV of SALT II.

As discussed in chapter five, there are previous instances where Soviet encryption practices were alleged to be violations of SALT. In 1980, Soviet encryption during testing of the SS-18 was reportedly such an instance. Subsequently, the State Department publicly stated that the SS-18 encoded telemetry did not constitute a violation of SALT.

The Arms Control Association paper observed that:

> The fact that a good deal of telemetry from a missile test is being encrypted does not necessarily constitute a violation. Only if channels are being blocked that impede the ability of the U.S. to verify Soviet Compliance with SALT II could a violation be alleged. The Soviets contend this is not the case. In March, 1983, Air Force Chief of Staff Charles Gabriel testified before Congress that "it is misleading to use the level of encryption as a guide for determining how well we can verify what they (the Soviets) are doing." More critical is the "nature" of the encryption, that is, what missile functions are being encrypted and what functions are being transmitted in the clear.
>
> While monitoring electronic signals from missile tests is one means the U.S. has for gathering intelligence on Soviet missiles, it is by no means the only one. The U.S. has multiple, redundant capabilities for this purpose, and these capabilities are good, despite telemetry encryption.

Observations. Each side has raised concerns in the SCC about actions by the other that impede verification. The term "impede," however, is not precisely defined. Negotiations on this question are usually a test of skill wherein the two countries try to get as many concessions as possible from each other without revealing precise information in order to protect their intelligence capabilities. Experts refer to revealing a limited amount of intelligence information as a "slippery slope" problem: take one step and find yourself much further than you wanted to be. Providing information about which channels may be illegally encoded could jeopardize sources and reveal sensitive information about U.S. methods for collecting data which might undermine U.S. security. Precisely what impedes verification is one of the continuing gray areas which could be explored and addressed at the SCC. (See discussion in chapter five.)

Testing Two New Types of ICBMs

The U.S. alleges that Soviet testing of the SS-X-25 ICBM "is a probable violation of the Soviets" political commitment to observe the SALT II provision limiting each party to one new type of ICBM.' The issue is whether the SS-X-25 is indeed a second new missile, or an allowed modified version of an older missile, the SS-13, as the Soviets claim.

Background. Article IV, paragraph nine of the SALT II Treaty states:

> Each Party undertakes not to flight test or deploy new types of ICBMs...except that each Party may flight test and deploy one new type of light ICBM.

FIGURE 3. **An artist's conception of what the alledged new Soviet SS-X-25 ICBM may look like.** The U.S. has charged that this missile is a violation of the SALT II Treaty. (Department of Defense)

The Soviets informed the U.S. that their one new type of ICBM, allowed under SALT II, is the SS-X-24. In October 1982, they began testing it at Plesetsk. In early 1983 at the same test center, the Soviets began testing what appeared to the U.S. to be another missile. Whereas the 1982 missile had several reentry vehicles (RVs) or warheads, the 1983 missile had a single warhead. U.S. intelligence named the second missile the SS-X-25.

According to the Soviets, the original U.S. intelligence gathered on the SS-13 is inaccurate, otherwise the U.S. could verify their claim. The U.S.S.R. maintains that U.S. intelligence in the 1960s underestimated the missile's throw-weight or payload, i.e., the maximum weight of the warheads, post-boost vehicle or "bus" which dispenses the reentry vehicles, guidance unit, etc., that can be delivered by the missile over a particular range and trajectory. Therefore, they say that the U.S. is now overestimating the difference between the SS-13 and the one tested in 1983. The Soviets state that the throw-weight of the latter falls within the range of changes in payload allowed under Article IV's Common Understandings and Agreed Statements. Reportedly, Reagan Administration officials have acknowledged privately that early intelligence collected on the SS-13 is inadequate for determining whether the 1983 missile payload exceeds Article IV's five percent limit.

The U.S. asserts further that even if this Soviet explanation is correct, they have violated another section of Article IV with the 1983 test. One part of Article IV's Third Agreed Statement apparently requires that a missile with a bus not be tested with a warhead less than one-half the total throw-weight. This provision prevents either country from converting single warhead missiles into ICBMs with several RVs. Apparently, U.S. intelligence has determined that the SS-X-25's warhead weighs less than 50 percent of its throw-weight. However, it is not perfectly clear that the Third Agreed Statement provision applies in this situation. There are other clauses of SALT II which could be interpreted as more or less favorable to the Soviet Union. For example, a different clause and interpretation more favorable to the Soviets may apply since the SS-13 doesn't have a post-boost vehicle and the Treaty's restrictions are less stringent for missiles tested before May 1, 1979.

Observations. Slight modifications of older ICBMs are allowed under SALT II according to specific criteria given in the Common Understandings and Agreed Statements. One question is whether the data collected during the SS-13 flight test program are sufficient to make a definitive judgment. The language of the finding, "probable violation," indicates some U.S. uncertainty about this judgment. Another question is precisely which provisions of SALT II apply. This latter question is technical and apparently subject to interpretation. The U.S. and U.S.S.R. disagree on the accuracy of the U.S.'s information and on matters of definition. Thus, the issue of the 1983 missile test is (1) complex, (2) open to different interpretations, and, therefore, (3) not clear cut.

The SS-16 Soviet ICBM

Has the Soviet Union deployed the SS-16 at the Plesetsk test facility? The U.S. report states that: "While the evidence is somewhat ambiguous and we cannot reach a definitive conclusion, the available evidence indicates that the activities at Plesetsk are a probable violation of their legal obligation not to defeat the object and purpose of SALT II prior to 1981 during the period when the Treaty was pending ratification and a probable violation of a political commitment subsequent to 1981."

Background. The SS-16, a land-mobile ICBM, is an older Soviet missile of relatively small size and poor accuracy last tested in 1976. According to the testimony of several high-ranking Carter Administration officials in 1979, the Soviet's SS-16 test program was very unsuccessful. Because of the similarity between the SS-16, a three-stage missile, and the deployed highly accurate SS-20, a two-stage intermediate-range ballistic missile, and the possibility that the availability of SS-16 third stages might mean ready conversion of the SS-20 to an ICBM without assurance of detection, the older missile was banned by SALT II. The First Common Understanding of Article IV, paragraph eight of the SALT II Treaty states "...the Union of Soviet Socialist Republics will not produce, test or deploy" SS-16s.

Observations. In testimony before Congress on March 1, 1983, Air Force Chief of Staff Charles Gabriel stated that "We do not believe mobile SS-16s are operational at the Plesetsk Test Range." Apparently some number of SS-16s (the most authoritative sources place it between 30 and 80) are at Plesetsk and were not operational as of March 1983. If they are non-operational, are they deployed as the U.S. charge implies?

The U.S.'s assertion is vague and weakly phrased. It was probably written that way deliberately. The U.S. report stated: "The study examined the evidence whether the Soviets have deployed the SS-16 ICBM." Its finding that "available evidence indicates that the activities at Plesetsk are a probable violation," however, can be interpreted in a variety of ways. The language of the Reagan Administration suggests that it is correctly hedging on its conclusion.

Underground Testing in Excess of 150 Kt Threshold

Is it true that, since 1978, the U.S.S.R. conducted a number of underground tests (as many as 14) the yields of which have exceeded the 150 kiloton limit set by the 1974 Threshold Test Ban Treaty?

Reportedly, several have been above 250 kilotons. The Reagan Administration found:

> While the available evidence is ambiguous, in view of the ambiguities in the pattern of Soviet testing and in view of verification uncertainties, and we have been unable to reach a definitive conclusion, this evidence indicates that Soviet nuclear testing activities for a number of tests constitutes a likely violation...."

The Soviets contend that if the U.S. would ratify the TTBT allowing the geological and calibration data to be exchanged, the U.S. would find that the U.S.S.R. is in compliance.

Background. The Threshold Test Ban Treaty (TTBT) prohibits the U.S. and the U.S.S.R. from carrying out underground nuclear tests with yields exceeding 150 kilotons. A threshold at 15 percent of a megaton yield is militarily significant since it eliminates the opportunity to test large-yield new or existing weapons. Prior to the Treaty, many tests conducted by both countries were well above 150 kt. The rationale behind the TTBT was that mutual threshold restraint will reduce the explosive force of new weapons and perhaps bring the reliability of older untested larger ones into question, thereby lessening both countries' first-strike capabilities.

The Treaty provides for exchange of information between the two countries on the location of tests, geological and geophysical data of the regions around the test sites, and calibration seismic data on the yields of two nuclear tests. Signed in 1974, the Treaty was submitted for approval to the U.S. Senate in 1976. Senate action was delayed. When the Reagan Administration assumed power in 1981, it decided not to pursue ratification of the Treaty unless the U.S.S.R. agreed to changes. The Soviets rejected the idea and called upon the U.S. to resume the suspended Comprehensive Test Ban Treaty negotiations. As a result, the exchange of data has not occurred.

The principal method of verifying the yields of underground tests is seismic monitoring. According to the White House Compliance report, "In view of the technical uncertainties associated with predicting the precise yield of nuclear weapons tests, the [U.S. and Soviet] sides agreed that one or two slight unintended breaches per year would not be considered a violation." The U.S. implies that the breaches are numerous. The reports state that "The U.S. is seeking to negotiate improved verification measures for the Treaty."

Observations. Seismologists have disagreed about whether the yields of Soviet weapons tests have exceeded the 150 kiloton limit. (See the extensive discussion of the issue in chapter four.) Some calculated yields over the threshold, others did not. More recently, seismologists have narrowed their technical differences which lead to these different conclusions. Noted scientist, Dr. Lynn Sykes of Columbia University who served on the TTBT negotiating team, concludes that calculations that show the Soviets exceeding the 150 kiloton limit "are based on a systematic overestimation of the relation between seismic magnitude and explosive yield." Based on his own study, Sykes concludes that "Over the past five years, the size of the largest Soviet tests come very close to 150 kilotons but none appear to have exceeded the limit."

The Reagan Administration's conclusion that Soviet...activities... constitute a likely violation" does not seem to follow from its finding that the "available evidence is ambiguous" and "we have been unable to reach a definitive conclusion."

Chemical Weapons and Yellow Rain

Is the Soviet Union "maintaining an offensive biological warfare program" and transferring to its allies "toxins and other chemical warfare agents that have been used in Laos, Kampuchea, and Afghanistan," in violation of the 1972 Biological Weapons Convention (BWC) and the 1925 Geneva Protocol as the U.S charges?

Background. The charge of the illegal use of chemical warfare agents in Southeast Asia was first made by Secretary of State Alexander Haig in 1981. It has been called "yellow rain" because of the description natives gave of how it falls from the sky and the yellow spots found on samples (leaves) from the region. The U.S. State Department identified the agent as tricothecene mycotoxin, a toxin that is produced from a fungus that attacks decaying material. In addition, the U.S. has officially queried the Soviet Union about an outbreak of pulmonary anthrax, following an accident at a suspected biological weapons facility at submitted for ratification, it was clearly stated that verification might be difficult. However, since the U.S. had already made the unilateral decision to forego its biological weapons program, the Senate concurred that the agreement would nonetheless be in our national security interest.

Observations. To some observers, there is persuasive evidence that yellow rain is not a natural phenomenon and that an arms control violation has occurred. However, not all of the evidence is in and there are enough questions about the extent and nature of the existing evidence that many observers remain very skeptical about the case for a violation.

Skeptics include a number of respected members of the U.S. scientific community. Most prominent of these is the noted Harvard biologist Matthew Messelson, an expert on chemical warfare. His study of this problem has included trips to the jungles of Thailand with other scientists to examine this problem. He has presented information which suggests that the yellow rain per se may be a natural phenomenon. (He reported being caught in a five-minute shower of pollen-rich bee droppings, which he thinks is the source of yellow rain samples being examined by the U.S. government.)

At present, scientific evidence is inadequate to support a conclusion that mycotoxin weapons are in use in Southeast Asia. The latest in a series of State Department Bulletins, submitted in a report to the United Nations on February 21, 1984, says that "there appears to be a diminution of attacks in Afghanistan....at the same time, however, there is evidence of continuing use in Laos and Kampuchea of an as yet unidentified, non-lethal agent or agents." Noted experts and informed observers draw different conclusions. Some, such as Messelson, attribute the toxins in samples to natural sources. Others point out that so far no evidence has been found of the extensive systems that would be logistically required to disperse the magnitude of attack needed for relatively low toxicity mycotoxins to be lethal. Thus, many believe that the government's case is not made.

The absence of a consultative mechanism associated with the 1972 Convention (similar to the SCC) and the early U.S. public accusation of a Soviet violation may partly explain why this issue seems so difficult to resolve.

While not directly pertinent to the verification of strategic nuclear arms agreements, the reported use of chemical warfare agents, including so-called yellow rain, in Afghanistan and Southeast Asia has an effect on U.S. attitudes about Soviet compliance with agreements. Although the circumstances and verifiability of the agreements on nuclear and chemical weapons are quite different, were this charge clearly proven to be a violation, American willingness to negotiate any arms limitations with the Soviets might be severely reduced.

Observations on the U.S. Compliance Charges

All of the charges are serious and the language of the Administration's January 1984 report indicates the difficulty of citing a definitive violation of an agreement. The strength of the charges in the report varies from "...the evidence is somewhat ambiguous and we cannot reach a definitive conclusion...(but it is) a probable violation..." (deployment of SS-16s); to "...a probable violation of the Soviet's political commitment..." (testing of the SS-X-25) to "...almost certainly constitutes a violation of legal obligations under the Anti-Ballistic Missile Treaty of 1972..." (Soviet construction of the Krasnoyarsk radar). The phrases "probable violation," "somewhat ambiguous" and "ambiguous" occur in other findings in the report as well.

Three issues in the Administration's report relate to the SALT II Treaty, which was signed in June 1979 with the understanding that it would remain in force through December 1985. In 1981, the United States made clear its intention not to ratify the Treaty. Both countries, however, affirmed their intention to continue abiding by its provisions. In May of 1982, President Reagan gave a speech about his START proposals in which he said:

> As for existing strategic arms agreements, we will refrain from actions which undercut them so long as the Soviet Union shows equal restraint.

The report stipulates that SALT II infractions are "violations of political commitment" rather than of an agreement. The SALT II issues raised by the United States are similar to issues raised in the past in the SCC. They include questions of throw-weight and precise specifications of allowed and banned missiles (which arose under the SS-19 issue) and of impeding verification (which arose under the issues of expanding patterns of concealment). Since similar issues have been previously resolved in the SCC, perhaps the current issues could have been more profitably handled through this private diplomatic channel.

Krasnoyarsk Radar. The Krasnoyarsk radar issue is a vexing one, with fewer ambiguities than other charges in the U.S. report. Information provided about the radar by the national technical means appears to be clear and specific, if incomplete. The precise function of the radar is open to some interpretation. The language of the ABM Treaty governing early warning radars is also quite specific. Whether it is a violation as the U.S. asserts or more of a "gray area" matter as some observers argue, the Krasnoyarsk construction is a serious compliance matter with important arms control and strategic military implications. The issue appears to be the most serious one in the Administration report.

Issues of non-allowed radars with a possible ABM purpose have arisen previously in the SCC with the Soviet SAM-5 radar and the U.S. Cobra Dane radar. The body of information developed there could be helpful for resolving the Krasnoyarsk radar issue.

The resolution of this issue is crucial for Soviet-American relations. If the Krasnoyarsk radar does turn out to be a violation of the ABM Treaty (as increasingly appears to be the case), then it would support the often heard contention that "the Soviets cheat even when they know they will be caught," since the radar could not have been hidden from U.S. satellites. Resolving the matter before the radar becomes operational is, therefore, of major importance for both countries.

Issues Raised by the Soviet Union

Briefly, the Soviet report charges that the U.S. (1) failed to ratify SALT II and pursue its obligations under the Treaty's Protocol to negotiate limitations on long-range cruise missiles; (2) violated a provision of SALT II by deploying in Western Europe long-range cruise missiles and Pershing II intermediate-range missiles which the Soviets see as "strategic" weapons since they are capable of reaching targets in the U.S.S.R.; (3) has taken a negative approach to limiting nuclear testing, failed to ratify the 1974 TTBT and 1976 PNE Treaties, and repeatedly violated the TTBT 150 kiloton limit; (4) unilaterally blocked arms negotiations on a comprehensive test ban on anti-satellite systems, disorganized the established process of arms control talks, and not kept its commitment under the Nuclear Nonproliferation Treaty to negotiate a CTB; (5) violated SALT I by using shelters over its Minuteman II silos and Titan II silos, and concealing retrofit work on the Minuteman II which converted them to MIRVed Minuteman III missiles; (6) violated the 1972 ABM Treaty in a number of ways including deploying a large phased array radar on Shemya Island, conducting

FIGURE 4. **The Pave Paws radar.** It is a phased array system with the dual purpose of protecting the U.S. from submarine-launched ballistic missiles and monitoring satellites in low earth orbit. (Raytheon Corporation)

work to create a space-based ABM system, and deploying the "Pave Paws" radars in a manner which could serve as a basis for an ABM defense; and (7) systematically violated the principle of confidentiality in bilateral talks on compliance. The U.S. rejected all Soviet charges as being without technical or legal basis.

Observations on the Soviet Charges

Several of the Soviet charges need no further explanation. The "tit-for-tat" Soviet approach mentioned in chapter five is at work in several of their countercharges. For example, in 1976, the U.S. began construction of two radars for SLBM early warning and space tracking, called Pave Paws. In 1978, the Soviets raised the question in the SCC of whether these radars were consistent with Article VI of the ABM Treaty. The U.S. responded and the matter rested. Since the U.S. initiated construction of two new Pave Paws sites in Georgia and Texas, whose coverage includes portions of the U.S., the Soviets, in their January 1984 countercharges, have, in fact, questioned whether these early warning radars comply with the ABM Treaty. They have also reopened the question of compliance of the Cobra Dane radar on Shemya Island.

The Soviet Union also accused the U.S. of violating Article VI of the ABM Treaty when, in a recent U.S. Homing Overlay Experiment (HOE) a modified Minuteman I ICBM was used to intercept an incoming Minuteman. Article VI prohibits giving ABM capabilities to a non-ABM missile. The experiment involved a fixed, land-based system in the middle of the Pacific Ocean on Kwajalein Island, a designated test range, all of which is allowed by the Treaty. The U.S. may have erred in how it described the HOE, calling its interceptor a Minuteman instead of just a test vehicle, but does not appear to be in violation of the Treaty. According to Sidney Graybeal, former Standing Consultative Commissioner, since the U.S. has called this ABM interceptor a Minuteman I, any future deployment at other than permitted sites would then violate the Treaty's Article VI.

At least three of the Soviet charges are identifiable as "tit-for-tat" responses to the U.S. charges, including the charge of deploying a phased array radar in violation of the ABM Treaty, which was previously raised and presumably dealt with.

The shelters-over-silos is another such response. The Soviet charge that the United States is impeding verification (see chapter five) appears to counter the U.S. charge that the Soviets are impeding verification by encrypting telemetry. This matter was discussed in the SCC in the mid-1970s and resolved when both sides agreed in SALT II not to use environmental shelters over missile silos.

The charge that Soviet "data" show "repeated instances" when the U.S. violated the 150 kt Threshold Treaty limit is probably another. A more serious concern, however, is the accompanying charge of "a negative" approach to limiting nuclear testing and failure to ratify the 1974 and 1976 test ban treaties. (See discussion in chapters four and five.)

The charge that the United States has violated SALT II by circumventing "the treaty through other state or states" by deploying the Pershing II in Western Europe is based on a Soviet interpretation of the new U.S. IRBM as a strategic missile since it can reach well into the U.S.S.R. heartland and perhaps to Moscow. By the standards previously used by both countries, the Pershing II is not a strategic missile.

Confidentiality. The charge that the U.S. violated SCC confidentiality rules is a long-standing Soviet concern which has been raised before. (See chapter five for an extensive discussion.) It is important that this charge not be dismissed lightly since violations by either side tend to undermine the SCC.

The charges that the U.S. has failed to ratify SALT II or to negotiate limitations on long-range cruise missiles as it pledged to do are, first, examples of the Soviets chiding the U.S. about its unreliability in following through on commitments and, second, reminders that the Treaty is a fragile agreement and important weapons limitations negotiations have not moved forward in the last four years.

These five issues involve past activities covered by or related to the SALT Treaties. The other two issues involve suspended or future arms negotiations.

CTB & ASAT Negotiations. The Soviets appear more interested in resuming the CTB and the ASAT negotiations than the U.S. The Soviet Union has tabled draft treaties for a ban on anti-satellite weapons. Prior to 1985, the U.S. has said that such an agreement cannot be verified. The U.S. Congress has passed measures urging the Administration to move toward anti-satellite arms control. The technical case that a CTB Treaty can be verified is strong (see chapter four). However, the Reagan Administration has shown little interest in resuming the talks.

Conclusions. A number of the Soviet charges are serious, but not as compliance matters. The most serious may be the one that the U.S. is blocking negotiations of a treaty banning anti-satellite weapons.

The major concerns can be listed as the consequences of (a) three unratified treaties (two test ban and one weapons system); (b) no negotiations on limiting long-range cruise missiles or other strategic nuclear weapons systems; (c) no negotiation of a comprehensive test ban; (d) no negotiation of an ASAT ban; and (e) neglect of an effective private discussion channel.

"Star Wars" and the ABM Treaty

Is the U.S. heading for a violation or termination of the ABM Treaty? Some observers think so.

In March of 1983, President Reagan gave a speech in which he called upon the scientific community to help develop the means of rendering nuclear weapons "impotent and obsolete." Dubbed "Star Wars" by Senator Edward Kennedy, a name quickly adopted by the popular press, the President's concept included space-based ABM systems designed to completely protect the U.S. and its allies from Soviet missiles. In this scheme, Soviet missiles and warheads would be destroyed after launching and before reaching their targets. Land-based ABM systems are also part of this defensive scheme.

The Strategic Defense Initiative

To support his initiative, President Reagan created in the fall of 1983 a long-term research program of land- and space-based advanced anti-ballistic missile technologies called the Strategic Defense Initiative (SDI). The program's goal is to develop options for ballistic missile defense (BMD) systems from which the President may choose in the early 1990s.

The SDI is similar to previous ABM research with substantially greater funding. Inheriting programs that were funded at about $50 million in FY1984, the SDI is budgeted at about $3 billion in FY1986 and is scheduled go up to $7.4 billion in FY1989. Both the U.S. and the U.S.S.R. have had exploratory research programs, for example, examining the capabilities of laser or particle beam devices that might be developed into offensive or defensive weapons. Many experts agree that it would be prudent for the U.S. to continue research at some level, e.g., around $2 billion, in this area, while expressing concern at the size and "ramp-up" rate of the SDI budget plans.

SDI Purpose. The purpose of the SDI program differs significantly, however, from earlier efforts. It is directed towards a stated presidential goal and based on a concept that breaks with the previous premises of the U.S. and Soviet strategic relationship, deterrence, and with that of the ABM Treaty. The President's goal is "eliminating the threat posed by (Soviet) strategic missiles" and thereby completely protecting the U.S. and allied strategic nuclear forces, territory, and population. This approach is in marked contrast to the mutual deterrence policy of the past two decades.

The candidate technologies examined in the SDI include both "kinetic energy," e.g., interceptor missiles, and "directed energy," e.g., laser, weapons. Other elements of the research program include development of surveillance, acquisition, tracking, and kill assessment capabilities as well as technologies for battle management/command, control and communications systems.

Assessment of SDI Goals

Great technical problems must be overcome before actual systems are proven effective. The projected costs of these defensive systems are quite large. Economic and technical advantages appear to tilt strongly toward offensive weapons. Since they are much less expensive, overwhelming numbers could be produced and still not cost as much as the defensive weapons systems. Furthermore, it seems that various plausible countermeasures can be effected relatively cheaply to neutralize these systems.

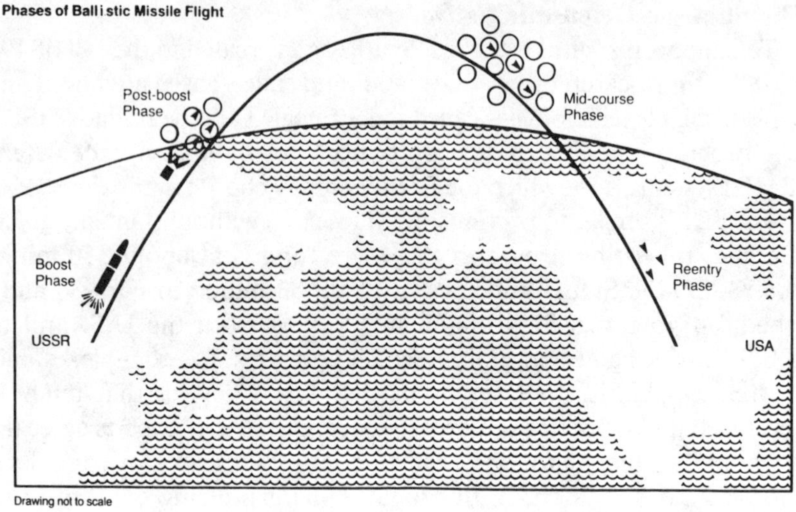

FIGURE 5. **Shown are the four phases of a ballistic missle trajectory.** Various penetration aids — schematically represented as balloon decoys, some concealing warheads — could be deployed in the post-boost phase. Discriminating warheads from decoys would be difficult until the latter burn up during reentry. Reportedly, a Soviet ICBM attack launched from 1000 missile silos could include deployment of more than 100,000 decoys. (Union of Concerned Scientists; adapted from Space-Based Missile Defense)

Protection of Cities. Many experts doubt that a BMD system can be developed to provide the degree of protection that is the goal set forth in the President's speech. Even if a system could be produced that was as unrealistically effective as 99.9%, about ten reentry vehicles would still "get through" the defenses, assuming only current levels of land- and sea-based ballistic missiles. These nuclear warheads, each a fraction of a megaton, would lead to unacceptable loss of human life and damage in the U.S.

Defense of Silos. Some experts think that ABM defense of missile silos, however, could be a viable proposition with a system that was only 70 or 80 percent effective. Some people directly involved with SDI have indicated that this is the reason why the U.S. should pursue BMD, contrary to the President's purpose. The possibility of a totally disabling first-strike by an adversary would thereby be less likely than it is at present, since even if the offense targeted many more warheads per silo the defense would ensure that some MIRVed missiles survived. Of course, this scenario could be played out with moves and countermoves by the adversary as well, such as its developing its own ABM defense.

FIGURE 6. **An artist's conception of the Pushkino radar which is part of the Moscow ABM system.** A phased-array radar; it reportedly provides 360° strategic defense coverage. (Department of Defense)

The point is that a perfect defense which protects people and cities appears to be unfeasible and, from a military strategy point of view, an ABM defense of missile fields could raise the stakes for any aggressor considering a pre-emptive strike. However, even this more limited goal of ICBM retaliatory strike survivability (1) is questionable in light of the U.S.'s existing submarine-based, bomber, and cruise missile retaliatory force; and (2) was in any event rejected over ten years ago during the ABM debates because of recognition that such a move would almost certainly stimulate the arms race by fostering the creation of greater numbers of warheads on both sides and destabilizing the nuclear balance between the superpowers.

Compliance With the ABM Treaty

Critics of the President's program assert that the SDI, if pursued, will lead to either a violation or the termination of the ABM Treaty. Further, they argue that such a serious violation or termination of the Treaty, which many think is the best so far negotiated, would be too costly, given the likelihood that the SDI goals cannot be achieved and that strategic instability would result if they were. They fear that pursuing the SDI could unravel the entire fabric of arms control painstakenly developed over the past twenty years. The Reagan Administration responds to such criticism by emphasizing that SDI is only a "research program" and the ABM Treaty does not limit even goal-directed research.

While most experts will acknowledge that the goal of SDI is at least inconsistent with the purpose of the ABM Treaty, there is disagreement about how far the program can proceed without coming into serious conflict with the Treaty. At some point, research on space weapons and development of support systems may move into field-testing and it would then be in violation of the Treaty.

Perhaps even more serious are the "signals" sent by this activity. If the United States is moving aggressively in a direction that will sooner or later conflict with the ABM Treaty, why should the Soviet Union be scrupulous about its compliance? Why wouldn't the U.S.S.R. accelerate its BMD research programs also? The short-term arms control implications of proceeding with the SDI have to date been given too little attention.

Summary and Observations

Two of the U.S. charges dealing with strategic nuclear issues appear to be of greater compliance concern than the others and one of these, the radar construction at Krasnoyarsk, is the most serious. If this issue is not satisfactorily resolved, major negative consequences for arms control will no doubt result. The other is the nagging concern of Soviet encryption practices.

The Soviet charges do not seem to be of comparable compliance concern. In fact, several of them appear to be largely old issues once thought to be resolved and reopened by the U.S.S.R. to counter charges made by the Americans.

However, several other issues the Soviets raise regarding U.S. ratification procedures, willingness to negotiate, and adherence to agreed confidentiality rules are serious. If not changed by current arms control negotiation explorations, they could become extremely serious matters.

What can one make of these charges and countercharges? The following conclusions seem inescapable: the Soviets appear to have acted in ways that tend to undermine the political viability of arms control agreements; to a lesser extent and for different reasons, the same can be said about the United States. At times, both the U.S. and the U.S.S.R., have acted in ways that suggest they are not as interested in securing meaningful nuclear arms reductions as in keeping open options to gain weapons advantages. However, following Ronald Reagan's reelection as U.S. President, the willingness of both sides to engage in a new and comprehensive set of strategic arms control negotiations beginning in March of 1985, raises the hope that another period of sustained arms control progress may be in store for the next several years.

Reflection upon the charges and findings in this chapter raises an important question: What constitutes adequate proof that a violation has occurred? The answer is complex and elusive. Both premature release of information indicating noncompliance and attempts to delay have consequences. The 1983 "Final Report" of the Carnegie Endowment for International Peace series **Challenges for U.S. National Security** noted:

> Evidence may be simultaneously both inadequate for serious action and sufficient, when leaked, to create a major embarrassment for the process (and possibly the administration of the moment). Efforts to conceal compliance information from the public have been dismal failures, succeeding only in giving critics a free (and sometimes irresponsible) ride.

Public Charges of Noncompliance

There are many who question the certainty of the U.S. charges and the approach used by the Reagan Administration. Whatever the actual merits of each of the charges, some of the following consequences may result from their being made public: (1) in the short-term, the Soviets, ever sensitive to public airing of what they consider to be information only for diplomatic channels, may be slow to use the SCC; (2) also in the short-term, arms control negotiations will be more difficult to continue; and (3) public trust in arms control treaties and the effectiveness of verification methods to insure compliance will decrease, and so, consequently, will public support for negotiated agreements with the U.S.S.R.

Chapter 7

Verification in the Future

There will have to be more cooperation and cooperative measures to strengthen verification by National Technical Means, and such measures will require clear treaty language and compliance procedures. Both are difficult; neither is impossible.

Challenges for U.S. National Security
Carnegie Endowment for International Peace
1983

A worrisome question for the 1980s is, will future weapons technologies be verifiable? Since monitoring capabilities will also advance, another question might be, will monitoring technology and other verification approaches keep pace with weapons advances such as small size and mobility?

Many weapons technologies are moving in directions that may make future agreements more difficult to verify. These include technologies for anti-satellite weapons, mobile missiles, dual capable systems and cruise missiles. In the future, verification of arms limitations will depend to a greater extent on cooperative measures built into the agreements, as well as the advances in weapons and surveillance technologies. For example, collateral constraints, additions to treaty provisions to mutually enhance verification by eliminating actions that might otherwise make monitoring more difficult, may figure more prominently in future agreements.

While the specifics of future arms control agreements are unknown, it is possible to deduce information about future verification requirements by examining the monitoring requirements posed by current proposals. Proposals at various stages of discussion include (1) banning certain anti-satellite (ASAT) weapons, (2) limiting and reducing strategic and intermediate weapons (START and INF) including cruise missiles, (3) a "freeze" on all nuclear weapons systems including a cut-off of the production of fissile material, and (4) a comprehensive test ban.

This chapter deals with the verification of proposed limitations on reductions of existing or future weapon systems as well as verification of a comprehensive nuclear test ban. It focuses primarily on U.S. weaponry and verification technology since more is known about them. The purpose here is to illustrate verification and monitoring problems and possibilities.

FIGURE 1. **An artist's conception of a high-energy laser facility at the Sary Shagan test facility in the Soviet Union.** The beam is directed at a space target. The U.S. is constructing a similar facility at White Sands (New Mexico) missile range. Laser ASAT weapons provide a serious challenge for verification. (Department of Defense)

Anti-Satellite (ASAT) Technology and Verification

In the past five years, the Soviet Union has put forward two draft treaties that would limit anti-satellite activity. The second of these was proposed in August 1983. The U.S. and U.S.S.R. spent two years, 1978-79, in negotiations aimed at achieving an ASAT treaty. Negotiations were suspended in 1980. Preventing the spread of weapons into space continues to be a subject of intense political debate in the U.S., with the Congress pressing for a consideration of the possibilities for arms control ASAT limitations before the U.S. deploys its first (non-nuclear) anti-satellite weapon.

In the 1960s, the U.S., and reportedly the U.S.S.R., had nuclear-armed missiles with ASAT capability. ABM systems based on nuclear-armed missiles may also have ASAT capability. However, the use of nuclear explosives against satellites has many disadvantages, including

FIGURE 2. **This U.S. aircraft (a modified Boeing NKC-135) has a laser generator on board** and is used to test ASAT lasers, as well as beam weapons that can be used against other aircraft. These are currently being tested for use in anti-satellite and anti-ballistic missile warfare. (U.S. Air Force)

the likelihood that an attack would damage "friendly" and enemy satellites alike. The U.S. nuclear-armed system was retired in 1975.

Currently, both the U.S. and the U.S.S.R. are developing anti-satellite systems with sophisticated homing devices which destroy relatively fragile space craft by high-speed impact.

Soviet ASAT

The Soviets have deployed an ASAT. It is a large and relatively crude interceptor that is launched into approximately the same orbit as the target satellite, maneuvers close to it, and then explodes, destroying the target with a shotgun-like blast of metal pellets. Since 1968, all Soviet tests have used launchers at Tyuratam in Kazakhstan and orbits within a very narrow range of inclinations, 62 to 65 degrees. While the approximately 20 tests conducted have given mixed results, the Department of Defense declared the Soviet system operational in 1977.

The 2.5-foot long interceptor weighs three tons and consists of the explosive anti-satellite warhead and its maneuvering engine. It is launched with the SS-9 booster, the predecessor of the SS-18 ICBM booster. The interceptor can only reach low-orbiting satellites. The highest altitude reached thus far is reported to be about 1,400 miles.

Since the Soviet ASAT is ground based, an interceptor may have to sit on the launch pad up to 24 hours until the earth turns to bring the target satellite's orbit over the launch site. Using the co-orbital mode of attack, the interceptor can destroy a target during its first two revolutions. From ASAT launch, which would be detected by U.S. NTM, to target destruction could take several hours. The system is not suited for a sudden attack.

FIGURE 3. **An artist's conception of a Soviet ASAT weapon.** The weapon would use small metal pellets to destroy a rival satellite. (Department of Defense)

U.S. ASAT

The U.S. ASAT system is considerably smaller and based on different principles than the Soviet one. Advanced laser and infrared technologies are used in the launch, guidance, and tracking systems of the interceptor. Development of the system began seven years ago. It is now entering its initial test phase. Reportedly, if tests are not further delayed and they work as well as expected, the U.S. could deploy its ASAT system before 1988.

The U.S. ASAT is an air-launched system designed to intercept a target satellite by "direct ascent." The actual interceptor itself is a Miniature Homing Vehicle (MHV), which is a small metal cyclinder about one foot in diameter and one foot in length. It is launched from an F-15 fighter plane and carried into space by a 17-foot two-stage rocket. The F-15 is maneuvered under the target satellite's orbit, and when the target passes overhead the interceptor is launched. The interceptor is guided to the proper general location in space with an inertial guidance system in the second stage, after which it separates from the rocket. As the booster falls away, the intercepter follows a ballistic trajectory until it approaches the target. An infrared homing device in the cylindrical MHV guides it into collision with the target. The MHV destroys its target by direct impact at high velocity. The U.S. ASAT system can reach target satellites in a variety of orbits and close on them very quickly. The entire process would take ten to twenty minutes. Because the U.S. ASAT is plane borne, destruction of a satellite can take place anywhere. Currently, the MHV is only able to reach low-orbiting satellites.

FIGURE 4. **An F-15 aircraft carrying a U.S. ASAT weapon underneath the fuselage.** (Department of Defense)

The MHV would be launched from specially modified F-15s, with squadrons based on both the East and West coasts of the U.S. If deployed, the U.S. ASAT will have greater versatility to attack a variety of targets than the present Soviet system. It will also be easier to modify for attacks on satellites in higher orbits.

The Satellites at Risk

The attractiveness of satellites as targets stems from the vital roles that they play in modern military systems. They are used for intelligence gathering, navigational assistance, missile-launch detection and warning, strategic targeting, and meteorology. Much overseas military communication is by satellite. If war broke out between the superpowers, bringing it quickly to an end would depend entirely on each side's command, control, communications, and intelligence systems, of which satellites are crucial elements.

The satellites potentially at risk in the near future are those in low-altitude orbits: photoreconnaissance, ocean surveillance, meteorological, and some navigation satellites. However, unconstrained ASAT competition would eventually put satellites in higher synchronous orbits at risk, including communications and early warning satellites, which are an even more serious matter.

Suggestions for protective measures have been made. One is to move more satellites out of reach in higher orbits. This is not possible for photoreconnaissance satellites. Another is to duplicate important satellites. Other protective measures are to "harden" satellites against certain kinds of attack, to distribute military functions among a larger set of satellites, and to give certain satellites sensing ability to detect a possible attack and maneuvering ability to avoid it.

Congressional Pressure for ASAT Limitations

The U.S. Congress has made further development of the U.S. ASAT system conditional on new arms control efforts by the Administration. The Senate passed an amendment to the fiscal year 1985 defense authorization bill requiring the Reagan Administration to demonstrate its willingness to negotiate before carrying out the first test of the F-15 system against a moving target in space. In the House, the release of $19.4 million in anti-satellite procurement funds was tied to the submission of a report by the Administration on its ASAT arms control plans.

Sticking points in the suspended U.S.-U.S.S.R. ASAT negotiations included verifiability, the role of the U.S. space shuttle, and the fact that the Soviet system is deployed and the American system is not yet deployed.

U.S. ASAT Test

In August, 1985, the White House informed Congress of a planned ASAT test. In justifying the move, the Reagan Administration cited "good faith" anti-satellite arms control negotiation efforts, that "no arrangements. . . have been found to date that. . . meet the congressionally mandated requirements of verifiability. . .," that "the Soviet Union has. . . the world's only operational" ASAT system, and "a growing threat from present and prospective Soviet satellites." Many congressional and technical experts think that Moscow's advantage is minimal, and that the best hopes for effective and verifiable ASAT limitations lie in test restrictions and other measures to prevent each country from moving to the next generation of small, quick and accurate anti-satellite weapons. They think that Washington would be better off not to proceed with the final testing stages of its system. Since it would occur just two months before a planned U.S.-Soviet Summit meeting of the two countries' leaders, there was heated debate over whether the United States should go ahead with the test.

Despite some congressional opposition, the test occurred in September of 1985. A six-year-old still-active solar research satellite was the target for destruction. An F-15 from Edwards Air Force Base, flying at about 35,000 feet and directed by a radar command center at Vandenberg, launched the rocket carrying the homing vehicle. It was aimed at the oncoming satellite, which was traveling over the Pacific in a north-south polar orbit. When the MHV hit, "both telemetry signals ceased at exactly the same time." Administrative officials termed the test "absolutely flawless" and themselves "delighted" by the outcome. Moscow stated that, because of the U.S. test, the U.S.S.R. may break its self-imposed two-year moratorium on testing anti-satellite weapons.

Administration Position on ASAT Verification

The Reagan Administration states that a treaty banning the possession of ASATs would be unverifiable. Responding to the 1983 Soviet proposal, the U.S. State Department said that "our preliminary examination suggests that inadequate verification is one of its major weaknesses."

In particular, the U.S. Administration cites the near impossibility of verifying dismantling and destruction of the Soviet ASAT because its SS-9 booster is used for other missions. In the cover letter of his March 31, 1984 report to the Congress on the Administration's policy on arms control for anti-satellite systems, President Reagan said that "The factors that impede the identification of effective ASAT arms control measures include significant difficulties of verification...." The report concluded:

> The fact that anti-satellite capabilities are inherent in some systems developed for other missions or are amenable to undetected or surreptitous development makes it impossible to verify compliance with a truly comprehensive testing limitation that would eliminate tests of all methods of countering satellites.

Limits on ASAT Testing

Proponents of an ASAT treaty emphasize that an agreement which bans further deployment of such weapons should also limit testing. The time for prohibiting the current slow and questionably effective Soviet

ASAT behemoth has passed. However, improvements in reliability and significant upgrades, e.g., to reach geosynchronous orbit or achieve intercept in less than two orbital revolutions, require new testing by the Soviets. Testing of an extended-range upgrade of the Soviet ASAT would be relatively easy to detect with U.S. NTM. Testing for upgrading for a so-called "pop up" or fast intercept, which takes less than a full orbit, could also be monitored. Soviet NTM could, in turn, monitor whether the U.S. was observing test limitations on ASAT development.

Verifying a Ban on Deployed ASATs

The verification of a ban on deploying ASAT systems, once tested, presents different and more difficult problems. For example, the Soviet SS-9 booster used with their present ASAT is also used to launch a variety of other satellites. Verification could require determining whether the payload on top of the SS-9 were an ASAT or a reconnaissance satellite. Other problems arise if changes were made in the recognizable pattern of past Soviet ASAT tests, for example, a target launched from Plesetsk with an SS-5 missile and an interceptor launched from Tyuratam with a similar orbital inclination. It is not clear that complete dismantling of the Soviet system would be verifiable. The SS-9 would probably continue in production and a small number of ASAT payloads

FIGURE 5. **An artist's conception of an F-15 firing an ASAT weapon.** (Department of Defense)

could be hidden on-site or moved off-site during any verification inspections.

The Soviets would have similar difficulties verifying by their NTM that the U.S. was not deploying its F-15 ASAT system once it is fully tested. In fact, the problems might be more severe since the U.S. ASAT is small enough that the entire system (booster, second stage, and interceptor) can be carried under an F-15, and the MHV interceptor itself is small enough to fit into a breadbox.

Extended-Range ASAT and Lasers

Although there are only two systems acknowledged to be operational or near operational, many verification questions have also been raised about possible future ASAT systems. Two of these are extended-range ASAT capable of reaching the highest satellites and ground- and space-based directed energy beams, or lasers.

Extended-range anti-satellite systems require more powerful booster rockets than those currently used by the U.S. and U.S.S.R. Such modifications could be achieved relatively quickly by using the interceptors presently available. It would be easier to verify this extra capability for the Soviet ASATs. The booster needed for the small U.S. ASAT would be relatively small, while the one needed for the much heavier Soviet ASAT would be as large as the biggest boosters they have built. The Soviets may well be working on a system similar to the U.S. air-launched ASAT, which could pose more difficult verification problems.

Both countries have been developing high-powered laser weapons for at least a decade. Future ASATs could be ground-based lasers or space-based lasers. Technical success of a laser weapon is not fully certain, but it is generally agreed that the earliest deployment would most likely be as a ground-based ASAT weapon. The March 31, 1984 White House Report to Congress states that "The current Soviet ASAT capabilities include...ground-based test lasers with probable ASAT capabilities..." Methods are under study for "hardening" satellites against ground-based lasers. Laser ASAT weapons could present new verification problems, since their testing could be difficult to monitor.

FAS Study

A panel of prominent scientists, organized under the auspices of the Federation of American Scientists, analyzed the verifiability of an ASAT ban. They testified before the Senate Foreign Relations Committee on May 18, 1983 that a ban was verifiable. The group pointed out that covert Soviet attempts to test the present ASAT with the extended capability necessary to reach important military satellites in geosynchronous orbit would likely be detectable because the booster required would be "massive rockets with long preparation times, whose launches would be unmistakable."

The panel concluded:

> [T]here are no obvious reasons why an arms control agreement banning space tests and use of ASAT weapons could not be adequately verifiable. There may be some areas of uncertainty, but not so great as to permit the Soviets to pose a significant, unanticipated threat to U.S. security if we take prudent steps towards improving intelligence capabilities and diversifying and protecting vital satellite functions.

DOD Conclusion

The conclusion of the Defense Department review of the question was just the opposite. According to congressional testimony of Richard Perle, Assistant Secretary of Defense for International Security, "we cannot now foresee the means of verification" because the small size of an ASAT interceptor makes it easy to conceal and even a ban on testing would be difficult to monitor because the components of a full-fledged system could be tested surreptitiously. In its response to the Soviet proposal of August 1983, the State Department elaborated on this point as follows:

> We do not know how many ASAT interceptors have been manufactured, and it would be relatively easy for the Soviets to maintain a covert supply of interceptors for use in a crisis. Since satellites which serve U.S. and allied national security are very few in number, any Soviet cheating on an ASAT agreement, even on a small scale, could pose a prohibitive risk.

As with many other arms control questions, there is a sharp difference of opinion on the verifiability of an ASAT treaty. Those who conclude it is unverifiable focus on the possibility of covert deployment of a few weapons. Those who conclude it is verifiable cite the strategic significance of potential threats from a full Soviet ASAT capability and the desirability of eliminating that threat.

Verification and Strategic Nuclear Weapons

The Reagan Administration initiated the Strategic Arms Reduction Talks (START) in May 1982 in place of the interrupted third phase of the SALT process, SALT III. The goal of START was to achieve substantial reductions in strategic arms. The initial phase of the two-phase U.S. proposal included the following: First, it called for a reduction of ballistic missile warheads by at least a third (to 5,000 warheads each) as well as reductions in the total number of ballistic missiles by about half (to an equal level of 850 missiles for each side); second, it stipulated that each side have not more than 2,500 warheads on land-based ballistic missiles; third, it stipulated that at least half of each side's forces (specifically warheads) be at sea; fourth, it required that in the second phase the throw-weight of the two nations' forces be reduced to equal levels, below the current levels of U.S. forces and far below the current levels of Soviet forces.

SALT II Background

The background for the START negotiations was the SALT II Treaty, which specified equal limits, category by category, on the numbers of launchers. The SALT II Treaty, however, dealt with MIRVed missiles only indirectly by adopting a rule which counted every missile tested with MIRVs as being MIRVed, whether it was eventually deployed that way or not.

This rule eased verification although it fostered a situation where each side increased rather than decreased the MIRVed fraction of its forces. SALT II did put a verifiable upper limit on the number of warheads each missile type could carry, i.e., the maximum number tested as of the date of the Treaty. Thus, no missile type could be tested with a greater number, and, of course, no missile would be deployed without testing. For example, the huge Soviet SS-18 missile is capable of carrying at least 24 warheads, but is limited under SALT II to ten.

START Suspended

The START negotiation, with limits on warheads, took a different approach. It sought to achieve deeper reductions in strategic missile systems relative to SALT II. (SALT II did specify reductions but these never came into force because the Treaty was not ratified by the U.S.) The Reagan Administration proposals, however, put no limitations on long-range, air-launched cruise missiles. After NATO began deploying medium-range Pershing II missiles in Europe in the fall of 1983, the Soviet delegation walked out of the negotiations saying that this step had changed "the overall strategic situation." The START negotiations were suspended.

a b c

FIGURE 6. **A Ground-Launched Cruise Missile (GLCM) launcher** (a). **A GLCM being fired** (b). **A cruise missile in the air** (c). (Department of Defense)

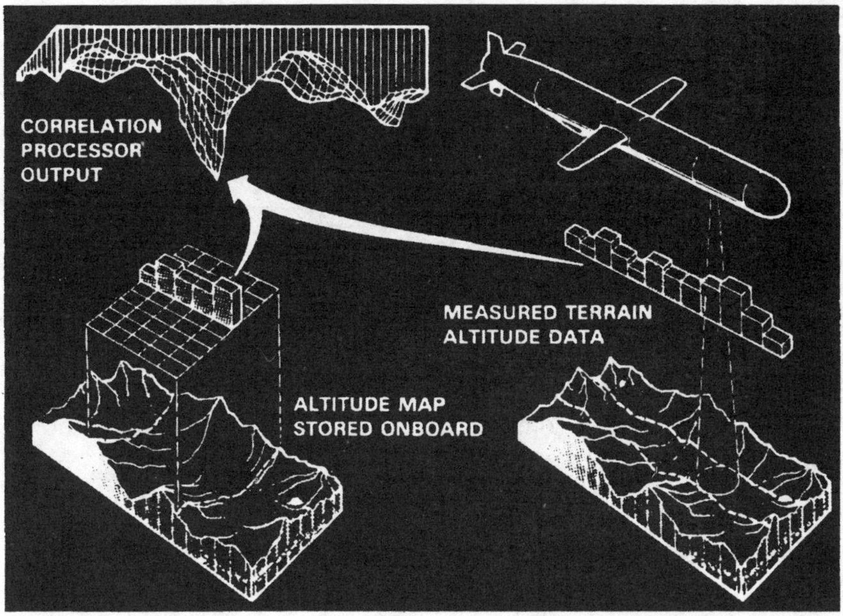

FIGURE 7. **A cruise missile's terrain contour matching (Tercom) guidance system.** (Aviation Week and Space Technology)

The START negotiations went through two rounds of proposals and counterproposals before they were suspended by the Soviets. During this time different formulations of "build-down" proposals were discussed in the Congress. These proposals and others sought to create a formula for reductions and a disincentive for MIRVing strategic forces.

Build-Down

The build-down is a nuclear arms reduction proposal, introduced in early 1983 by Senators William Cohen and Sam Nunn, calling for the United States and Soviet Union each to eliminate "two (older) nuclear warheads for each newly deployed nuclear warhead." The general idea of a build-down is not new. According to Senator Cohen, it provides for reductions with modernization. While its proponents have argued that a build-down increases "the survivability and reliability of deployed systems," this is not true in all cases.

On October 4, 1983, President Reagan announced that the United States would incorporate a more detailed form of the build-down proposal into the U.S. START negotiating position. Ambassador Rowny, head of the U.S. team, had only conceptually presented the position to the Soviets shortly before they broke off the negotiations. It reportedly called for a reduction of the number of missile warheads to 5,000 by eliminating two old warheads for each new MIRVed land-based warhead, three old warheads for every two new submarine-based missile warheads, and one old warhead for every new single-warhead, land-based ICBM. Such a proposal appears to foster decreased dependence on MIRVed land-based ICBMs and increased dependence on submarine-based and single-warhead forces. It is not clear how it would work in practice. The U.S. indicated that it was also prepared to discuss a build-down of bombers and tradeoffs since the two sides' force structures are different. The Soviets rejected the proposal as being in the U.S.' favor and a ploy to secure congressional approval of the MX missile. They offered, instead, a comprehensive nuclear freeze proposal without details.

While the build-down could lead to a more stable superpower nuclear relationship, such a result is critically dependent on the details of particular missile replacement scenarios and may not be possible without also restricting weapons modernization. Critics point out that as framed the START build-down position did favor the U.S. by not taking into account the Soviet dependence on land-based forces. Domestic critics, including many freeze supporters, add that while some reductions would occur under the build-down, the nuclear arms race would nonetheless continue.

Cutbacks in various weapons systems as would be prescribed in a build-down agreement could be readily verified. Monitoring would focus on destruction of launchers or silos and verifying replacement missiles would use the SALT II counting rule that the number of warheads assigned to a missile would be the maximum with which it was tested by the date that the Treaty was signed.

L + RV Formula

An early formulation, different from the one used in START, is the so-called "launcher plus reentry vehicle" (L + RV) formula for both reducing and "deMIRVing" strategic forces. It is based on an accounting system for missiles that, for example, would make MIRVed missiles such as the MX and the Soviet SS-18 extremely "expensive," relative to a fixed quota, while making single warhead missiles, such as the proposed Midgetman, quite "cheap." The goal of this formulation is to decrease the number of missiles with the greatest first-strike capability and increase those with single warheads. The L + RV plan illustrates an approach to devising a system for equitably reducing each side's strategic forces.

Under the proposal, each delivery system would be given an L + RV count of one plus the number of reentry vehicles. Negotiations would be based on each side having the same L + RV quota for strategic systems, i.e., land-based and sea-launched ballistic missiles and long-range bombers. For example, Sidney Drell of Stanford University proposed an L + RV quota of 8,000 plus SALT II restrictions on modernization of land-based ICBMs as a "simple and powerful combination for effective arms control." Such a quota represents a reduction by almost a factor of two relative to the maximum deployments of 2,250 launchers and 13,000 reentry vehicles permitted by SALT II.

What weapons systems would be the most restricted if L + RV accounting were applied? The following table gives some examples:

TABLE 1. Examples of L + RV Accounting

U.S. Weapons		L + RV Number	U.S.S.R. Weapons		L + RV Number
Missile or Delivery Vehicle	Reentry Vehicles (Warheads)		Missile	Reentry Vehicles (Warheads)	
MX	10	11	SS-18	10	11
Trident I (C4)	8	9	SS-19	6	7
Single-Warhead	1	2	Single-Warhead	1	2
B-52	20 ALCM	21			

The most expensive missiles under this accounting scheme would be the massive Soviet SS-18 and the U.S. MX missiles.

The L + RV proposal formed one of the bases for the build-down proposal and its more complicated variations. The proposal was concrete and tried to create an incentive for deMIRVing, while retaining the straightforward verification approach of monitoring numbers of launchers used by SALT.

Verification of an agreement based on an L + RV formulation would be approximately the same as with SALT II. Such an agreement would retain the SALT counting rules for the number of reentry vehicles on each missile.

There are drawbacks to this proposal. Only survivable missiles, SLBMs and mobiles, have primarily retaliatory capability and the L + RV proposal does not promote these. Other measures of force effectiveness, in particular throw-weight, would be ignored in this proposal, in the interest of flexibility and simplicity. Of course, explicit limits on throw-weight and destructive potential could be addressed subsequently for any future systems.

FIGURE 8. **A U.S. Los Angeles Class submarine (the USS Los Angeles).** SLCMs have been deployed on these attack submarines. SLCMs are difficult to verify because they are designed to be launched from conventional torpedo tubes. (U.S. Navy)

Advocates of this approach argue that it would (1) improve stability by making it quite costly, relative to a fixed quota, for either country to deploy large numbers of the weapons systems that are most threatening to the other's forces; and (2) provide an equitable and flexible basis for reductions.

This proposal, unlike Phase I of the START proposal, also incorporates cruise missiles launched from heavy bombers. Verification of limitations on cruise missiles is discussed later in this chapter.

Nuclear Weapons Freeze

In its broadest form, the freeze proposal calls for a mutual and verifiable halt to the production, testing, and deployment of nuclear weapons and their means of delivery. The freeze would stop the modernization of nuclear arms, regarded by the proposal's adherents as one of the principal driving forces of the arms race, and ban the production of nuclear warheads and new weapons-usable fissionable material.

FIGURE 9. **A Soviet SLCM.** This artist's conception illustrates how a Soviet SLCM would attack its target. (Department of Defense)

In the past few years, proposals for a joint U.S.-U.S.S.R. nuclear weapons freeze have been considered in several forums, including the U.S. Congress in 1982 and 1983 and the U.N. General Assembly. The Soviet Union proposed a freeze during the START negotiations.

This proposal is also the basis of a political movement active in the 1980s. It is a relatively simple and comprehensive approach to limiting nuclear arms: halt then reverse the arms race. Opponents in the U.S. and western Europe argue that halting now could permanently establish Soviet leads in certain weapons categories.

IS A FREEZE VERIFIABLE?

The following excerpt of an Op-Ed article by Herbert Scoville, Jr., formerly Deputy Director of the Central Intelligence Agency for Research (Science and Technology), appearing in **The New York Times**, October 25, 1984, indicates that at least the important provisions of a freeze could be verified.

Consider a freeze on the testing, production and deployment of new long-range ballistic missiles, the most dangerous type of weapons being developed by either superpower today. Our intelligence capabilities can easily determine whether or not the Soviet Union is secretly acquiring such weapons. For example, our infra-red satellites can observe any testing of them, whether launched from land or a submarine. What's more, if the Russians tested any new missile—a weapon with characteristics different from those already seen—this could be determined by ground observation after it was launched and also on re-entry.

Even without intercepting Soviet telemetry, we can easily count the number of warheads on a tested missile, while also determining their weight and whether they are "terminal guided" for accuracy in hitting their targets. With telemetry, we can get even more detailed information, and presumably the encoding of any telemetry needed for verification would be forbidden by a freeze. Such encoding would in itself provide evidence of a violation of the freeze.

We have also been able to observe the deployment of new missiles, usually several years before they are operational. Even were the Russians to develop mobile missiles, which almost certainly would be picked up in testing, it is highly probable that we would detect their existence before significant numbers were deployed.

Adding verification of a ban on production to a ban on testing and deployment increases our overall confidence that the Soviet Union is not acquiring an important new missile capability. The monitoring of production is difficult, but public testimony indicates that we know where all Soviet missiles are built today. Any significant secret production would most likely also be spotted.

To verify a freeze on the production of nuclear explosives, as opposed to warheads and delivery systems, we can keep track of the Soviet Union's fissionable material. Twenty years ago, our intelligence was good enough to locate the plants that produced all Soviet fissionable material, and it certainly has improved since then. Since the Soviet Union already has more than 100,000 kilograms of weapons-grade uranium-235 and plutonium, any secret production would have to be quite large in order to be significant. There is virtually no chance that this would escape our eyes.

Yet another essential element of a freeze would be a comprehensive test ban treaty, along the lines of the agreement that was being worked out with the Soviet Union in 1978. This, too, could be satisfactorily monitored: verification provisions, including inspections and unmanned seismic stations, have been agreed upon. These, together with our vastly improved seismic discrimination techniques, would permit the identification of tests as low as a kiloton of explosive force or less. Herbert York, chief United States negotiator of the agreement, has testified that with the political will, we could have had a verifiable test ban in less than six months.

Verification Controversy

The proposal's verifiability is a contentious issue. Some aspects of the freeze proposal appear to be less verifiable than others. Critics point to these as indications of major weaknesses in the proposal. However, like the comprehensive test ban (CTB) proposal, this proposal has the advantage that if just one of the activities prohibited by a freeze agreement were detected, it would constitute an unambiguous violation. Proponents in the U.S. assert that all of its important provisions are readily verifiable and, in any event, there is a margin of safety since any covert Soviet action of strategic importance would be readily detected before the U.S.S.R. could gain any significant advantage.

An important feature of the comprehensive freeze proposal is a ban on the assembly of new warheads. Advocates of a warhead ban want to impose ceilings on nuclear weapons stockpiles and prevent further technological innovations in warheads. The ban is controversial. Some believe it would eliminate our technological edge over the Soviets.

Freeze Advocates

Advocates of the freeze point out that matters of verification of testing and deployment of strategic systems were largely worked out in the SALT II negotiations, and verification of a total freeze should be even easier when programs are completely halted. Monitoring halts to modifications of Soviet SS-18 and SS-19s and U.S. Minuteman IIIs, however, might be more difficult. Verifying a production halt would be more difficult than monitoring deployment. However, if both sides "declared" the locations of plants where the major components of frozen weapons systems were produced and agreed to simply shut them down, the task would be eased. In general, advocates say the U.S. would have no trouble verifying most parts of a freeze. Herbert Scoville, Jr., former Deputy Director of the Central Intelligence Agency for Research (Science and Technology) wrote in the fall of 1984:

> The truth is that we could indeed verify the important provisions of a freeze and could certainly detect any violation that would significantly threaten our security.

If a freeze agreement were in place now, could the U.S. verify that the Soviets were complying with a missile test moratorium? Could the U.S. determine the characteristics (number, weight, guidance systems, etc.) of Russian warheads in spite of their encryption practices? Could the U.S. verify the number of warheads on Soviet missiles without on-site inspection? The answer to all three questions based on information contained in chapters two through six seems clearly to be "yes." Could the U.S. determine whether, in fact, the Soviets had halted the production of nuclear explosives? See the box, "Is a Freeze Verifiable?," and the next section on fissile material cutoff.

Freeze Skeptics

Skeptics about the ease of verifying a freeze point out that many of the production facilities are multi-purpose plants. Furthermore, a complete halt of production at known plants does not foreclose covert production at alternative facilities. There are several other problems cited by the skeptics. They say that it may be difficult to (1) distinguish missile components manufactured for replacement purposes from those manufactured for deploying prohibited delivery systems; (2) monitor deployment of small mobile missiles and cruise missiles because they are easy to conceal; (3) guard against the conversion of non-nuclear versions of cruise missiles and tactical aircraft to nuclear ones; and (4) distinguish permitted safety modifications from prohibited improvements in performance. However, these concerns are also true of the START, build-down, and other proposals. In other words, many of the contentious verification issues in a comprehensive freeze are also contained in other proposals. Setting those aside, monitoring and verification of a freeze are much like other arms control proposals, such as START.

Important verification questions related to a nuclear freeze are, for example, what methods are available to verify a warhead production ban? and what should be done about the stockpile of obsolete warheads on each side? The following section addresses these and other questions.

FIGURE 10. **The Oak Ridge, Tennessee, nuclear weapons production plant.** Proposals for a ban on fissionable material as a means of arms control would require careful monitoring of plants such as this one in all countries possessing nuclear weapons. (Department of Energy)

Fissile Material Production Cutoff

Fissionable material, either the isotope of uranium with atomic weight 235 (U-235) or of manmade plutonium at 239 (Pu-239), is necessary to make a nuclear weapon.* In contrast to proposals limiting launchers, warheads, or delivery vehicles, a ban on further production of fissile material would freeze both countries' stockpiles of the crucial ingredients for making nuclear warheads.

Proposals for a fissile material cutoff are also not new. United States President Dwight Eisenhower recommended a mutual cutoff to Soviet Premier Nikolai Bulganin in his 1956 "open skies" inspection proposal. Presidents John Kennedy and Lyndon Johnson each proposed versions

*Nuclear chain reactions and hence nuclear weapons are made possible by the existence of fissile nuclei, i.e., those which can be fissioned by a low-energy or "slow" neutron. Isotopes are chemically indistinguishable variations of the same element whose nuclei contain the same number of protons and a different number of neutrons. The sum of the number of protons and neutrons is the element's atomic weight. Other isotopes of a heavy nuclei may be fissionable but not fissile, and some may be fertile, capturing neutrons and converting into new, and fissile, nuclei. Fissile Pu-239 is created from the fertile uranium isotope U-238 in this way.

of a cutoff. In 1969, President Richard Nixon repeated the Johnson proposal to the Soviets. The U.S. proposals have never been formally withdrawn. The Soviet Union rejected earlier proposals, but stated at the 1982 Special Session of the United Nations on Disarmament that the "initial stages (to nuclear disarmament) could be a cessation of production of fissionable material." Advocates of this proposal argue that approaches which merely limit weapons systems are intrinsically difficult because of asymmetries in U.S. and Soviet delivery systems, and that a cutoff offers a way around this difference.

Enrichment and Reprocessing

Verification of a cutoff would require monitoring the sources of production of enriched uranium and plutonium. Uranium for nuclear weapons is extracted from hard-rock ore and "enriched" from its naturally occurring concentration of 0.7 percent of the fissile U-235 to a form with a more than 90 percent concentration of that isotope. The resultant highly-enriched uranium is often called "weapons grade." The mining, milling and other operations could all be highly visible from satellites, even if the enrichment process were not.

Currently, uranium enrichment plants, such as the one at Oak Ridge, Tennessee (see figure 10) use the gaseous diffusion technology. These plants are large with distinctively shaped and arrayed buildings covering tens of acres and recognizable delivery and other support activities. Through collateral constraints in a freeze agreement these activities could be required to be "transparent," e.g., deliveries and pickups unloaded and loaded in the open at specified times.

Plutonium for weapons is produced first at special purpose "production" nuclear reactors, such as the L reactor at Savannah River, South Carolina, and the N reactor at Hanford, Washington. It is then reprocessed to eliminate most of the undesirable isotopic contaminants, resulting in a material consisting of almost pure fissionable Pu-239 isotope. Reprocessing facilities are not necessarily large but do have a distinct building design which is especially apparent during construction, e.g., some operations require very thick walls.

Verification Tasks

The tasks for verification would be to detect (1) existing military production and refining facilities still in operation, (2) the construction or operation of clandestine production facilities, and (3) any diversions of fissionable material from civilian nuclear facilities. Since a cutoff could be a first step toward reduction, keeping track of material taken out of existing fissile material stockpiles and its purpose would be important.

Verification of the size of existing fissile material stockpiles may also be needed. Currently, the buildings and general performance for uranium and plutonium weapons material production facilities are large, their locations well known, and they have distinctive characteristics. Advocates of a cutoff, such as W.K.H. Panofsky, think that national technical means would "probably be adequate" to monitor whether existing production had been entirely discontinued. In addition, both parties to a cutoff might request that existing facilities be dismantled and destroyed, which are verifiable activities readily monitored by national technical means.

Verification Complexities

New technologies, especially for uranium enrichment, could make verification more difficult. Centrifuge enrichment plants, while large facilities, are considerably smaller than the older gaseous diffusion plants. Laser enrichment plants, a technology currently under development, could be much smaller. Various "observables" and agreements to make operations transparent would probably make it possible to monitor centrifuge plant production. Not enough is known to predict the nature of monitoring of laser technologies. Such technologies are still very much in the developmental stage and their technical and commercial success is not certain. If smaller-scale enrichment emerges, it could make monitoring more difficult.

Commercial nuclear fuel facilities are not always easily distinguishable from military ones. This identification problem could be a complicating factor in monitoring a ban on fissionable material production for weapons. Quite possibly, however, cooperative agreements could be developed to designate specific production areas in each country. Furthermore, monitoring of pickups and deliveries over a period of time is likely to distinguish whether an operation is commercial or military.

Highly-Enriched Uranium

Some civilian research reactors and most U.S. naval nuclear propulsion systems, e.g., those in submarines, use highly-enriched uranium as fuel. A fissile material cutoff agreement would have to include cooperative measures to either forego such uses, which is not difficult in the cases cited, or to enhance the ability of monitoring to determine precisely the amounts of uranium produced and consumed for research and other non-weapons uses, which is also not difficult. In fact, conversion of research reactors, which exist in many countries, to medium-enriched uranium is already underway primarily for nonproliferation reasons.

Plutonium Diversion

Modern nuclear warheads use plutonium. Some people worry about the diversion of plutonium from commercial to weapons use. There is cause for concern that such a diversion might occur in one of the eight or so countries in the Middle East, Asia, and Africa possessing the requisite technology and which sometimes seem apparently eager to demonstrate a nuclear explosion capability. However, commercial plutonium, while usable for weapons, has some very significant drawbacks. It includes more isotopes of plutonium mixed with the Pu-239, resulting in a material which is more difficult to handle and machine, and for which there is greater uncertainty about its explosive yield than for weapons grade or production reactor plutonium. These yield uncertainties and handling difficulties make it very unlikely to be used by either U.S. or Soviet government weapons designers.

The Stockpile Problem

A particular problem is the determination of the size of the existing stockpiles of fissionable material. Approximate sizes of the stockpiles can be determined from information gained from national technical means and calculations based on known Soviet practices. It is believed that the military nuclear materials stockpiles of the U.S. and U.S.S.R. are reasonably well-balanced. However, it is easier to verify changes than to precisely assess the current size of the stockpiles. If large decreases were contemplated, then knowing the actual stockpile sizes before reduction would be very important since the U.S. would want assurance that the Soviet's reserves would be as small as its own. Advocates of a cutoff suggest that cooperative measures such as establishing an agreed data base, as was done for strategic vehicles in SALT II, would facilitate this task.

Of course, a production cutoff of fissile material would not necessarily stop new weapons from being produced. In the long term, a comprehensive nuclear test ban might have that effect. The fissile material in a country's existing nuclear weapons stockpile could be exploited or "mined" to meet new weapons requirements.

Significant Covert Production

The important consideration, however, is whether any undetected covert production of fissile material could produce enough highly-enriched uranium or refined plutonium to allow a strategically significant number of weapons to be manufactured and stockpiled. Assessments of whether enough fissile material could be clandestinely produced for a significant number of weapons differ primarily over what constitutes "significant." One analysis shows that material for some 25-50 weapons could be produced clandestinely. Given the present size of our nuclear arsenal, that number is said to be of marginal significance at most. If someday both sides reduce their aresenals to a few hundred weapons apiece, such an amount of unaccounted for fissile weapons material could be very important. By then, however, cooperative measures may be developed to reduce the amount of material that could go unaccounted to such a low level that it would correspond to only a few weapons at most.

Turn In and Destroy

A proposal that explicitly eliminates nuclear weapons and their fissile material is the "turn in and destroy" proposal, whose most visible proponent is Admiral (USN, Ret.) Noel Gayler. This proposal, part of the Deep Cuts approach advocated by the American Committee on East-West Accord, would require the U.S. and U.S.S.R. to each turn in their nuclear weapons at a facility under international supervision. The fissionable material would be removed and refabricated as reactor fuel for use in the peaceful nuclear power industry or stored under international control and the other components of the weapon would be mechanically destroyed. Such a facility could be built explicitly for this purpose at a neutral country site. Soviet and American teams, under international supervision, would identify each device, count them, and weigh the fissionable material turned in. Since the proposal is designed to effect large reductions in the superpowers' arsenals, a fissile material production cutoff and a system of civilian reactor safeguards against diversion are included. A great deal of institutional experience with the Nuclear Nonproliferation Treaty and the role of the International Atomic Energy Agency in Vienna would be applicable in developing a regime to manage, monitor, and verify the results of such a turn in and destroy operation.

A Comprehensive Test Ban

The concept of a comprehensive nuclear test ban is nearly forty years old. It was part of the Baruch plan of 1946 and was the focus of the early test ban negotiations of the late 1950s and early 1960s. In those negotiations it was dropped in favor of the achievable Limited Test Ban Treaty. Under the Carter Administration, negotiations for a Comprehensive Test Ban Treaty took place from 1977-80. The negotiations are suspended, and the Reagan Administration has refused to resume them, citing lack of confidence in its ability to verify such an accord.

CTB: PRO AND CON

A halt to all nuclear weapons testing was the original goal of the negotiations that led to the 1963 Limited Test Ban Treaty. A comprehensive nuclear test ban (CTB) in one form or another has been the subject of negotiations from 1954 to 1980. In spite of substantial progress in resolving verification problems and achieving agreement on in-country seismic sensors, the U.S. did not resume the suspended test ban negotiations with the U.S.S.R. and Great Britain in July of 1980. The Reagan Administration cited lack of confidence in methods of verifying compliance as the primary reason for not continuing the negotiations.

Proponents of a CTB argue that it (1) can be verified; (2) would end the technological modernization of nuclear explosives, which they contend is a factor driving the arms race; (3) would follow through on a commitment made by the nuclear weapon states in the Nonproliferation Treaty (NPT) of 1970 to negotiate such a ban and thereby strengthen the NPT and reduce the likelihood that additional countries will acquire nuclear weapons; and (4) would lead to greater stability in the world and enhanced international security. The principal argument in support of a comprehensive test ban is its essential role in bolstering a world-wide nonproliferation regime.

Opponents argue that it (1) is not verifiable and, if the Soviets successfully cheated, they would then have a strategic advantage; (2) would weaken and undercut America's nuclear weapons scientific and technological base and our advantage over the Soviets in that area; (3) would lead to uncertainty over the quality of our nuclear weapons giving us less confidence in the reliability of our nuclear arsenal; and (4) would thereby result in a Soviet advantage and a less stable world.

Throughout the debate, the U.S.'s ability to verify a CTB has been a contentious issue. As indicated in this chapter and chapter four, it appears possible to negotiate the in-country installation of a monitoring system capable of detecting even muffled explosions smaller than one kiloton.

Despite this capability, many nuclear weapons experts think that as long as the U.S. maintains a stockpile of such weapons it will be necessary to conduct periodic tests to assure that they still work. The issue of "stockpile reliability" continues to be the principal basis for opposition to a comprehensive test ban by the Joint Chiefs of Staff, the Defense Nuclear Agency, the Departments of Defense and Energy, and the nuclear weapons laboratories.

History of 1977-80 Negotiations

Ambassador Herbert F. York, who headed the U.S. Comprehensive Test Ban negotiating team in 1979 and 1980, wrote in an article entitled "Bilateral Negotiations and the Arms Race," which appeared in the October 1983 issue of **Scientific American**, that:

> In 1977, President Carter included the negotiation of a comprehensive test ban among his top arms-control priorities. By that time the position of the U.S.S.R. with regard to on-site inspections had evolved to the point where it was willing to accept a voluntary form of on-site inspection; meanwhile, the U.S. position had evolved to the point where it was willing to accept a carefully hedged form of voluntary on-site inspections instead of mandatory ones. In addition the Russians indicated their willingness to accept a substantial number of specially designed and constructed "national seismic stations" on their territory. Between 10 and 15 of these stations were to be built according to agreed specificiations and provided with cryptologic systems that would guarantee that the data stream received from them was continuous and unmodified.
>
> The details of a treaty were only about half worked out when external events slowed the negotiations to such an extent that it became impossible to complete the process before the end of President Carter's term. Among the external factors were unanticipated difficulties in the second phase of the strategic arms limitation talks (SALT II), which were going on at the time, the seizure of U.S. hostages in Iran, and the Russian intervention in Afghanistan. The Carter round of test-ban negotiations was adjourned indefinitely a week after the 1980 elections.
>
> The Reagan Administration decided immediately after taking office not to resume the negotiations, but it continued to debate for almost a year

and a half its reasons for not doing so. One group argued that the administration should simply declare that as long as the U.S. relied on nuclear weapons as an important element of its defense strategy, it would be necessary to continue testing them, and so a comprehensive test ban would not be in the nation's interest for the foreseeable future. A second group argued that the main problem was that there still was no adequate system for verifying a ban on underground tests (the implication being that if there were, the U.S. might then be willing to negotiate an agreement). The second group eventually won the internal debate, and the current official position is that a comprehensive test ban remains a "long-term goal" of the U.S. but that "international conditions are not now propitious for immediate action on this worthy project."

The verification issue remains highly controversial. In brief, large- and moderate-yield nuclear explosions can be readily detected and identified by means of remote sensors but very small ones cannot. The boundary separating the two classes of events is indistinct, however, and that leads to widely varying interpretations of the data, depending on the predisposition of the person interpreting them.

Verification Questions

Several questions are raised by the prospect of a comprehensive test ban. Would the national technical means be sufficient to monitor such a ban? What level of detection is necessary? What is the nature of the seismic network necessary to achieve such a level? Would on-site inspections be necessary to supplement seismic methods? There is some disagreement about how small a test could be detected with seismic methods (see chapter four). Estimates range from a fraction of a kiloton to 10 or 20 kilotons, depending on whether an in-country or external network of seismic sensors is envisioned. As indicated, the CTB negotiations included provisions for an in-country network of unmanned seismic stations.

Most scientists agree that with a 25 to 30 station in-country network and using proven techniques, tests with yields at least as small as a few kilotons could be detected with high confidence, even if cavity-decoupling measures were taken to muffle the seismic signal (see chapter four). Comparably confident detection of lower-yield explosions is possible, according to seismologist Willard J. Hannon writing on "Seismic Verification of a Comprehensive Test Ban" in the January 18, 1985 issue of **Science**, and "would require networks of more than 30 high-quality in-country arrays." Seismologists disagree, however, about how extensive these stations or arrays would have to be. Recent documented

FIGURE 11. **A U.S. ALCM in flight.** It is currently launched from the wing pylon of B-52 bombers. It has a range of 6,000 km. which allows it to be launched outside Soviet air space. (U.S. Air Force)

research indicates that by using higher frequencies, a 25 station in-country network could detect muffled yields well below one kiloton.

There are some people who think that only on-site inspection can provide unequivocal identification of a nuclear explosion through, for example, radiological sampling. Others think that the national technical means are sufficiently powerful that such inspections, while possibly useful, are not necessary. They cite examples of tests where no radiological contamination of the surface occurred and teams sent to find the test site were not successful. One group argues that on-site inspection is essential and the other that it could lead to a false sense of security. Both agree, however, that on-site inspections could be useful as deterrents and as confidence building measures.

Bomber and Cruise Missile Limitations

The cruise missile operates entirely within the earth's atmosphere, maintaining thrust throughout its flight. Both the U.S. and U.S.S.R. deploy them. The U.S. cruise missile is about 15 feet long and less than 2 feet in diameter. Soviet cruise missiles are considerably larger. U.S. cruise missiles are technologically more advanced, of smaller size, and equipped with better guidance systems. They can be launched from land (GLCM for ground-launched cruise missile), sea (SLCM), and air (ALCM).

Cruise missiles present new verification problems. They are much smaller than ballistic missiles, yet can deliver a nuclear warhead to a long-range target with great accuracy. They are mobile and can be

FIGURE 12. **A Soviet Missile on a Transporter-Erector-Launcher (TEL).** The TEL allows the missile to move from one place to another, thereby increasing its survivability but also making it more difficult to verify. (Department of Defense)

FIGURE 13. **An artist's conception of a Soviet SS-20 missile being fired.** (Department of Defense)

FIGURE 14. **The U.S. Pershing II missile.** This is one of the new intermediate-range nuclear weapons that NATO has deployed in Europe in response to the Soviet build up of SS-20s. (Department of Defense)

deployed in several modes. Both nuclear and non-nuclear cruise missiles already exist in both U.S. and Soviet forces. Military planners call them "dual purpose" systems. Since cruise missiles fly close to the ground and can be tested at less than full range, their tests are more difficult to monitor than those of ballistic missiles.

The task of verifying limitations on ground-launched cruise missiles is similar to that for mobile ballistic missiles such as the American Pershing IIs and the Soviet SS-20s. These intermediate-range missiles are small enough to travel on vehicles similar to a large flat-bed truck. They are launched from transporter-erector-launchers (TELs) which carry, raise, and fire the missiles. Because TELs can be reloaded and fired much faster than ICBM silos, "rapid reload" is also a verification issue with mobile and cruise missiles.

Verification

In SALT II, verification of air-launched cruise missiles was dealt with by means of specific cooperative measures. SALT II restricted the current heavy bombers (the American B-52 and B-1 and the Soviet Bear and Bison) to carry no more than 20 cruise missiles. It also set a maximum for all heavy bombers of 28 cruise missiles per airplane. Any aircraft that is equipped with long-range cruise missiles is counted as an ALCM-carrying heavy bomber and is included in the SALT II numerical aggregates.

Because the Soviets also used their Bison aircraft as tankers, a potential verification problem arose in the SALT II negotiations. It was agreed, however, that heavy bombers not carrying cruise missiles would also be modified with functionally related observable differences (see chapter two). Bison tankers were modified so that they no longer had bomb bay doors. Both the U.S. and U.S.S.R. have considerable experience verifying numbers of heavy bombers. Deployment of sea- and ground-launched cruise missiles could be even more difficult to verify.

One view is that since cruise missiles are small, easy to conceal and require limited logistical support, they are difficult to verify. The problem is further complicated by their dual purpose deployment. Another view is that any efforts to conceal deployment of a significant number of cruise missiles would likely be observed and raise questions. Thus, according to this view, verification must be good enough to avoid military disadvantages but need not provide absolute certainty about the total number of cruise missiles deployed. A total ban on sea- or ground-launched cruise missiles would be comparatively easy to verify.

Counting Problems

These systems also present special counting problems. They could be deployed in hard-to-count ways such as placing sea-launched cruise missiles in submarine torpedo tubes. To supplement NTM, special counting rules and cooperative procedures could be used. These would be comparable to those in SALT II for cruise-missile equipped heavy bombers. For example, sea-launched cruise missiles could be required to be deployed in distinctive launchers. The United States has or will soon modify some Iowa class battleships to carry SLCMs. Reportedly, the modifications will be visible since some guns will be removed and the SLCMs will be deployed in in special "boxes" called vertical launch tubes.

These systems are more readily concealed than ICBM silos, but perhaps not more than many other military systems such as tanks or tactical aircraft which seem to be easily monitored. Mobile IRBMs are regular targets for intelligence. Soviet SS-20s are mobile intermediate-range ballistic missiles successfully counted in the past, as are the large Soviet (and U.S.) complements of relatively short-range cruise missiles. Reportedly, these weapons have signatures that are independent of their individual size.

Sea-launched cruise missiles, in particular, present formidable challenges for verification. Reportedly, Tomahawk cruise missiles have been deployed for torpedo launch on a few Los Angeles class U.S. submarines. A new Oscar class Soviet submarine is reported to be equipped with cruise missiles. Furthermore, the U.S. plans to deploy more cruise missiles on submarines and surface ships using the vertical launching system. Thus, some are concerned that virtually any ship or submarine could become a carrier and launch platform for SLCMs.

Verification Aids

One method to aid verification of deployment quotas for cruise missiles or mobile missiles would be the adoption of cooperative measures to allow national technical means to monitor the missiles as they were produced. Both countries could agree that certain production functions at designated facilities would be kept transparent to satellite surveillance. For example, completed missiles could be displayed for observation and specifically made available for satellite inspection at points of exit by mutually agreed procedures.

Other, more ambitious devices could be used. For example, mobile missiles might also be tagged in some manner, say by a device which sends out a radio signal that allows a sampling by some challenge procedure such as a demand that all signals be activated. In this way total counts and deployment locations could be periodically checked. While such methods are not absolutely foolproof, they would so complicate any efforts to cheat and raise the risk of detection of any covert action to such a level that they would almost certainly effectively eliminate the threat of deception.

Dual Purpose Systems

Dual purpose systems are not a new problem in arms control. Tactical aircraft may be conventionally- or nuclear-armed. The Soviet medium-range Backfire bomber was a difficult problem in SALT II. It was thought to be capable, under some circumstances, of delivering a nuclear weapon on an intercontinental mission, even though that was not its principal combat purpose.

The problems with cruise missile verification are further compounded by the fact that it would be relatively easy to shift from non-nuclear to nuclear warheads. It is probably impossible to know whether a particular dual-capable missile has a nuclear or a conventional warhead at a particular moment. No one has yet devised a FROD that is truly functionally related to distinguish between the two. Advocates of cruise missile limitations say it is important to know what fraction of a cruise missile force is nuclear-armed. Nuclear-armed cruise missiles do require special procedures in handling such as tight security which could make deployment easier to monitor. Nuclear-armed cruise missiles might be restricted to certain planes and ships and not others. Counting rules of so many missiles per allowed type of plane or ship could then be used to attribute total numbers. Essentially this approach was used in SALT II for cruise missile-equipped heavy bombers.

In summary, there are many potential ways of dealing with verifying limitations on cruise missiles. It is, however, still a complicated, formidable, and uncertain proposition needing more careful attention.

Speculations on Advances in Verification Technologies

At the beginning of this chapter, we asserted that monitoring and verification capabilities would probably advance in the future. What capabilities might the U.S. have five or ten years from now that it doesn't have now? This section addresses that question.

In this and the six preceeding chapters, a great deal has been said about the U.S.'s monitoring capacity, its technologies and their capabilities and limitations, and the current state-of-the-art of information processing. In some cases, more detail, available elsewhere, is excluded from this book. There are many reasons for these exclusions. Some of that information is wrong, garbled or misleading. Some is not confirmed by other information in official open sources.

As we have repeatedly stressed, there are good reasons for the U.S. intelligence community not to want the Soviets to know the full extent of our capabilities. For example, Washington has reportedly gained useful information in the past because Moscow was not fully aware of the U.S. monitoring ability.

Technological Advances

Since the early 1960s, U.S. satellite photoreconnaissance and related data processing have steadily improved in resolution—the ability to see and distinguish small objects—in integrated search and find and close look capabilities, in the "real-time" availability of information, and in computer enhancement of images allowing yet more information to be recovered.

Satellite Photoreconnaissance. It is reported in a number of open sources that the current limit of resolution for U.S. photoreconnaissance satellites is about 10 cm. There is no official confirmation of this figure and such specifications are usually highly classified for the reasons already given. If this is indeed the approximate resolving ability of close look satellites, then objects as small as chairs, benches, and large suitcases as well as human beings could often be distinguished in photographs, and under some conditions, using computer enhancement techniques, smaller objects might also be identifiable. Optical scientists and other experts suggest that, at least theoretically, that level of resolution is not the limit of what might be possible in the future.

Radar. Radar systems have become much more sophisticated over the last twenty years. It is now possible, for example, for some radars to produce "pictures" which are not blips on a screen, but rather clear accurate maps showing buildings, bridges, roads, vehicles, etc. Phased array radars contain no moving parts. They are made up of many individual radars from which information is electronically integrated to allow very small objects, much smaller than warheads, in the atmosphere or space to be readily detected at thousands of miles. During Soviet missile tests where the impact zone is on the Kamchatka Peninsula, the U.S. Cobra Dane radar on Shemya Island, Alaska, is reportedly able to not only distinguish the missile's bus from its warheads but also each of the bus's reactions as it dispenses them.

Currently, the United States does not deploy radars in satellites. The Soviet Union does. Radars, of course, can "see" through cloud cover. In the future the U.S. may also deploy radar satellites to augment its photoreconnaissance coverage.

SIGINT. Electronic intelligence is gathered from many sources. Continuous refinement of collection satellites, ferrets, and improvements in listening posts as well as better processing are all predicted.

Seismic. The state of seismic technology and prospects for refinements were discussed extensively in chapter four and earlier in this chapter. Given large enough in-country networks of seismic detectors, cavity-decoupled explosions of less than a kiloton can be readily detected. Current research indicates that measurements at higher frequencies could move this limit much lower.

Information about improvements in monitoring capability five years hence is necessarily sketchy and speculative. Official information about this issue is classified. Available facts suggest that these capabilities will continue to improve. At this time, however, improvements in technology seem less important than (1) commitment by both countries to negotiate mutually satisfactory agreements and (2) cooperative measures of various sorts built into any agreements to facilitate verification.

Can Agreements Be Verified in the Future?

There is a temptation to say simply, probably yes! However, the answer to this question is not simple. Different observers have come up with different answers. One's answer depends heavily on whether one believes that (1) the verification-related complexities are insurmountable, and (2) current monitoring capabilities are inadequate for the challenge or, on the other hand, whether one believes (A) many possibilities exist for cooperative measures in new agreements, and (B) U.S. monitoring and verification capabilities are sufficient to meet the challenge.

Possible new agreements pose special problems for verification. While the technology for monitoring is likely to improve, weapons technologies are moving in directions that could make verification more difficult, i.e., small size, dual capability, mobility, and more widespread deployment.

There may be no way to achieve verification of the "coming generation of weapons" such as small anti-satellite weapons, as some critics argue. (If true, however, this raises the question, why don't the two countries agree not to deploy them?) It is probably true that verification will be even more challenging in the future. The weapons systems that have previously been limited by strategic arms control agreements have principally been large, single-purpose systems such as long-range ICBMs which, in retrospect, did not pose extreme problems of verification.

New steps in arms control may, for example, require agreements to limit the military use of space to such essential functions as communications, surveillance and reconnaissance, early warning, navigation, weather and geodesy. To verify agreements banning ASAT weapons, the signatories would have to establish new common understandings and deploy new space-based systems for monitoring of space activities. Such understandings would cover the use of space by all nations. They may cover such items as space mines, chaff, pre-notification of test activities, etc., as well as how ASAT agreements would be monitored.

The technologies used for verification have improved steadily, and further improvements can be expected. Some experts fear that, as weapons technologies advance, the gap between monitoring capabilities and verification requirements may be widening.

Agreements banning new weapons or the testing of new weapons technologies may be easier to verify than limits upon deployment. Furthermore, agreements that include restraints on testing of existing or new systems can ease some verification problems.

As the Carnegie report noted, progress in arms control will require more cooperation and greater use of cooperative measures to strengthen verification. These steps will require thorough planning, creative negotiation, clear treaty language, and the commitment to making nuclear arms agreements work.

Chapter 8

Concluding Observations

If we are trying to trick one another, why do we need a piece of paper?

U.S.S.R. General Secretary
Leonid Brezhnev
to U.S. President Richard Nixon
at the 1972 Moscow Summit

Verification involves a complex set of technical, institutional, and political factors. There is no simple, universally accepted, definition of what constitutes adequate or effective verification. The judgment of adequacy is highly subjective.

National Technical Means

The process of verification begins before a negotiation and continues as long as an agreement is in force. It involves monitoring and evaluation. Each nation's principal tool for monitoring is its national technical means. In the future, NTM could be augmented by various negotiated cooperative measures.

The exact capabilities of most of the national technical means are secret. From what we do know of them, their monitoring and detection capabilities are impressive. Photographic reconnaissance satellites can easily count individual ICBM silos and many weapons-related activities far smaller; radars can count individual warheads released from missiles undergoing tests; and seismic detectors, if deployed in in-country networks, are capable of detecting nuclear explosions of a kiloton or less. (Before the CTB negotiations were suspended in 1979, the negotiating countries made considerable progress toward agreement on deploying a network of seismic sensors in each country. Those deployed in one country would have been part of the other's NTM.) As impressive as these technologies may be, there is far more to verification than just their capability.

Each side's national technical means collect a large amount of information. An important part of the verification process consists of sifting through this information to determine what is significant, suspicious, or a possible violation.

While the national technical means are extensive, their coverage has limits. For example, clouds can interrupt photographic surveillance, and operational difficulties can shut down some systems for periods of time. However, verification of arms control agreements rarely, if ever, requires rapid response. NTM are deployed in ways that are redundant, complementary, and synergistic, so that confidence in the detection capability of the overall technical network is enhanced.

On-Site Inspection

Beginning in 1946, on-site inspection has been repeatedly proposed as a method for verification of nuclear arms control agreements. The Soviets have consistently rejected it on the grounds that it would be too intrusive, fearing that it would also lead to espionage in addition to verification. In recent years, they have shown more willingness to accept on-site inspections for verification of nuclear test bans. For example, such rights are incorporated in the unratified 1976 Peaceful Nuclear Explosions Treaty.

As surveillance technologies became more sophisticated, the extra information made available in some cases from on-site inspection might be of only marginal value. Conceivably, on-site inspections could provide false information, since modifications hiding actual operations could be made before an inspector arrived. Some people believe that to improve significantly upon the verification information available from NTM for current agreements, on-site inspections would have to be too intrusive for either the U.S. or the U.S.S.R. to accept.

While on-site inspection is not a panacea for verification and, in fact, would be informationally valuable in perhaps only a few kinds of agreements, its potential to operate if needed could have a deterrent benefit and substantially enhance mutual confidence. Some forms of on-site inspection make sense as part of the verification package for some kinds of arms control proposals such as nuclear test bans. For other kinds of agreements, where inspection would provide little additional verification information, insisting on such rights could be an unnecessary source of negotiating conflict.

On U.S.-Soviet Negotiation

Verification in the bilateral context is the product of mutual agreement by adversaries to allow one another to gain knowledge about what, in the absence of agreement, would often be closely protected. Gaining Soviet acceptance of many verification measures is not easy. The Soviet penchant for secrecy is well known. Whether their motive is to conceal strengths, weaknesses or both, the Soviets believe they have more to gain by preserving tight controls on information and access to their territory than by agreeing with the western notion that openness promotes stability and security.

Herbert York, head of the U.S. delegation on the Comprehensive Test Ban Negotiations from 1977 to 1980 noted in a 1983 **Scientific American** article on "Bilateral Negotiations and the Arms Race" that:

> (O)ne of the general problems which has persisted throughout the entire postwar period of bilateral negotiations is that the Americans always ask for more intrusive means of verification than the Russians are willing even to discuss, much less accept, and the Russians are always complaining that the Americans persist in trying to spy on them, to undermine their sovereignty and to otherwise interfere in their internal affairs. This problem will, I believe, continue into the indefinite future, and important elements of the American body politic will continue to harbor grave doubts about the adequacy of any conceivable verification system.

An even greater obstacle may be the Soviet belief that cooperative measures should not provide more information about Soviet military activities than is absolutely necessary to verify treaty obligations. Early in the SALT II negotiations, Moscow agreed for the first time to share with the U.S. official information on the numbers of its strategic weapons. This was data considered highly secret by the Soviet authorities. At that time, Soviet negotiator Vladimir S. Semenov reportedly told his American counterpart, Paul Warnke, that "you must realize you have just repealed 400 years of Russian history." While Semenov's exaggerated remark may have been intended to make the data exchange seem as if it were a more radical departure than perhaps it was, it illustrates the entrenched Soviet resistence to such information sharing. The United States will have to be persistent and resourceful in negotiating measures that can ensure access to treaty-related information needed for adequate verification.

There are differences in the ways that the two superpowers make treaties legally binding. A treaty negotiated by the United States must be approved by a two-thirds Senate vote before the President can certify ratification. This requirement contributes to the tension between the executive and legislative branches over arms control policy. In the ten years since 1974, three nuclear arms control treaties have been signed but not ratified by the U.S. In the U.S.S.R., by contrast, ratification of a negotiated treaty is a formality. Most Soviet internal political and military differences are resolved long before a treaty is signed and perhaps even before it is negotiated.

Not every nuclear arms control initiative may require a negotiated agreement or depend on verification. Joseph S. Nye, of the John F. Kennedy School of Government at Harvard University and former State Department official, recently observed that:

> It would be a tragedy if we interpret arms control so narrowly that the only steps we take would be those that are negotiable and verifiable. In some cases, it might be in our interest to take certain arms control steps unilaterally regardless of what the Soviets do. Withdrawal of battle-field nuclear weapons in Europe is a good example.

FIGURE 1. **The negotiators shaking hands.** (AP/Wide World Photos)

US.–SOVIET ARMS NEGOTIATIONS AND NEGOTIATORS

September 1985

Soviet Union	**United States**
Country Leaders	
General Secretary of the Communist Party	President
Mikhail Gorbachev	Ronald Reagan
Senior Advisors	
President Andrei A. Gromyko	Secretary of State George P. Shultz
Foreign Minister Eduard Shevardnadze	Secretary of Defense Caspar Weinberger
	National Security Advisor Robert C. McFarlane
	Arms Negotiations Advisors Paul Nitze Edward Rowny
	Director, Arms Control and Disarmament Agency Kenneth Adelman
Bilateral Negotiations and Negotiators	
Strategic Nuclear Arms Reductions	
Viktor Karpov (also overall head of the Soviet negotiating team)	John G. Tower
Defense and Space Arms Limitations	
Yuli Kvitsinsky	Max M. Kampelman (also overall head of the U.S. negotiating team)
Intermediate-Range Nuclear Arms Limitations	
Alexei Obukhov	Maynard W. Glitman

Alliance and Multilateral Negotiations

Mutual and Balanced Force Reductions (MBFR)

Valerian Mikhailov	Robert Blackiwell

Conference on Disarmament in Europe (CDE), Stockholm

Oleg Grinevsky	James Goodby

Conference on Disarmament (CD), Geneva

Victor Issraelyan	Donald Lowitz

See Appendix II for further explanation.

Risks of Noncompliance

Some risk is inherent in almost any approach to verification because information is usually incomplete. The level of uncertainty can be assessed and decisions made about the level of risk that is acceptable. It is important, however, not that verification be absolute but that it be adequate to maintain or enhance each party's security. In addition, the risks of non-compliance must be weighed against the risks of not having a treaty at all.

In the United States, arms control and national security issues are highly visible and political issues. An arms control negotiation often represents a major presidential initiative. While there have been shifts in emphasis of different administrations from 1968 through 1980, all had the same general approach to strategic nuclear arms limitations and verification. The SALT process spanning the Nixon, Ford and Carter administrations was remarkably continuous and consistent. A significant break seemingly occurred in 1980 with the Reagan Administration which appeared to view previous arms control approaches and verification standards as inadequate.

That a shift in the Reagan Administration's views on verification may have occurred was detected during a White House Press conference on January 9, 1985 following the Geneva talks between Secretary of State George Shultz and Soviet Foreign Minister Andrei Gromyko. In response to a question about whether the U.S. can adequately verify arms control agreements with the Soviet Union, President Reagan replied in part:

> We know also that absolute verification is impossible. But verification to the extent possible is going to be a very necessary feature in our negotiations.

The acceptance of less than pefect verification and the apparent willingness to work within some limits of verification may signal more flexibility in the Reagan Administration's approach to verification.

Certain safeguards or means of cross-checking the results of monitoring are in the verification process. These include the overall intelligence capabilities such as ongoing monitoring of new weapons development and cooperative measures agreed during the drafting of the treaty. Provisions for continuing consultations after a treaty is signed are an essential component of the overall verification and compliance process.

Possible Violations: Response and Compliance Policy

Not all activities that appear to be inconsistent with a treaty are necessarily violations, and not all violations are equally grave in their consequences. Many verification issues are ambiguous. The sources of the ambiguity include incomplete information, imprecise treaty language, and the implications of actions not forseen when a treaty was signed.

Appropriate channels must be used for clarification of suspected violations. Private channels of communication were used during the 1970s; increasingly, in the 1980s, public channels have been used.

Raising a suspected arms control violation in public, rather than through established private channels, reduces the subsequent options for diplomatic solutions and political response. After the President personally makes an accusation, a position is taken and national pride is at stake. Thus, there is not only little flexibility but also no further means of increasing diplomatic pressure, and positions tend to become rigid.

The extensive record of compliance questions raised privately in the SCC, as examined in chapter five, shows that it is possible to resolve most issues in such a forum. In some instances, merely raising a concern in such a forum about some questionable action was sufficient to halt it. These kinds of results are, after all, the purpose of verification: to ensure that agreements continue to work. Robert Buchheim, U.S. Commissioner at the SCC from 1977-1980 has noted that:

> The initial requirement of (the work of the SCC) is to raise potential problems before they get out of hand and become causes for undesired reconsideration of an entire agreement. Lying in the grass and building a comprehensive case for eventually jumping up and shouting "gotcha" might be fun for some of the grass-dwellers but it would not be a sensible way to sustain a desired agreement.

Final Observations

There is no special mystique to the verification process. Some parts of the process must be kept secret, but the principles described in this book apply to most verification questions.

Intelligence gathering and monitoring of new weapons developments will continue to be necessary to assure U.S. national security whether or not the information gathered is used for monitoring of specific provisions of arms control agreements or new arms control treaties are negotiated in the future.

Questions will continue to arise about whether some particular approach to limiting a weapon system can be verified. However, when combined with carefully drafted arms control proposals, including cooperation among countries to facilitate required monitoring, verification capabilities do not appear to be a limiting factor in achieving new and significant nuclear arms control and weapons reductions agreements.

Appendices

Appendices

I Text of the Anti-Ballistic Missile Treaty

Treaty Between the United States of America and the Union of Soviet Socialist Republics on the Limitation of Anti-Ballistic Missile Systems

Signed at Moscow May 26, 1972

The United States of America and the Union of Soviet Socialist Republics, hereinafter referred to as the Parties,

Proceeding from the premise that nuclear war would have devastating consequences for all mankind,

Considering that effective measures to limit anti-ballistic missile systems would be a substantial factor in curbing the race in strategic offensive arms and would lead to a decrease in the risk of outbreak of war involving nuclear weapons,

Proceeding from the premise that the limitation of anti-ballistic missile systems, as well as certain agreed measures with respect to the limitation of strategic offensive arms, would contribute to the creation of more favorable conditions for further negotiations on limiting strategic arms,

Mindful of their obligations under Article VI of the Treaty on the Non-Proliferation of Nuclear Weapons,

Declaring their intention to achieve at the earliest possible date the cessation of the nuclear arms race and to take effective measures toward reductions in strategic arms, nuclear disarmament, and general and complete disarmament,

Desiring to contribute to the relaxation of international tension and the strengthening of trust between States,

Have agreed as follows:

Article I

1. Each party undertakes to limit anti-ballistic missile (ABM) systems and to adopt other measures in accordance with the provisions of this Treaty.

2. Each Party undertakes not to deploy ABM systems for a defense of the territory of its country and not to provide a base for such a defense, and not to deploy ABM systems for defense of an individual region except as provided for in Article III of this Treaty.

Article II

1. For the purpose of this Treaty an ABM system is a system to counter strategic ballistic missiles or their elements in flight trajectory, currently consisting of:

(a) ABM interceptor missiles, which are interceptor missiles constructed and deployed for an ABM role, or of a type tested in an ABM mode;
(b) ABM launchers, which are launchers constructed and deployed for launching ABM interceptor missiles; and
(c) ABM radars, which are radars constructed and deployed for an ABM role, or of a type tested in an ABM mode.

2. The ABM system components listed in paragraph 1 of this Article include those which are:

(a) operational;
(b) under construction;
(c) undergoing testing;
(d) undergoing overhaul, repair or conversion; or
(e) mothballed.

Article III

Each Party undertakes not to deploy ABM systems or their components except that:

(a) within one ABM system deployment area having a radius of one hundred and fifty kilometers and centered on the Party's national capital, a Party may deploy: (1) no more than one hundred ABM launchers and no more than one hundred ABM interceptor missiles at launch sites, and (2) ABM radars within no more than six ABM radar complexes, the area of each complex being circular and having a diameter of no more than three kilometers; and
(b) within one ABM system deployment area having a radius of one hundred and fifty kilometers and containing ICBM silo launchers, a Party may deploy: (1) no more than one hundred ABM launchers and no more than one hundred ABM interceptor missiles at launch sites, (2) two large phased-array ABM radars comparable in potential to corresponding ABM radars operational or under construction on the date of signature of the Treaty in an ABM system deployment area containing ICBM silo launchers, and (3) no more than eighteen ABM radars each having a potential less than the potential of the smaller of the above-mentioned two large phased-array ABM radars.

Article IV

The limitations provided for in Article III shall not apply to ABM systems or their components used for development or testing, and located within current or additionally agreed test ranges. Each Party may have no more than a total of fifteen ABM launchers at test ranges.

Article V

1. Each Party undertakes not to develop, test, or deploy ABM systems or components which are sea-based, air-based, space-based, or mobile land-based.
2. Each Party undertakes not to develop, test, or deploy ABM launchers for launching more than one ABM interceptor missile at a time from each launcher, nor to modify deployed launchers to provide them with such a capability, nor to develop, test, or deploy automatic or semi-automatic or other similar systems for rapid reload of ABM launchers.

Article VI

To enhance assurance of the effectiveness of the limitations on ABM systems and their components provided by this Treaty, each Party undertakes:

(a) not to give missiles, launchers, or radars, other than ABM interceptor missiles, ABM launchers, or ABM radars, capabilities to counter strategic ballistic missiles or their elements in flight trajectory, and not to test them in an ABM mode; and

(b) not to deploy in the future radars for early warning of strategic ballistic missile attack except at locations along the periphery of its national territory and oriented outward.

Article VII

Subject to the provisions of this Treaty, modernization and replacement of ABM systems or their components may be carried out.

Article VIII

ABM systems or their components in excess of the numbers or outside the areas specified in this Treaty, as well as ABM systems or their components prohibited by this Treaty, shall be destroyed or dismantled under agreed procedures within the shortest possible agreed period of time.

Article IX

To assure the viability and effectiveness of this Treaty, each Party undertakes not to transfer to other States, and not to deploy outside its national territory, ABM systems or their components limited by this Treaty.

Article X

Each Party undertakes not to assume any international obligations which would conflict with this Treaty.

Article XI

The Parties undertake to continue active negotiations for limitations on strategic offensive arms.

Article XII

1. For the purpose of providing assurance of compliance with the provisions of this Treaty, each Party shall use national technical means of verification at its disposal in a manner consistent with generally recognized principles of international law.

2. Each Party undertakes not to interfere with the national technical means of verification of the other Party operating in accordance with paragraph 1 of this Article.

3. Each Party undertakes not to use deliberate concealment measures which impede verification by national technical means of compliance with the provisions of this Treaty. This obligation shall not require changes in current construction, assembly, conversion, or overhaul practices.

Article XIII

1. To promote the objectives and implementation of the provisions of this Treaty, the Parties shall establish promptly a Standing Consultative Commission, within the framework of which they will:

(a) consider questions concerning compliance with the obligations assumed and related situations which may be considered ambiguous;
(b) provide on a voluntary basis such information as either Party considers necessary to assure confidence in compliance with the obligations assumed;
(c) consider questions involving unintended interference with national technical means of verification;
(d) consider possible changes in the strategic situation which have a bearing on the provisions of this Treaty;
(e) agree upon procedures and dates for destruction or dismantling of ABM systems or their components in cases provided for by the provisions of this Treaty;
(f) consider, as appropriate, possible proposals for further increasing the viability of this Treaty, including proposals for amendments in accordance with the provisions of this Treaty;
(g) consider, as appropriate, proposals for further measures aimed at limiting strategic arms.

2. The Parties through consultation shall establish, and may amend as appropriate, Regulations for the Standing Consultative Commission governing procedures, composition and other relevant matters.

Article XIV

1. Each Party may propose amendments to this Treaty. Agreed amendments shall enter into force in accordance with the procedures governing the entry into force of this Treaty.
2. Five years after entry into force of this Treaty, and at five-year intervals thereafter, the Parties shall together conduct a review of this Treaty.

Article XV

1. This Treaty shall be of unlimited duration.
2. Each Party shall, in exercising its national sovereignty, have the right to withdraw from this Treaty if it decides that extraordinary events related to the subject matter of this Treaty have jeopardized its supreme interests. It shall give notice of its decision to the other Party six months prior to withdrawal from the Treaty. Such notice shall include a statement of the extraordinary events the notifying Party regards as having jeopardized its supreme interests.

Article XVI

1. This Treaty shall be subject to ratification in accordance with the constitutional procedures of each Party. The Treaty shall enter into force on the day of the exchange of instruments of ratification.
2. This Treaty shall be registered pursuant to Article 102 of the Charter of the United Nations.

DONE at Moscow on May 26, 1972, in two copies, each in the English and Russian languages, both texts being equally authentic.

FOR THE UNITED STATES OF AMERICA

President of the United States of America

FOR THE UNION OF SOVIET SOCIALIST REPUBLICS

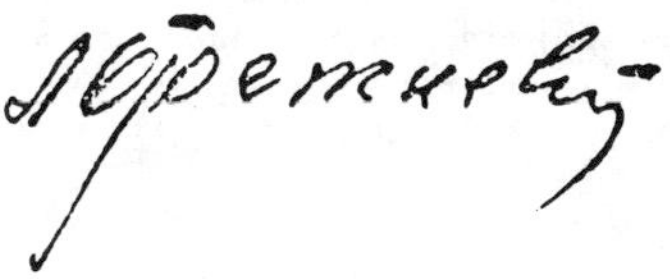

General Secretary of the Central Committee of the CPSU

SALT: AGREED INTERPRETATIONS AND UNILATERAL STATEMENTS

1. AGREED INTERPRETATIONS

(a) Initialed Statements. — The texts of the statements set out below were agreed upon and initialed by the Heads of the Delegations on May 26, 1972.

ABM TREATY

[A]

The Parties understand that, in addition to the ABM radars which may be deployed in accordance with subparagraph (a) of Article III of the Treaty, those non-phased-array ABM radars operational on the date of signature of the Treaty within the ABM system deployment area for defense of the national capital may be retained.

[B]

The Parties understand that the potential (the product of mean emitted power in watts and antenna area in square meters) of the smaller of the two large phased-array ABM radars referred to in subparagraph (b) of Article III of the Treaty is considered for purposes of the Treaty to be three million.

[C]

The Parties understand that the center of the ABM system deployment area centered on the national capital and the center of the ABM system deployment area containing ICBM silo launchers for each Party shall be separated by no less than thirteen hundred kilometers.

[D]

The Parties agree not to deploy phased-array radars having a potential (the product of mean emitted power in watts and antenna area in square meters) exceeding three million, except as provided for in Articles III, IV and VI of the Treaty, or except for the purposes of tracking objects in outer space or for use as national technical means of verification.

[E]

In order to insure fulfillment of the obligation not to deploy ABM systems and their components except as provided in Article III of the Treaty, the Parties agree that in the event ABM systems based on other physical principles and including components capable of substituting for ABM interceptor missiles, ABM launchers, or ABM radars are created in the future, specific limitations on such systems and their components would be subject to discussion in accordance with Article XIII and agreement in accordance with Article XIV of the Treaty.

[F]

The Parties understand that Article V of the Treaty includes obligations not to develop, test or deploy ABM interceptor missiles for the delivery by each ABM interceptor missile of more than one independently guided warhead.

[G]

The Parties understand that Article IX of the Treaty includes the obligation of the US and the USSR not to provide to other States technical descriptions or blueprints specially worked out for the construction of ABM systems and their components limited by the Treaty.

INTERIM AGREEMENT

[H]

The parties understand that land-based ICBM launchers referred to in the Interim Agreement are understood to be launchers for strategic ballistic missiles capable of ranges in excess of the shortest distance between the northeastern border of the continental U.S. and the northwestern border of the continental USSR.

[I]

The Parties understand that fixed land-based ICBM launchers under active construction as of the date of signature of the Interim Agreement may be completed.

[J]

The Parties understand that in the process of modernization and replacement the dimensions of land-based ICBM silo launchers will not be significantly increased.

[K]

The Parties understand that dismantling or destruction of ICBM launchers of older types deployed prior to 1964 and ballistic missile launchers on older submarines being replaced by new SLBM launchers on modern submarines will be initiated at the time of the beginning of sea trials of a replacement submarine, and will be completed in the shortest possible agreed period of time. Such dismantling or destruction, and timely notification thereof, will be accomplished under procedures to be agreed in the Standing Consultative Commission.

[L]

The Parties understand that during the period of the Interim Agreement there shall be no significant increase in the number of ICBM or SLBM test and training launchers, or in the number of such launchers for modern land-based heavy ICBMs. The Parties further understand that construction or conversion of ICBM launchers at test ranges shall be undertaken only for purposes of testing and training.

(b) Common Understandings. — Common understanding of the Parties on the following matters was reached during the negotiations:

A. INCREASE IN ICBM SILO DIMENSIONS

Ambassador Smith made the following statement on May 26, 1972:

> The Parties agree that the term "significantly increased" means that an increase will not be greater than 10-15 percent of the present dimensions of land-based ICBM silo launchers.

Minister Semenov replied that this statement corresponded to the Soviet understanding.

B. LOCATION OF ICBM DEFENSES

The U.S. Delegation made the following statement on May 26, 1972:

> Article III of the ABM Treaty provides for each side one ABM system deployment area centered on its national capital and one ABM system deployment area containing ICBM silo launchers. The two sides have registered agreement on the following statement: "The Parties understand that the center of the ABM system deployment area centered on the national capital and the center of the ABM system deployment area containing ICBM silo launchers for each Party shall be separated by no less than thirteen hundred kilometers." In this connection, the U.S. side notes that its ABM system deployment area for defense of ICBM silo launchers, located west of the Mississippi River, will be centered in the Grand Forks ICBM silo launcher deployment area. (See Initialed Statement [C].)

C. ABM TEST RANGES

The U.S. Delegation made the following statement on April 26, 1972:

> Article IV of the ABM Treaty provides that "the limitations provided for in Article III shall not apply to ABM systems or their components used for development or testing, and located within current or additionally agreed test ranges." We believe it would be useful to assure that there is no misunderstanding as to current ABM test ranges. It is our understanding that ABM test ranges encompass the area within which ABM components are located for test purposes. The current U.S. ABM test ranges are at White Sands, New Mexico, and at Kwajalein Atoll, and the current Soviet ABM test range is near Sary Shagan in Kazakhstan. We consider that non-phased array radars of types used for range safety or instrumentation purposes may be located outside of ABM test ranges. We interpret the reference in Article IV to "additionally agreed test ranges" to mean that ABM components will not be located at any other test ranges without prior agreement between our Governments that there will be such additional ABM test ranges.

On May 5, 1972, the Soviet Delegation stated that there was a common understanding on what ABM test ranges were, that the use of the types of non-ABM radars for range safety or instrumentation was not limited under the Treaty, that the reference in Article IV to "additionally agreed" test ranges was sufficiently clear, and that national means permitted identifying current test ranges.

D. MOBILE ABM SYSTEMS

On January 28, 1972, the U.S. Delegation made the following statement:

> Article V(1) of the Joint Draft Text of the ABM Treaty includes an undertaking not to develop, test, or deploy mobile land-based ABM systems and their components. On May 5, 1971, the U.S. side indicated that, in its view, a prohibition on deployment of mobile ABM systems and components would rule out the deployment of ABM launchers and radars which were not permanent fixed types. At that time, we asked for the Soviet view of this interpretation. Does the Soviet side agree with the U.S. side's interpretation put forward on May 5, 1971?

On April 13, 1972, the Soviet Delegation said there is a general common understanding on this matter.

E. STANDING CONSULTATIVE COMMISSION

Ambassador Smith made the following statement on May 22, 1972:

> The United States proposes that the sides agree that, with regard to initial implementation of the ABM Treaty's Article XIII on the Standing Consultative Commission (SCC) and of the consultation Articles to the Interim Agreement on offensive arms and the Accidents Agreement,* agreement establishing the SCC will be worked out early in the follow-on SALT negotiations; until that is completed, the following arrangements will prevail: when SALT is in session, any consultation desired by either side under these Articles can be carried out by the two SALT Delegations; when SALT is not in session, *ad hoc* arrangements for any desired consultations under these Articles may be made through diplomatic channels.

Minister Semenov replied that, on an *ad referendum* basis, he could agree that the U.S. statement corresponded to the Soviet understanding.

F. STANDSTILL

On May 6, 1972, Minister Semenov made the following statement:

> In an effort to accommodate the wishes of the U.S. side, the Soviet Delegation is prepared to proceed on the basis that the two sides will in fact observe the obligations of both the Interim Agreement and the ABM Treaty beginning from the date of these two documents.

In reply, the U.S. Delegation made the following statement on May 20, 1972:

> The U.S. agrees in principle with the Soviet statement made on May 6 concerning observance of obligations beginning from date of signature but we would like to make clear our understanding that this means that, pending ratification and acceptance, neither side would take any action prohibited by the agreements after they

*See Article 7 of Agreement to Reduce the Risk of Outbreak of Nuclear War Between the United States of America and the Union of Soviet Socialist Republics, signed Sept. 30, 1971.

had entered into force. This understanding would continue to apply in the absence of notification by either signatory of its intention not to proceed with ratification or approval.

The Soviet Delegation indicated agreement with the U.S. statement.

2. UNILATERAL STATEMENTS

(a) The following noteworthy unilateral statements were made during the negotiations by the United States Delegation:

A. WITHDRAWAL FROM THE ABM TREATY

On May 9, 1972, Ambassador Smith made the following statement:

The U.S. Delegation has stressed the importance the U.S. Government attaches to achieving agreement on more complete limitations on strategic offensive arms, following agreement on an ABM Treaty and on an Interim Agreement on certain measures with respect to the limitation of strategic offensive arms. The U.S. Delegation believes that an objective of the follow-on negotiations should be to constrain and reduce on a long-term basis threats to the survivability of our respective strategic retaliatory forces. The USSR Delegation has also indicated that the objectives of SALT would remain unfulfilled without the achievement of an agreement providing for more complete limitations on strategic offensive arms. Both sides recognize that the initial agreements would be steps toward the achievement of more complete limitations on strategic arms. If an agreement providing for more complete strategic offensive arms limitations were not achieved within five years, U.S. supreme interests could be jeopardized. Should that occur, it would constitute a basis for withdrawal from the ABM Treaty. The U.S. does not wish to see such a situation occur, nor do we believe that the USSR does. It is because we wish to prevent such a situation that we emphasize the importance the U.S. Government attaches to achievement of more complete limitations on strategic offensive arms. The U.S. Executive will inform the Congress, in connection with Congressional consideration of the ABM Treaty and the Interim Agreement, of this statement of the U.S. position.

B. LAND-MOBILE ICBM LAUNCHERS

The U.S. Delegation made the following statement on May 20, 1972:

In connection with the important subject of land-mobile ICBM launchers, in the interest of concluding the Interim Agreement the U.S. Delegation now withdraws its proposal that Article I or an agreed statement explicitly prohibit the deployment of mobile land-based ICBM launchers. I have been instructed to inform you that, while agreeing to defer the question of limitation of operational land-mobile ICBM launchers to the subsequent negotiations on more complete limitations on strategic offensive arms, the U.S. would consider the deployment of operational land-mobile ICBM launchers during the period of the Interim Agreement as inconsistent with the objectives of that Agreement.

C. COVERED FACILITIES

The U.S. Delegation made the following statement on May 26, 1972:

I wish to emphasize the importance that the United States attaches to the provisions of Article V, including in particular their application to fitting out or berthing submarines.

D. "HEAVY" ICBM'S

The U.S. Delegation made the following statement on May 26, 1972:

The U.S. Delegation regrets that the Soviet Delegation has not been willing to agree on a common definition of a heavy missile. Under these circumstances, the U.S. Delegation believes it necessary to state the following: The United States would consider any ICBM having a volume significantly greater than that of the largest light ICBM now operational on either side to be a heavy ICBM. The U.S. proceeds on the premise that the Soviet side will give due account to this consideration.

E. TESTED IN ABM MODE

On April 7, 1972, the U.S. Delegation made the following statement:

Article II of the Joint Text Draft uses the term "tested in an ABM mode," in defining ABM components, and Article VI includes certain obligations concerning such testing. We believe that the sides should have a common understanding of this phrase. First, we would note that the testing provisions of the ABM Treaty are intended to apply to testing which occurs after the date of signature of the Treaty, and not to any testing which may have occurred in the past. Next, we would amplify the remarks we have made on this subject during the previous Helsinki phase by setting forth the objectives which govern the U.S. view on the subject, namely, while prohibiting testing of non-ABM components for ABM purposes: not to prevent testing of ABM components, and not to prevent testing of non-ABM components for non-ABM purposes. To clarify our interpretation of "tested in an ABM mode," we note that we would consider a launcher, missile or radar to be "tested in an ABM mode" if, for example, any of the following events occur: (1) a launcher is used to launch an ABM interceptor missile, (2) an interceptor missile is flight tested against a target vehicle which has a flight trajectory with characteristics of a strategic ballistic missile flight trajectory, or is flight tested in conjunction with the test of an ABM interceptor missile or an ABM radar at the same test range, or is flight tested to an altitude inconsistent with interception of targets against which air defenses are deployed, (3) a radar makes measurements on a cooperative target vehicle of the kind referred to in item (2) above during the reentry portion of its trajectory or makes measurements in conjunction with the test of an ABM interceptor missile or an ABM radar at the same test range. Radars used for purposes such as range safety or instrumentation would be exempt from application of these criteria.

F. NO-TRANSFER ARTICLE OF ABM TREATY

On April 18, 1972, the U.S. Delegation made the following statement:

In regard to this Article [IX], I have a brief and I believe self-explanatory statement to make. The U.S. side wishes to make clear that the provisions of this Article do not set a precedent for whatever provision may be considered for a Treaty on Limiting Strategic Offensive Arms. The question of transfer of strategic offensive arms is a far more complex issue, which may require a different solution.

G. NO INCREASE IN DEFENSE OF EARLY WARNING RADARS

On July 28, 1970, the U.S. Delegation made the following statement:

> Since Hen House radars [Soviet ballistic missile early warning radars] can detect and track ballistic missile warheads at great distances, they have a significant ABM potential. Accordingly, the U.S. would regard any increase in the defenses of such radars by surface-to-air missiles as inconsistent with an agreement.

* * * * * * *

(b) The following noteworthy unilateral statement was made by the Delegation of the U.S.S.R. and is shown here with the U.S. reply:

On May 17, 1972, Minister Semenov made the following unilateral "Statement of the Soviet Side":

> Taking into account that modern ballistic missile submarines are presently in the possession of not only the U.S., but also of its Nato allies, the Soviet Union agrees that for the period of effectiveness of the Interim 'Freeze' Agreement the U.S. and its NATO allies have up to 50 such submarines with a total of up to 800 ballistic missile launchers thereon (including 41 U.S. submarines with 656 ballistic missile launchers). However, if during the period of effectiveness of the Agreement U.S. allies in NATO should increase the number of their modern submarines to exceed the numbers of submarines they would have operational or under construction on the date of signature of the Agreement, the Soviet Union will have the right to a corresponding increase in the number of its submarines. In the opinion of the Soviet side, the solution of the question of modern ballistic missile submarines provided for in the Interim Agreement only partially compensates for the strategic imbalance in the deployment of the nuclear-powered missile submarines of the USSR and the U.S. Therefore, the Soviet side believes that this whole question, and above all the question of liquidating the American missile submarine bases outside the U.S., will be appropriately resolved in the course of follow-on negotiations.

On May 24, Ambassador Smith made the following reply to Minister Semenov:

> The United States side has studied the statement made by the Soviet side of May 17 concerning compensation for submarine basing and SLBM submarines belonging to third countries. The United States does not accept the validity of the considerations in that statement.

On May 26 Minister Semenov repeated the unilateral statement made on May 24. Ambassador Smith also repeated the U.S. rejection on May 26.

Protocol to the Treaty Between the United States of America and the Union of Soviet Socialist Republics on the Limitation of Anti-Ballistic Missile Systems

Signed at Moscow July 3, 1974
Entered into force May 24, 1976

The United States of America and the Union of Soviet Socialist Republics, hereinafter referred to as the Parties,

Proceeding from the Basic Principles of Relations between the United States of America and the Union of Soviet Socialist Republics signed on May 29, 1972,

Desiring to further the objectives of the Treaty between the United States of America and the Union of Soviet Socialist Republics on the Limitation of Anti-Ballistic Missile Systems signed on May 26, 1972, hereinafter referred to as the Treaty,

Reaffirming their conviction that the adoption of further measures for the limitation of strategic arms would contribute to strengthening international peace and security,

Proceeding from the premise that further limitation of anti-ballistic missile systems will create more favorable conditions for the completion of work on a permanent agreement on more complete measures for the limitation of strategic offensive arms,

Have agreed as follows:

Article I

1. Each Party shall be limited at any one time to a single area out of the two provided in Article III of the Treaty for deployment of anti-ballistic missile (ABM) systems or their components and accordingly shall not exercise its right to deploy an ABM system or its components in the second of the two ABM system deployment areas permitted by Article III of the Treaty, except as an exchange of one permitted area for the other in accordance with Article II of this Protocol.

2. Accordingly, except as permitted by Article II of this Protocol: the United States of America shall not deploy an ABM system or its components in the area centered on its capital, as permitted by Article III(a) of the Treaty, and the Soviet Union shall not deploy an ABM system or its components in the deployment area of intercontinental ballistic missile (ICBM) silo launchers permitted by Article III(b) of the Treaty.

Article II

1. Each Party shall have the right to dismantle or destroy its ABM system and the components thereof in the area where they are presently deployed and to deploy an ABM system or its components in the alternative area permitted by Article III of the Treaty, provided that prior to initiation of construction, notification is given in accord with the procedure agreed to by the Standing Consultative Commission, during the year beginning October 3, 1977, and ending October 2, 1978, or during any year which commences at five year intervals thereafter, those being the years for periodic review of the Treaty, as provided in Article XIV of the Treaty. This right may be exercised only once.

2. Accordingly, in the event of such notice, the United States would have the right to dismantle or destroy the ABM system and its components in the deployment area of ICBM silo launchers and to deploy an ABM system or its components in an area centered on its capital, as permitted by Article III(a) of the Treaty, and the Soviet Union would have the right to dismantle or destroy the ABM system and its components in the area centered on its capital and to deploy an ABM system or its components in an area containing ICBM silo launchers, as permitted by Article III(b) of the Treaty.

3. Dismantling or destruction and deployment of ABM systems or their components and the notification thereof shall be carried out in accordance with Article VIII of the ABM Treaty and procedures agreed to in the Standing Consultative Commission.

Article III

The rights and obligations established by the Treaty remain in force and shall be complied with by the Parties except to the extent modified by this Protocol. In particular, the deployment of an ABM system or its components within the area selected shall remain limited by the levels and other requirements established by the Treaty.

Article IV

This Protocol shall be subject to ratification in accordance with the constitutional procedures of each Party. It shall enter into force on the day of the exchange of instruments of ratification and shall thereafter be considered an integral part of the Treaty.

Done at Moscow on July 3, 1974, in duplicate, in the English and Russian languages, both texts being equally authentic.

For the United States of America:

RICHARD NIXON

President of the United States of America

For the Union of Soviet Socialist Republics:

L. I. BREZHNEV

General Secretary of the Central Committee of the CPSU

II Some Strategic Nuclear Arms Control Treaties and Negotiations, 1963-1985

I. Major Nuclear Arms Control Agreements

Weapons Systems

SALT I – The first set of strategic arms talks between the U.S. and the U.S.S.R. Commencing in 1969, the discussions lasted until 1972 and resulted in two ratified agreements: the Interim Agreement on Strategic Offensive Arms and the Anti-Ballistic Missile (ABM) Treaty. Both of these agreements stipulated that verification was to be accomplished by national technical means.

The Interim Agreement on Strategic Offensive Arms – This agreement halted construction of new ICBM silos and placed ceilings on other strategic weapon launchers for five years. It was not a complete freeze because both the U.S. and the U.S.S.R. were permitted to expand their sea-based missile forces as long as they dismantled an equal number of old land- or sea-based missile launchers. The agreement did not limit the number of warheads on strategic weapons. It did, however, serve as a restraint on the build up of offensive weapons during the SALT II negotiations (at the expiration of the agreement in 1977, both sides stated they did not plan to take action inconsistant with the agreement pending the conclusion of SALT II). The Interim Agreement was signed and ratified in 1972.

The Anti-Ballistic Missile (ABM) Treaty – This Treaty was the result of SALT I's emphasis on the need to limit strategic defensive weapons systems. Both nations agreed to reduce their ABM deployment to two sites (subsequently reduced to one by the 1974 ABM Protocol) and to severely limit quantitative and qualitative improvements of ABM systems. Though research and development for new ABM systems, subject to specific constraints, were permitted, the development, testing and deployment of sea-based, air-based, space-based, and mobile land-based ABM systems and components were prohibited. The agreement also provided the framework for the Standing Consultative Commission (SCC). The ABM Treaty is reviewed by the participants every five years. Signed and ratified in 1972, it has remained unamended.

SALT II – In line with the Interim Agreement of SALT I these talks were directed towards a comprehensive agreement on strategic offensive weapons. Beginning in 1972, negotiations were unproductive until a breakthrough at the Vladivostok meeting in 1974. The final agreement, which was signed in 1979, set limits on the number of strategic offensive missiles, warheads, launchers and delivery vehicles, as well as constraining the deployment of new strategic offensive arms. Verification of the Treaty is through NTM. The Treaty, which was to last through 1985, was sent to the Senate for advice and consent in 1979, but was placed on hold after the Soviet invasion of Afghanistan. It remains unratified, and each side has declared that it will adhere to the principles and restrictions of the Treaty as long as the other does.

Nuclear Testing

Limited Test Ban Treaty (LTBT) – This Treaty prohibits any nuclear testing in the atmosphere, outer space or underwater. Underground testing is allowed as long as the radioactive debris from the test does not escape the territorial limits of the nation conducting the test. The agreement is of unlimited duration and open to all states. It also includes provisions for amendment of withdrawal. Compliance with the Treaty is monitored by national technical means. The Treaty was ratified by the U.S. in 1963.

Threshold Test Ban Treaty (TTBT) – This agreement limited the yield of underground nuclear weapon tests to 150 kilotons and also designated specific sites for the tests. It was signed in 1974 by the U.S., U.S.S.R. and U.K. All parties agreed to exchange detailed technical data such as geological and geographic information about the explosions. Verification was to be accomplished through national technical means, particularly seismic detection. The transmission of the TTBT (which has a five-year duration) to the Senate for advice and consent was held in abeyance until 1976 when the companion treaty on underground nuclear explosions for peaceful purposes had been successfully negotiated in accordance with Article III of the TTBT. The Treaty is unratified.

Peaceful Nuclear Explosions Treaty (PNET) – This Treaty, which resulted from Article III of TTBT, governs all peaceful nuclear explosions detonated outside the weapons test sites specified under TTBT. The agreement limits single explosions to a yield of 150 kt or less, and group tests to yields under 1,500 kt. Within the group test each individual explosion may not exceed the 150 kt yield maximum. Verification of the Treaty includes NTM and on-site access to explosion sites. The Treaty has a five-year duration and includes a provision that restricts withdrawal from the PNET while the TTBT remains in force. It was signed in 1976, the same year it was submitted to the U.S. Senate for advice and consent. It is as yet unratified.

Nonproliferation

Outer Space Treaty – This Treaty prohibits placing nuclear and other weapons of mass destruction in orbit around the earth, on the moon or any other celestial body, or stationing them in space. It also limits the use of the moon and other celestial bodies exclusively to peaceful purposes and expressly prohibits their use for establishing military bases, installations or fortifications, testing weapons of any kind, or conducting military maneuvers. Verification is carried out by space tracking systems. The Treaty was signed by the U.S., the U.S.S.R., and 87 other countries. It was ratified by the U.S. in 1967.

Nonproliferation Treaty (NPT) – This multilateral Treaty prohibits the transfer of nuclear weapons to non-nuclear weapons countries by countries that possess nuclear weapons. It also prohibits the acquisition of nuclear weapons by non-nuclear weapons countries that have signed the Treaty. As of 1985, 136 countries have signed the NPT, including the U.S., U.K., and the U.S.S.R. The International Atomic Energy Agency (IAEA) plays an important role in nuclear material accountancy, containment and surveillance associated with this Treaty. The Treaty was signed by the U.S. in 1968 and ratified in 1969.

II. Suspended Nuclear Arms Control Negotiations, 1980-1984

Comprehensive Test Ban Treaty (CTBT) – This proposed agreement would prohibit all nuclear weapons testing. Since the LTBT outlaws all but underground testing, the problems of verification of a CTB primarily concern the degree of accuracy of national techical means in detecting underground nuclear explosions of very small yields. The treaty has been debated internationally for twenty years, but negotiations have been suspended since 1980.

Strategic Arms Reduction Talks – Arms control talks, begun by the Reagan Administration, that emphasized strategic arms reduction, not limitation. Negotiations were suspended in December 1983 after the NATO INF deployment began.

Intermediate-Range Nuclear Force (INF) Talks – Negotiations between the U.S. and the U.S.S.R. on limiting intermediate-range nuclear weapons. The talks were terminated in December 1983 when NATO began deploying Pershing II and cruise missiles.

Anti-Satellite (ASAT) Weapons Talks – Talks between the U.S. and U.S.S.R. that sought to eliminate ASAT weapons. Negotiations were suspended in 1979. In 1984, initiation of a new round of ASAT talks was discussed by the U.S. and Soviets.

III. Renewed Nuclear Arms Control Negotiations, 1985

Strategic Nuclear Arms – On January 8, 1985, the United States and Soviet Union agreed to resume negotiations beginning March 12, 1985, toward the goal of reducing the number and destructive power of the offensive strategic nuclear weapons possessed by both nations. A joint U.S.-Soviet statement calls for these talks to deal with "limiting and reducing nuclear arms" with the goal of "complete elimination of nuclear arms everywhere." The Soviet negotiator, Victor Karpov, was the head of the Soviet delegation to START, 1982-1983, and was chief Soviet negotiator in the final phase of SALT II. The American negotiator, John G. Tower, was a U.S. Senator (R-TX) and Chairman of the Senate Armed Services Committee from 1981 to 1984.

Defense and Space Arms – This is a new category of negotiations that will focus on the limitation of space- and land-based anti-ballistic missiles and anti-satellite weapons. The talks convened on March 12, 1985. A joint U.S.-Soviet statement established these negotiations "aimed at preventing an arms race in space." The Soviet negotiator, Yuli Kvitsinsky, was head of the Soviet delegation to INF talks, 1981-1985. The U.S. negotiator, Attorney Max M. Kampelman, headed the U.S. delegation to Madrid for the multilateral talks on Security and Cooperation in Europe from 1980 to 1983.

Intermediate-Range Nuclear Arms – The purpose of these negotiations, which resumed on March 12, 1985, is to seek elimination of, or reductions in the number of intermediate-range nuclear missiles in Europe. A joint U.S.-Soviet agreement called for intermediate-range weapons questions to be "resolved in their interrelationship" with space weapons and strategic nuclear arms questions. The Soviet negotiator, Alexei Obukhov, was deputy head of Soviet START delegation, 1982-1983. The U.S. negotiator, Maynard W. Glitman, was deputy head of the U.S. INF delegation, 1981-1983, and headed the U.S. delegation to Vienna negotiations on conventional force reductions.

IV. Alliance and Multilateral Negotiations

The mutual and balanced force reductions (MBFR) are negotiations between the NATO and Warsaw Pact countries (see MBFR in the Glossary). The Conference on Disarmament in Europe (CDE) takes place in Stockholm and is a multilateral negotiation involving 35 nations. It is part of the Conference on Security and Cooperation in Europe. The Conference on Disarmament (CD) takes place in Geneva and is a multilateral negotiation involving 40 nations. It is part of the UN.

III Glossary of Strategic Nuclear Arms Control Verification Terms and Concepts

A

ABM (Anti-Ballistic Missile) A defensive missile designed to intercept and destroy a strategic offensive missile or its reentry vehicle(s). Often used interchangeably with BMD (Ballistic Missile Defense), current ABM systems typically consist of (1) interceptor missiles of short or long range, (2) launchers for the interceptor missiles (either in above-ground cannisters or in below-ground silos), (3) radars for identifying and tracking targets which then guide the interceptors to them, and (4) support equipment. Deployment of ABM systems is limited by the ABM Treaty of 1972 and its 1974 Protocol to one site per side. The Soviet deployed system (known as Galosh) defends Moscow. The U.S. system (Safeguard), now deactivated, was located at Grand Forks, North Dakota. The consensus of experts is that ABM systems of the early 1970s would not have provided an effective defense. These ABM systems would have been ineffective for defense of cities, could be overwhelmed by large numbers of incoming warheads, and, if deployed widely, might further stimulate each country to greatly increase their deliverable warhead capability to overwhelm the ABM system deployed by the other. Both the U.S. and the U.S.S.R. are doing research on advanced ABM technologies, including space-based systems. (See also BMD, SDI)

ABM Treaty This 1972 Treaty, part of the SALT I agreements between the U.S. and the U.S.S.R., limits the deployment of anti-ballistic missile systems in several ways. Each country may deploy ABMs at only two sites (subsequently reduced to one site in the ABM Treaty's 1974 Protocol). Neither side may deploy more than 100 interceptors and 100 launchers at its site. Certain improvements are prohibited, most importantly the development, testing or deployment of sea-, air-, or space-based ABM systems and their technology. Mobile, land-based ABM systems are also banned as are ABM systems using MIRVed warheads. The agreement is of unlimited duration and subject to review every five years. The Treaty also provides for the creation of the Standing Consultative Commission (SCC). (See also ABM, SCC)

ACDA (See Arms Control and Disarmament Agency)

Acoustic Detection A technique used to detect and identify nuclear explosions by the detection of sound waves associated with the detonation. It is used in conjunction with seismic detection to verify compliance with the test ban treaties. (See also Seismology, Seismic Coupling)

Adaptive Optics A system capable of measuring and compensating for atmospheric phenomena that lie in the optical path and degrade the performance of imaging systems. The purpose is to allow a better resolved image of the target. The atmospheric phenomena, known technically as wavefront phase error, include haze and thermal variations. These cause twinkling and shimmering in photos without the adaptive optic process. Adaptive optics have three main components: a wavefront sensor, a wavefront processor and a deformable or flexible mirror. They can be used in ground-based, airborne and satellite observation systems.

AEDS (See Atomic Energy Detection System)

Aerodynamic Missile An air-breathing, unmanned missile that uses aerodynamic forces (lift, drag, and propulsion) to maintain its flight path. Thus, it is very different in operation from a ballistic missile. Examples are air-, sea-, and ground-launched cruise missiles. (See also ALCM, Ballistic Missile, Cruise Missile, GLCM, SLCM)

Agreed Data Base Information provided by the U.S. and U.S.S.R. during the SALT II negotiations about their respective weapons systems under discussion. Prior to that time the SALT process had previously relied only on U.S. data. In SALT II, each party's data base had to be accepted by the other party before it was incorporated into the agreed data base. Assuming ratification of SALT II, the information was to be updated twice yearly. This exchange would enhance verification by allowing each side to measure its monitoring capabilities through cross-checking of independent information. (See also SALT II)

Agreed Statements Clarifying statements in a treaty or executive agreement that reflect the joint views of the negotiating parties on an issue. Agreed statements are usually more specific elaboration of a general provision in an agreement, often more narrowly defined by common understandings which are very specific. (See also Common Understandings, Treaty)

Agreement Usually a formal, negotiated agreement between two or more nations. An arms control agreement may take any one of several forms: treaty, protocol, executive agreement, etc. (See also Executive Agreement, Negotiation, Protocol, Ratification Process, Treaty)

Air Defense Systems designed to destroy attacking aircraft or cruise missiles. These systems are distinct in performance and operation from ABM or BMD systems. Air defense systems usually consist of radar, interceptor aircraft and surface-to-air missiles (SAMs). Examples of older surface-to-air missiles include the U.S. Nike, Patriot and Hercules. More modern air-to-air missiles are mounted on interceptor jets.

Air-Launched Ballistic Missile (ALBM) Any ballistic missile launched from aircraft or lighter-than-air vehicles such as balloons or dirigibles. Although experimental ALBMs have been tested, neither the U.S. nor the U.S.S.R. currently have any deployed. The most recent U.S. test, in 1974, was in connection with a possible airborne basing mode for the MX ICBM. To test the method a Minuteman I ICBM was air-launched from a C-5A aircraft. (See also MX)

Air-Launched Cruise Missile (ALCM) An air-breathing aerodynamic missile designed to be launched from an aircraft. As with all cruise missiles, ALCM range is a function of payload, propulsion, and fuel volume and therefore can vary greatly. Range variance is typically between 300 km and several thousand kilometers. Newer generations of cruise missiles, such as ALCM-B or the Tomahawk, show a trend toward smaller size and increased performance. Under the provisions of SALT II, planes equipped to carry ALCMs must be distinguished by functionally related observable differences (FRODs). (See also Aerodynamic Missile, Cruise Missile, FRODs, GLCM, SLCM)

ALBM (See Air-Launched Ballistic Missile)

ALCM (See Air-Launched Cruise Missile)

Anti-Satellite Weapons (ASAT) These weapons are designed to destroy space-based satellites. As of early 1985, the U.S.S.R. has deployed ASAT weapons of limited capability and questionable effectiveness. The U.S. has not deployed a more advanced ASAT it has developed. Since many satellites are used for military communication and early warning of a missile attack, this disruption capability could destabilize the strategic balance and weaken the confidence of a superpower in its ability to adequately anticipate or deter a nuclear strike from the other side, or support a nuclear strike against the other side. (See also Soviet ASAT Weapon, U.S. ASAT Weapon)

Arms Control Any unilateral or multilateral action or process that is based on international agreement and that limits or regulates any aspect of the weapon systems and/or the armed forces of the involved parties. Aspects of weapon systems include: production, numbers, size, and performance characteristics, as well as logistics and other supporting activities. Arms control arrangements between two or more countries usually involve unilateral and cooperative means to verify compliance with the rules of the agreement. Where a country plans to take a unilateral arms control action deemed to be in its national interest, whether or not other nations follow, verification per se may be less important, and existing intelligence collection and assessment will provide information about other parties' actions. Where strategic military and important political aspects are involved, adequate or effective verification is essential and particular arms control arrangements are formulated by negotiators in such a way as to be verifiable. (See also Agreement, Cooperative Measures, NTM)

Arms Control and Disarmament Agency (ACDA) Created in 1961 by the Arms Control and Disarmament Act, it is the principal agency of the U.S. government responsible for arms control policy. Other agencies involved in shaping arms control policy and whose influence may even override that of ACDA are the Departments of State and Defense. The Agency's Bureau of Verification and Intelligence is responsible for assessments of verification, information pertaining to compliance, requirements for intelligence data and assessment of new verification methods. The ACDA Director is the chief advisor to the President and Secretary of State on arms control and disarmament policy. In addition to responsibilities for the executive direction and coordination of ACDA activities, Directors sometimes serve as the head of U.S. delegations at arms control negotiations. (See also National Security Council)

ASAT (See Anti-Satellite Weapons)

Atomic Energy Detection System (AEDS) A U.S. system, comprised of an array of acoustic, seismic and radioactivity monitors used to detect Soviet nuclear tests. The sensors are deployed at 23 stations around the world and ring the Soviet Union. The system was installed for intelligence purposes after World War II and detected the first Soviet nuclear test in 1949. (See also NTM)

B

B-1 A U.S. long-range supersonic bomber currently undergoing testing and not yet deployed. Its range is approximately 9,800 km or 6,000 miles. (See also Long-Range Bomber)

B-1B A modified version of the B-1 bomber not yet deployed. It would carry up to 30 nuclear bombs. Current plans call for 100 B-1B bombers to be produced. The first 15 are to be deployed in 1986. (See also B-1, Cruise Missile)

B-52 A U.S. intercontinental-range bomber. First introduced in the 1950s, several models, incorporating various modernizations, have been deployed. As of July, 1985, these include approximately 263 B-52 G/Hs, which typically carried four bombs and six to eight short-range attack missiles (SRAMs), and many of which are modified to carry ALCMs. These planes have ranges estimated between 5,300 and 10,000 miles in unrefueled flight. (See also Bear, FB-111A, Long-Range Bomber)

Backfire The NATO name for the Soviet variable-wing, subsonic TU-26 (or T-22M) bomber. This aircraft entered service in 1974. It is deployed with the Soviet Air Force and Navy and its missions include nuclear weapon delivery, conventional attack, anti-ship strikes, and reconnaissance. During the SALT II negotiations there was much debate as to whether the plane's unrefueled range classified it as an intercontinental or intermediate-range bomber. In the "Soviet Backfire Statement" given to President Carter by President Brezhnev on June 16, 1979, two days before the signing of SALT II, the Soviet leader stated that the Backfire was a medium-range bomber and that its radius of action would not be increased to allow it to strike U.S. targets. Brezhnev also stated that intercontinental range would not be given to the plane by other methods such as in-flight refueling. If the Backfire were refueled in flight, its range would include almost all of the U.S. In the Backfire Statement, the Soviets also agreed not to produce more than 30 of the TU-26 planes per year. In response, President Carter stated that he considered this to be an obligation assumed by the Soviets and binding under the Treaty. Recent intelligence reassessments significantly lower the estimates of the Backfire's unrefueled range to about 2,500 miles. Reportedly, the Backfire lacks the special probes needed for in-flight refueling, and the Soviet Union does not have enough aerial tankers to refuel this and other aircraft on very long-range missions. (See also Bear, Medium-Range Bomber, SALT II, Vladivostok Accord)

Backscatter That part of the radar signal that is reflected back from the object (such as an aircraft or ICBM) toward which it was originally transmitted. (See also Frontscatter, OTH Radar, Radar Cross Section)

Ballistic Missile An unmanned missile propelled into space by one or more rocket engines. Thrust is terminated at a predesignated time and/or position, after which the payload, including at least one reentry vehicle (RV), is released. The RVs travel through space following trajectories that are governed primarily by gravity, reentry and drag. Midcourse corrections and terminal guidance permit only minor modifications to the ballistic flight path. (See also ICBM, Launcher, Minuteman, MX, MaRV, MIRV)

Ballistic Missile Defense (BMD) A system, or measures, designed to intercept and destroy hostile ballistic missiles or their components (e.g., reentry vehicles). Typical equipment includes interceptor missiles, target acquisition, tracking, and guidance radars, and support vehicles and structures. (See also ABM, SDI)

Ballistic Missile Early Warning System (BMEWS) The system of radar used by the U.S. for detection and early warning of attack by enemy intercontinental weapons. Operational since 1962, BMEWS consists of large radars at three sites: Thule, Greenland; Clear, Alaska; and Fylingdales Moor, England. The system is undergoing modernization. The Soviet Union has a larger number of ballistic missile early warning radars, some older and some newer than those of the U.S.

Baruch Plan A U.S. proposal in June 1946 for an international authority to own and manage all nuclear materials. Named for Bernard Baruch, an advisor to President Truman, the proposal was based on the Acheson-Lilienthal Report which urged that atomic resources be placed under the ownership and control of an independent international authority.

Beam Weapons Weapons that employ directed-energy beams of either laser light, atomic or sub-atomic particles to destroy targets. (See also Laser, SDI)

Bear NATO name for the Soviet TU-95 intercontinental-range bomber. First deployed in 1956, approximately 100 Bears are now in service. Each has a range of about 8,000 km. (See also Backfire, Bison, Long-Range Bomber, B-52)

Big Bird This U.S. satellite photographs land and ocean objects. The film is reportedly processed on board and a television image is transmitted to earth. Big Bird also drops pods containing film to earth for direct processing. It operates at an altitude of 100 to 200 miles. (See also Close Look Satellite, KH-11, Search and Find Satellite)

Biological Warfare (BW) Use of living organisms, toxic biological products, and plant growth regulators to produce death, disease or incapacitation in man, animals, or plants. Use of BW agents is prohibited by the Geneva Protocol of 1925 and the Biological Weapons Convention of 1972. (See also Biological Weapons Convention of 1972)

Biological Weapons Convention of 1972 An agreement to ban the development, stockpiling, or acquisition of biological agents or toxins 'of types and in quantities that have no justification for prophylactic, protective, and other peaceful purposes.' It also bans biological weapons and means of their delivery. Agreement was reached in 1972 after three years of negotiation under the auspices of the United Nations; the convention has been signed by 111 countries. The U.S. signed in 1972 and ratified in 1974. Verification of the treaty provisions was known to be difficult. At the time of signing, however, the U.S. had already decided to forego its BW program and therefore thought that an agreement which placed limitations on all signatories even if they were not verifiable would be in the national security interest. The Convention culminated efforts begun after World War I to ban biological and chemical weapons. (See also Biological Warfare)

Bison NATO name for the Soviet M-4 intercontinental-range bomber. About 40 Bisons are currently deployed as bombers while others have been modified as air refueling tankers. Each has a range of about 6,000 km. (See also Bear)

BMD (See Ballistic Missile Defense)

BMEWS (See Ballistic Missile Early Warning System)

Breakout A sudden change in the military balance caused when one party to an arms control treaty quantitatively or qualitatively improves its forces by violating treaty provisions, either before being detected by the other treaty adherent(s) or after abrogating an arms limitation agreement. In general, the term is used to express the concern that either the U.S. or the U.S.S.R. could be surprised by a sudden advance in the nature or quantity of a strategic weapon system deployed by the other side.

Build-Down A nuclear arms reduction proposal, introduced in early 1983 by Senators William Cohen and Sam Nunn, and later incorporated into the U.S. START negotiating position, calling for the U.S. and Soviets each to eliminate two old warheads for each new MIRVed land-based warhead, three old warheads for every two new submarine-based missile warheads, and one old warhead for every new single-warhead land-based ICBM. Such a proposal appears to foster decreased dependence on MIRVed land-based ICBMs and increased dependence on submarine-based and single-warhead forces. It is not clear how it would work in practice. While the build-down could lead to a more stable superpower nuclear relationship, such a result is critically dependent on the details of particular missile replacement scenarios and may not be possible without also restricting weapons modernization. According to Senator Cohen, it provides for reductions with modernization. While proponents argue that build-down increases 'the survivability and reliability of deployed systems', that is not true in all cases. Domestic critics, including many freeze supporters, add that while some reductions would occur under the build-down, the nuclear arms race would nonetheless continue. Cutbacks in various weapons systems as would be prescribed in a build-down agreement could be readily verified. Monitoring would focus on destruction of launchers or silos and verifying replacement missiles would use the SALT II counting rule that the number of warheads assigned to a missile would be the maximum with which it was tested. (See also Freeze, INF, SALT II, START)

Bus Shorthand term for the Post-Boost Vehicle (PBV), the final stage of a Multiple Reentry Vehicle (MRV) missile payload. The bus carries the reentry vehicles (warheads and perhaps decoys) and consists of a guidance package, fuel, and thrust devices. The thrusters enable the bus to maneuver in space. As it maneuvers, the bus sequentially launches the RVs toward different targets. (See also Decoy, ICBM, MRV, MaRV, MIRV)

C

C3I (See Command, Control, Communication and Intelligence)

CBMs (See Confidence-Building Measures)

CCD (See Charge-Coupled Device)

Charge-Coupled Device (CCD) A light-sensitive semiconductor device that stores electrical charges in individual small regions (pixels) proportional to the amount of light falling on them. CCDs are read directly by computers, eliminating film retrieval, developing and digital conversion of images. A CCD is more efficient and sensitive to a broader spectral range of light than is film and does not saturate or overexpose. (See also Digital Image Processing, Image Enhancement)

CIA Central Intelligence Agency. (See Intelligence Community)

Close Look Satellite High resolution satellites that provide detailed photographs from orbits 80-100 miles above the earth. They use less fuel and film and have a shorter orbiting span than search and find satellites. (See also NTM, Search and Find Satellite)

Cobra Dane A six-story high, missile-tracking, phased array radar located on Shemya Island, Alaska. The radar faces northwest toward the Soviet Union where it can monitor Soviet missile tests. It can track Soviet missiles from a few minutes after launch until they reach the Kamchatka Peninsula, where the missiles impact. The radar cannot, however, monitor the impact. In its tracking mode, Cobra Dane can follow as many as 200 objects simultaneously. (See also Phased Array Radar, Cobra Judy)

Cobra Judy A three-and-one-half story, missile-tracking, phased array radar that is stationed on the deck of the U.S. Navy Ship Observation Island. The radar is housed in a rotating box that allows it to monitor the final, near-earth paths of Soviet ICBM tests. The information Cobra Judy analyzes allows experts to determine missile characteristics such as size, shape and radar 'signature.' (See also Phased Array Radar, Cobra Dane)

Cold-Launch A missile launch technique that leaves the silo launcher undamaged for re-use. The missile pops up or is ejected from the silo before the rocket engines are fired. (See also MX, Rapid Reload, SS-18, Silo)

Collateral Constraint An elaboration of a treaty provision which enhances verification by constraining actions that might otherwise make monitoring of that provision difficult. These qualifications are most often contained in Agreed Statements or Common Understandings, which are added to the treaty. One example of a collateral constraint is the SALT I prohibition on increasing silo dimensions beyond 32% of the original internal volume. Another is the requirement in SALT II that certain weapons have functionally related observable differences (FRODs). (See also FRODs, ODs)

Collection Strategy The plan used to target and direct intelligence collection systems for arms control agreement monitoring (as well as general intelligence collection).

COMINT (See Communication Intelligence)

Command, Control, Communication, and Intelligence (C3I) The systems and procedures used to ensure that the President and senior civilian and military officials remain in communication with U.S. nuclear forces and each other. The Soviets also have C3I systems and procedures. C3I enables decision makers to plan for the use of nuclear weapons, choose among options, deliver orders to the forces in the field, and receive word that the forces have executed or attempted to execute their orders during the course of peacetime or wartime operations. Elements of C3I include: military communication satellites, the National Command Authority and Strategic Air Command (SAC).

Commonality The attribute of two different weapons or weapon systems that, while having widely different missions, nonetheless share similar characteristics or hardware that make it difficult to clearly distinguish one from the other for the purpose of verification. An example is the similarity between the transporter-erector-launcher (TEL) of the Soviet SS-16 intercontinental ballistic missile (ICBM) and that of the SS-20 intermediate-range ballistic missile (IRBM). (See also FRODs, ODs)

Common Understanding An ancillary statement in a treaty that modifies or clarifies the obligations contained in a particular provision. In interpreting what treaty obligations are, the treaty's provisions usually come first, followed by Agreed Statements, then Common Understandings. Common Understandings are often the most specific.

Communication Intelligence (COMINT) Intelligence information derived from interception of communications by a party other than the intended recipients. (See also NTM)

Compliance The adherence of a signatory country to the limits of an arms control agreement. Compliance is based on the broad intelligence capabilities of a country, in particular, its technical sensors. (See also Verification)

Comprehensive Test Ban Treaty (CTBT) A proposed treaty to prohibit all testing of nuclear weapons in all environments: underground, underwater, atmospheric and in space. Negotiations between the U.S., the U.S.S.R. and Great Britain toward a CTBT continued between 1962 and 1979. Substantial progress was made in the late 1970s toward agreement on monitoring with in-country sensors. Negotiations were suspended in 1980 and have not resumed. (See also LTBT, TTBT)

Compression Waves Seismic waves that vibrate through the solid body of the earth (the crust and mantle). They are known as P (for primary) waves because they are the first waves to arrive at a seismometer. An underground explosion is a source of nearly pure P waves because it applies a uniform pressure to the walls of the cavity it creates. (See also Seismology, Shear Waves)

Conference on Security and Cooperation in Europe (CSCE) The 1975 conference in Helsinki, Finland, in which the 35 participating states concluded agreements in three areas: principles governing relations between states (Basket 1); cooperation in economics, science and technology, and environment (Basket 2); and improved East-West governmental relations in human contacts, free information flow, increased cultural exchange, and education (Basket 3). Among other issues, CSCE 1 broke new ground by including Confidence-Building Measures (CBMs) in Basket 1. (See also CBMs)

Confidence-Building Measures (CBMs) Negotiated measures or actions designed to build faith in the political or military intentions of the parties as a prelude to concrete arms control. Originally developed during the Helsinki phase of the Conference on Security and Cooperation in Europe (CSCE), specific CBMs were included in Basket I of the Helsinki Accord. Examples of these include: notification of military maneuvers exceeding 25,000 troops; notification of troop movements within 250 km of a participating state's borders; and 21-day advance notice of maneuvers. CBMs have now been extended to nuclear arms control and include the prior notification of some missile tests. Recently the participants at the Madrid CSCE review conference, the first since the Helsinki agreement was signed, agreed to convene a Conference on Confidence and Security Building Measures and Disarmament in Europe (CDE). This conference was convened on January 17, 1984, and its CBM goals included militarily significant and politically binding measures that will reduce the high level of tension and risk of surprise attack in Europe.

Confidence Levels Intelligence judgments about monitoring confidence that are expressed in terms of high, moderate and low confidence. Percentage probabilities are commonly attached to these confidence levels, but for the most part they represent an optimistic or pessimistic consensus among experienced professionals rather than quantitative calculations. High confidence would mean that, having weighed their potential assets and problems, monitoring experts are very optimistic that the particular monitoring task can be performed, moderate would mean fairly optimistic, and low would mean pessimistic. In practice, the intelligence experts usually forecast monitoring confidence by hypothesizing plausible, representative cheating programs that would add to military power in some substantial way. Intelligence forecasts about monitoring confidence are intentionally conservative in two respects. First, if the chances of noncompliance were thought to be no better than 50-50, then monitoring confidence would be judged to be low. The reason is that the U.S. seeks to minimize the risk that the Soviets could gain advantages through noncompliance. Second, they are based solely on surveillance by programmable U.S. collection systems. Monitoring judgments anticipate no bonus such as a breach in Soviet security or access to a knowledgeable defector. (See also Compliance, NTM, and Verification)

Cooperative Measures Measures taken by one party to an agreement in order to enhance the ability of the other(s) to verify compliance. Such measures can be voluntary or negotiated. Some examples include data exchanges and unilateral dismantling and destruction of older weapons.

Cosmos A series of Soviet satellites. Numbered sequentially since the 1960s, Cosmos satellites perform a variety of functions including early warning, reconnaissance, navigation, communications, and military meteorological and scientific projects. (See also Molniya)

Counting Rules Rules designed to help verification of compliance with the numerical limitations in SALT. Examples include rules that require any missile tested with MIRVs to count as a MIRVed missile with the maximum number of MIRVs tested whether or not it is finally deployed with MIRVs.

Cruise Missile An unmanned missile propelled by an air-breathing engine that operates entirely within the earth's atmosphere and maintains thrust throughout its flight. Both the U.S. and U.S.S.R. deploy cruise missiles. Current U.S. systems are considered to be more technologically advanced, of smaller size, and equipped with better guidance systems. Current U.S. cruise missiles are subsonic. Cruise missiles may be launched from land (GLCM for ground-launched cruise missile), sea (SLCM for sea-launched cruise missile), and air (ALCM for air-launched cruise missile). Cruise missiles present a verification problem for future arms agreements because of their small size, dual capability (they can be armed with a nuclear or conventional warhead), mobility and deployment modes. (See also Aerodynamic Missile, ALCM, GLCM, SLCM)

Cruise Missile Carrier A platform (aircraft, submarine, ship, etc.) capable of carrying and launching cruise missiles. (See also Cruise Missile)

Cruise Missile Range The maximum distance that can be covered by the missile in its standard design mode flying until the fuel is exhausted. The range is determined by projecting the missile's flight path onto the earth from the point of launch to the point of impact. Thus, range is defined in terms of the odometer distance traveled, which includes deviations from a straight line. (See also Cruise Missile)

Cryptanalysis Translation and analysis of coded transmissions. (See also Encryption)

CSCE (See Conference on Security and Cooperation in Europe)

CTBT (See Comprehensive Test Ban Treaty)

D

DCI Director of Central Intelligence. (See Intelligence Community)

Declared Facilities Areas and facilities which have been designated by negotiated agreement as places where treaty-related (allowed) activities (missile production, testing, etc.) may take place.

Decoupling (See Seismic Coupling)

Decoy A device that accompanies a nuclear weapon delivery vehicle in order to mislead enemy defensive systems thereby increasing the probability of penetrating those defenses. It may be designed to simulate an aircraft or a ballistic missile reentry vehicle. An aircraft decoy can simulate a bomber's radar cross-section. An ICBM decoy usually simulates the radar signature of the RV. (See also Bus, MIRV, RV)

Deliberate Concealment Activities designed to conceal strategic weapons or related activities from National Technical Means (NTM) of verification. SALT I and II formally recognized that such concealment would be contrary to the interests of both parties to have confidence in verification. The SALT agreements prohibit any action which impedes verification by NTM. The negotiation record makes clear that deliberate concealment measures include use of camouflage, use of coverings, or deliberate denial of telemetry (such as through encryption) whenever these activities impede verification by NTM. (See also NTM)

Delivery System A system which includes a weapon (such as a warhead or gravity bomb), the means of propulsion (such as a missile, aircraft, or motorized vehicle) and associated mechanisms or equipment (such as silos and missile launchers). The components of a delivery system may be geographically dispersed as in the case of missile launchers and tracking and guidance radars.

Depressed Trajectory The trajectory of a ballistic missile fired at an angle to the ground significantly lower than the angle of a minimum energy trajectory (the usual ballistic missile trajectory). Such a trajectory causes the missile to rise above the line-of-sight radar horizon at a later stage of flight than traditionally launched missiles. This reduces flight time, makes the missile more difficult to detect and track, and diminishes warning time. Depressed trajectory is of particular concern with regard to submarine-launched ballistic missiles (SLBMs).

Deterrence A term usually meaning the dissuasion of an adversary from initiating an attack because of certain retaliation inflicting unacceptable damage. The concept of nuclear deterrence may be contrasted with that of nuclear defense (i.e., the strategy and forces for limiting damage if deterrence fails). Some believe that an effective nuclear defense of missile silos also would have a deterrent effect by making it less certain that an adversary could achieve a disabling 'first strike.' (See also MAD, SDI)

Development As used in SALT, it is the first stage in the process of producing a particular weapon system. Subsequent stages include testing, flight testing, production, and deployment. (See also SALT)

Digital Image Processing (DIP) A technique used to recover more information from an image than appears in an unenhanced photograph. For example, ground details that are obscured by clouds in a satellite photograph can be made sharper through this process. The DIP technique converts shadings on the film into corresponding numbers. When put through a digital computer, apparently lost or blurred lines are restored. (See also Charge-Coupled Device, Image Enhancement)

DIP (See Digital Image Processing)

Discrimination As used in nuclear test limitation verification, it is the ability to differentiate between underground nuclear explosions and earthquakes. This task is accomplished through the analysis of seismic and other data. (See also Resolution, Seismology)

Dismantlement and Destruction Treaty-related rules governing the removal of excess or banned weapon systems. The precise dismantlement and destruction rules for SALT-covered systems have been worked out in the SCC and remain classified. (See also SALT, SCC)

Dual-Capable Systems Systems capable of performing two different missions (such as delivery of both nuclear and non-nuclear weapons) using the same platform or vehicle. Examples include certain classes of artillery (e.g, NATO 155 howitzer), short-range missiles (e.g., NATO Honest John or Warsaw Pact SCUD missile), tactical aircraft (e.g., F-4 or Su-7), or cruise missiles (e.g, U.S. Tomahawk). (See also Commonality, FRODs, ODs)

E

Electromagnetic Spectrum In the context of verification, the set of bands of frequencies, wavelengths and/or energies over which electromagnetic sensors operate. Sensors detect radiated or reflected energy. The upper bands, including gamma, x-ray and ultraviolet, are used to monitor compliance with the Limited Test Ban Treaty (LTBT). The middle bands, including the visible (accessible to photography), infrared and microwave (used in radar) bands are used to monitor compliance with SALT. The lowest frequency spectral band, radio, is used for eavesdropping on communications and to intercept telemetry.

Electronic Intelligence (ELINT) A type of Signals Intelligence (SIGINT) that provides technical information by the collection of another country's electromagnetic emissions (usually radars). (See also NTM, SIGINT)

ELINT (See Electronic Intelligence)

Encryption Coding signals for the purpose of concealing information. In SALT II, this term applies to the practice of deliberately altering the telemetry transmitted from a weapon system under test so that, if it is intercepted, it cannot be deciphered. (See also NTM, Telemetry)

Endoatmospheric Refers to anti-ballistic missile defense systems that operate within the atmosphere, from the earth's surface to about 300,000 feet altitude. Within this category are high-altitude systems, which operate above approximately 100,000 feet, and low-altitude systems, which work below 50,000 feet. (See also ABM, BMD, Exoatmospheric)

Equivalent Megatonnage (EMT) The yield of a nuclear weapon in megatons, to the two-thirds power. For example, one 8 megaton (MT) weapon has an EMT of 4; a 1MT weapon has an EMT of 1; and a 125 kiloton (KT) or 0.125 megaton weapon has an EMT of 0.25. The principle behind EMT is that a single weapon of large megatonnage will have less destructive power, than several weapons of smaller megatonnage that together may not equal the megatonnage of the larger weapon. For example, four 125 KT weapons equal the destructive power of one 1 MT, and sixteen 125 KT warheads equal the destructive power of one 8 MT weapon. (See also Kiloton, Megatonnage)

Executive Agreement An international agreement, between the President of the U.S. and foreign heads of state, that does not require formal senatorial approval. Such agreements are concluded under the President's constitutional power as the Commander in Chief and his general authority in foreign relations, or under powers delegated to him by Congress. Executive agreements may be nullified by congressional action and are not binding on future presidents without their consent. Executive agreements include accords or agreements, interim agreements, conventions (usually agreements made at international conferences by many states), non-ratified protocols and pacts. (See also Treaty)

Exoatmospheric Refers to anti-ballistic missile systems that operate outside the atmosphere. Theoretically an 'exo' defense can destroy many RVs targeted on the same site because of the long flight times of RVs outside the atmosphere and the large battle space. (See also ABM, BMD, Endoatmospheric)

F

FB-111A A U.S. medium-range bomber first deployed in 1969. There are approximately 60 FB-111As currently deployed, each typically carrying either six bombs, or short-range attack missiles or some combination of both. The FB-111A has a range of approximately 5,000 miles. (See also B-52, Backfire, Medium-Range Bomber)

Ferret This type of U.S. satellite reportedly collects Soviet ground communications and other electronic signals. It operates at an altitude of about 400 miles. (See also ELINT)

Fixed ICBM Launcher There are two categories of ICBM launchers--fixed and mobile. A fixed launcher refers to the equipment used to launch an ICBM (either 'soft' above-ground launch pad, gantry, and associated equipment or buildings, or 'hard' underground silo; the terms soft and hard refer to the degree of vulnerability to a nuclear explosion). In both cases the launch equipment is fixed and cannot be transported. (See also Mobile ICBM Launcher, Hardened Silo)

Flight Test A test of any missile or air-breathing aerodynamic system. In SALT II, a missile flight test is any actual launch of a missile (as opposed to a static test) conducted for any purpose, including development, demonstration of the missile's capabilities, and training of crews.

FOBS (See Fractional Orbital Bombardment System)

Fractional Orbital Bombardment System (FOBS) A missile that achieves orbital trajectory but fires a set of retrorockets before completion of one orbit in order to slow down, reenter the atmosphere, and release the warhead it carries into a ballistic trajectory toward its target. A normal ICBM follows an arching, parabolic path and is highly visible to defending radars. A FOBS missile in low orbit (e.g., ten miles altitude) can make a sharp descent to Earth, substantially cutting radar warning time. These systems are banned by the SALT II Treaty (Article IX, Section C).

Fractionation The division of the payload of a missile into several warheads, as in the case of MIRVed ICBMs. The increase in the quantity of warheads that a payload can carry is achieved by reducing the size and weight of each RV. (See also MIRV, RV)

Freeze (See Nuclear Weapons Freeze)

FRODs (See Functionally Related Observable Differences)

Frontscatter Radar waves that are transmitted toward an object but continue beyond the target until received at another radar station receiver. (See also Backscatter, Radar)

Functionally Related Observable Differences (FRODs) A method developed in SALT II to deal with problems posed by weapons that perform different missions but have similar characteristics, thereby making them difficult to distinguish from each other by national technical means (NTM). FRODs are differences, which can be monitored by NTM, in the features of a weapon system. These observable features indicate whether or not the weapon system can perform specific missions. For example, FRODs are used to distinguish launchers of non-MIRVed ICBMs from MIRVed ones. For airplanes, FRODs are necessary differences in the externally observable design characteristics. These include the removal of bomb bay doors or the addition of strakelets. FRODs determine whether or not these delivery aircraft can perform certain missions such as carrying air-launched cruise missiles. (See also Commonality, ODs, Strakelets)

G

Geneva Protocol A 1925 international agreement restricting biological and chemical weapons. (See also Biological Weapons Convention, Protocol)

Geosynchronous Satellite (See High Altitude Satellite)

GLCM (See Ground-Launched Cruise Missile)

Ground-Based Electro-Optical Deep Space Surveillance (GEODSS) A monitoring system scheduled to be completed in 1987. It will augment ground- based radars and provide highly-detailed optical and orbital signature data on manmade objects in space, beyond 3,000 miles from earth. (See also ASAT, Space Object Catalogue)

Ground-Launched Cruise Missiles (GLCM) A cruise missile launched from ground installations or vehicles.

Ground Surveillance The use of earth-bound observation sites to monitor missile tests. There are two components in this type of monitoring-active radar and passive listening equipment. Active radar beams waves at the missile to determine certain characteristics and its flight path. Radar is able to identify the missile type by comparing the characteristics of the missile being flight-tested with characteristics of missiles already known to be deployed. Listening posts are used to intercept telemetry from the test missile. Because of range limitations caused by the curving of the earth, listening posts must be situated fairly close to the launch site. For example, the U.S. reportedly has listening posts in Turkey, Crete and elsewhere that are less than 1,000 miles from Soviet missile test ranges. (See also NTM)

H

Hardened Silo Launcher An ICBM silo that has been made less vulnerable to the blast, heat and radiation effects of nuclear explosions. Hardening is accomplished by surrounding the silo with earth, concrete and steel reinforcing rods. The purpose of hardening silos is to allow the ICBM contained within it to withstand the effects of a close nuclear detonation so that it will be able to launch and function properly in flight. The hardening of silos has been made necessary by the increasing accuracy of ICBM warheads, since the closer the warhead comes to scoring a direct hit on a silo, the more hardened a silo must be to withstand the effects. No amount of hardening, however, will allow a silo to withstand a direct hit by a nuclear weapon, yet this degree of accuracy is becoming possible. (See also ICBM, Launcher, Silo)

Helsinki Accords (See Conference on Security and Cooperation in Europe)

Heavy Bomber The term used in SALT II to describe nuclear-weapon-carrying aircraft included in the aggregate limitations of the agreement. These include current bombers (B-52 and B-1 for the U.S., and Bear and Bison for the U.S.S.R.), future bombers that can carry out the mission of a heavy bomber, and cruise missile carriers. (See also Long-Range Bomber, SALT II)

Heavy ICBM Heavy ICBMs have a launch weight or throw-weight that is greater than the heaviest 'light' ICBM deployed by the U.S. or U.S.S.R. at the time of the SALT II signing (i.e., the Soviet SS-19). Currently only the Soviet SS-18 is considered a heavy ICBM. (See also SS-19)

High Altitude Satellite These are special purpose satellites used for early warning and monitoring. Early warning satellites, which maintain a geosynchronous orbit, i.e., 23,000 miles above the earth and having an orbit velocity which maintains the satellite above the same part of the earth, use infrared sensors to detect the exhaust plumes of ICBMs and SLBMs. Nuclear explosion detection satellites maintain a very high orbit around the earth. They are able to detect the flash and radiation from a nuclear explosion above the ground and in space. Other satellites in high orbits have the ability to listen to ground communications, other satellites and telemetry from missile tests.

'Hot Line' Agreement An agreement between the U.S. and U.S.S.R. signed in June 1963 and updated in 1971 and 1984 that established an official communications link between Washington and Moscow for use by heads of government during crises. Originally a teletype link, the Direct Communications Link today consists of two satellite communications circuits served by terminals utilizing Intelsat (U.S.) and Molniya (U.S.S.R.) satellites.

Hotel The oldest class of Soviet nuclear ballistic missile submarines. First deployed in the early 1960s. It is deployed in three versions: the Hotel II with three missile launch tubes and the Hotel III and IV with six tubes. These submarines carry either SS-N-5 or SS-N-8 SLBMs. (See also Typhoon, SLBM)

Human Intelligence (HUMINT) The gathering of intelligence data by human sources. They include foreign nationals working for U.S. intelligence agencies and Americans abroad, usually employees of the U.S. government.

HUMINT (See Human Intelligence)

I

IAEA (See International Atomic Energy Agency)

ICBM (See Intercontinental Ballistic Missile)

Image Enhancement (or Image Processing) The computer process of extracting and clarifying information from imagery collected, stored, and transmitted in electronic form. Computers can manipulate these data (i.e., images in electronic digital form) to bring out detail and contrast that would otherwise be lost. The result can be exceedingly sharp color pictures.

Image Processing (See Image Enhancement)

Imagery The pictures produced by photographic and radar equipment that are used in the verification process. Imagery equipment is carried on special aircraft and satellites that monitor the territory and activities of a rival nation. (See also Photoreconnaissance)

In-Country Verification Usually refers to a means of unilateral verification in which tamper-resistant, unmanned detection sensors are placed on the territory of nations party to an arms control agreement. Networks of seismic sensors distributed over the U.S.S.R., the U.S., and Great Britain, have been discussed in connection with verification of a Comprehensive Test Ban Treaty. (See also CTBT, NTM, On-Site Inspection, Seismology)

INF (See Intermediate-Range Nuclear Forces)

Infrared Scanner An imaging sensor deployed on a satellite or aircraft that can detect heat radiation. Infrared scanners can penetrate cloud cover, nighttime darkness and camouflage. These scanners can detect underground silos and discriminate among test missiles by the way their propellants burn. (See also NTM)

Intelligence Community Includes the Director of Central Intelligence, the Central Intelligence Agency, the National Security Agency, the Bureau of Intelligence and Research in the U.S. Department of State, the White House Situation Room, Defense Intelligence Agency and the National Military Command Center. The Senate Select Committee on Intelligence and the House Permanent Select Committee on Intelligence are also members of the intelligence community although not involved in intelligence gathering or analysis. (See also DCI, Verification Community)

Interceptor In the context of anti-satellite weapons, the term used for the warhead and maneuvering or homing apparatus. In the context of the ABM Treaty, an interceptor missile deployed to counter strategic ballistic missiles or their elements in flight trajectory. (See also ABM, Soviet ASAT Weapon, U.S. ASAT Weapon)

Intercontinental Ballistic Missile (ICBM) A fixed or mobile land-based rocket-propelled missile capable of delivering a warhead to inter- continental ranges [defined in SALT II as 5,500 kilometers (km) or 3,000 nautical miles (nm)]. An ICBM consists of a rocket booster, one or more reentry vehicles, RV-associated objects (decoys, chaff, penetration aids) and in the case of MIRVed missiles, a post-boost vehicle (PBV) or 'bus.' (See also Bus, Launcher, Minuteman, MX, Silo, SS-17, SS-18, SS-19, Titan)

Intercontinental Bomber (See Long-Range Bomber)

Interference The U.S. and U.S.S.R. agreed in SALT I not to interfere with the National Technical Means (NTM) of verification of the other party. This means that neither side can destroy or attempt to negate the functioning of the NTM of the other party (e.g., blinding or attempting to blind photoreconnaissance satellites). SALT II extended the non-interference provision to forbid the encryption of missile performance data if such action would impede verification of specific parameters identified in the text of the Treaty. (See also Encryption, NTM)

Interim Agreement One of two agreements signed on May 26, 1972, known collectively as SALT I (the other being the ABM Treaty). This agreement established an interim freeze on ICBM and SLBM launchers for five years and was intended to set the stage for the SALT II discussions. The Interim Agreement expired October 3, 1977; however, both the U.S. and U.S.S.R. made independent statements that they did not plan to take any action inconsistent with the provisions of the Interim Agreement pending conclusion of the SALT II negotiations. The statements are still in effect. (See also SALT I, Vladivostok Accord)

Intermediate-Range Ballistic Missile (IRBM) A ballistic missile with a range capability between about 2,500 to 5,500 km. The Soviet Union's SS-20 is an example.

Intermediate-Range Bomber (See Medium-Range Bomber)

Intermediate-Range Nuclear Forces (INF) In general, a term used to emphasize the differences between strategic intercontinental nuclear weapon systems and those nuclear-weapon-carrying missiles and aircraft deployed in a particular theater (e.g., Europe or Asia). Intermediate-range nuclear forces have ranges less than 5,500 km. In the late 1970s, NATO officials agreed to modernize nuclear weapons in Western Europe and this was codified in the 1979 NATO dual track decision. This decision allowed for bilateral arms control talks, the Intermediate-Range Nuclear Force Negotiations, that were to be separate from the strategic arms talks between the U.S. and U.S.S.R. In the absence of an agreement, new long-range theater nuclear weapons would be deployed. The talks began in 1981 and ended inconclusively in December 1983, after NATO began its planned deployment of ground-launched cruise missiles (GLCMs) and Pershing II missiles in Italy, Britain and West Germany, and the Soviets suspended the negotiations. (See also INF Negotiations)

Intermediate-Range Nuclear Force (INF) Negotiations Talks between the U.S. and U.S.S.R. which began in Geneva in November 1981 on limiting INF. The talks were the direct result of the 1979 two-track NATO decision to modernize its INF (i.e., deploy new missiles) while seeking to negotiate with the Soviets. The decision was designed to reduce the strategic and political imbalances in INF weapons caused by the Soviet deployment of SS-20 missiles beginning in 1977. During the negotiating process many proposals were put forth by the two sides but none proved acceptable to both parties. The U.S. originally put forth a zero/zero proposal that called for the elimination of all U.S. and Soviet land-based INF missiles. The Soviets rejected this and countered with a half-zero proposal. This would allow the Soviets to keep some SS-20s but not allow any NATO missiles to be deployed. The U.S. then modified its position and offered to negotiate low but equal numbers of warheads. The Soviets found this unacceptable as they sought compensation for British and French nuclear forces. This was unacceptable to the U.S., whose position is that only American and Soviet weapons should be discussed in the negotiations. Another point of difference between the two parties was over the scope of the negotiations. The U.S. wanted the negotiations to cover all INF, worldwide, while the Soviets sought to limit discussion to those INF weapons stationed in Europe. The negotiations were terminated by the Soviets in December 1983 when NATO deployed Pershing II and cruise missiles. (See also Cruise Missile, Intermediate-Range Nuclear Forces, Pershing II, SS-20)

International Atomic Energy Agency (IAEA) A United Nations sponsored agency established in 1957 with a twofold purpose: to promote nuclear energy, and to establish and administer safeguards to ensure that peaceful nuclear energy not be used for military purposes. The IAEA inspects nuclear power plants to monitor the production and use of fissionable material. Headquartered in Vienna, the IAEA is the operating arm of the nonproliferation regime that includes: the Nonproliferation Treaty (NPT) (treaty commitments by non-nuclear weapon states not to acquire nuclear weapons); systems of safeguards and other monitoring to prevent misuse of commercial nuclear materials and technologies; informal commitments by nuclear supplier states to limit exports to the least dangerous nuclear technologies; and bilateral agreements between some nuclear supplier states and their clients.

IRBM (See Intermediate-Range Ballistic Missile)

K

KH-11 Digital Imaging Satellite This U.S. satellite reportedly takes enhanced color and infrared television pictures of land and ocean objects. The images are electronically signalled to earth. There are reported to be at least two of these satellites aloft at all times. They operate at an altitude of 170 to 300 miles. (See also Big Bird, Close Look Satellite, Search and Find Satellite)

Kiloton (KT) A measure of the yield of a nuclear weapon, equivalent to 1,000 tons of TNT. (See also Megaton)

L

Laser The name (acronym) for light amplification by stimulated emission of radiation. Lasers can produce an intense beam of monochromatic electromagnetic radiation. Some lasers produce emissions in the visible light range. (See also SDI, Beam Weapons)

Launch As used in SALT, a launch includes a flight of a missile for testing, training, or any other purpose. The term does not include 'pop-up' tests that test the launcher and ejection mechanism of cold-launch systems. (See also Cold-Launch, Silo)

Launcher The equipment which launches a missile. ICBM launchers are land-based and can be either fixed or mobile. SLBM launchers are the missile tubes on a ballistic missile submarine. A launcher for an air-to-surface ballistic missile is the carrier aircraft with associated equipment. Launchers for cruise missiles can be installed on aircraft, ships, or land-based vehicles or installations.

Launch-weight The weight of a fully loaded missile at the time of launch. This includes the aggregate weight of all booster stages, the post-boost vehicle, and the payload. (See also Bus, ICBM)

Light Spectrum The narrow band of the electromagnetic spectrum that is visible to the human eye. (See also Electromagnetic Spectrum)

Limited Test Ban Treaty (LTBT) A Treaty signed in 1963 by the U.S., U.S.S.R. and U.K. that prohibits the three parties from testing nuclear weapons in the atmosphere, outer space and underwater. Verification is by NTM. Underground tests are allowed as long as radioactive waste does not leave the territorial limits of the country conducting the test. The Treaty was signed in August 1963 and was ratified by the U.S. in September 1963. (See also CTBT, TTBT)

Line-of-Sight Radar A radar type sometimes used to monitor missile test flights. Because of its limited range, it must be stationed close to the Soviet Union and is able to track the missile undergoing testing only after it reaches a certain altitude (i.e., when it makes 'line-of-sight' contact). One line-of-sight radar has been operating in Turkey since the 1950s. Two others, which had been operational in Iran, are now closed down, although press reports state that new monitoring stations are compensating for the loss. Unlike over-the-horizon radar, line-of-sight does not extend its range capability through atmospheric reflection and refraction. (See also OTH Radar)

Long-Range Bombers Aircraft capable of delivering nuclear and non-nuclear ordnance at intercontinental distances and having an unrefueled range of 6,000 or more miles. (See also B-1, B-52, Bear, Bison, Heavy Bomber, Medium-Range Bomber)

M

MAD (See Mutual Assured Destruction)

Maneuvering Reentry Vehicle (MaRV) An independently targetable reentry vehicle that can maneuver to evade ballistic missile defense or to obtain better accuracy. (See also MRV, MIRV, RV)

MaRV (See Maneuvering Reentry Vehicle)

MBFR (See Mutual and Balanced Force Reductions)

Medium-Range Bomber An aircraft capable of delivering nuclear and non-nuclear ordnance and having an unrefueled range of between 3,500 and 6,000 miles. (See also Backfire, FB-111A)

Megatonnage (MT) A measure of the destructive power of nuclear weapons. A megaton has an explosive force equal to that generated by one million tons of TNT. A one-megaton nuclear bomb is about 50 times more powerful than the bombs dropped on Hiroshima and Nagasaki. The U.S. nuclear stockpile is estimated to have the destructive power of several thousand megatons while the Soviet stockpile is even larger. (See also Equivalent Megatonnage)

Miniature Homing Vehicle (MHV) (See U.S. ASAT Weapon)

Minuteman A three-stage, solid propellant, second generation U.S. ICBM. Currently, 450 Minuteman IIs are deployed with single warheads and 550 Minuteman IIIs are deployed with three MIRVed warheads. The single warhead Minuteman I was deployed in the early 1960s but is no longer in operation. Both Minuteman IIs and IIIs are undergoing modernization. (See also MIRV)

MIRV (See Multiple Independently Targetable Reentry Vehicle)

Mobile ICBM Launcher Movable equipment used to launch an ICBM. Mobile ICBM launchers can be mounted on wheeled vehicles (e.g., a tractor-erector-launcher), rail vehicles, as in the proposed Racetrack basing mode for MX, or aircraft. (See also Fixed ICBM Launcher)

Modernization The process of modifying a weapon system to improve performance capabilities. SALT II permits modernization and replacement subject to some limitations.

Molniya Soviet satellites whose function is military communication. (See also Cosmos)

Monitoring The starting point of the verification process, monitoring involves using intelligence capabilities to determine what the other side is and is not doing, first by collecting and then by evaluating raw intelligence. In the context of SALT II, monitoring meant collecting and analyzing information about Soviet weapon systems subject to SALT limits. (See also Intelligence Community, Verification)

MRV (See Multiple Reentry Vehicle)

MT (See Megatonnage)

Multiple Independently Targetable Reentry Vehicle (MIRV) Multiple reentry vehicles (RVs) carried as part of the payload of a ballistic missile. Each warhead can be directed to a separate and changeable target within a particular range. MIRVed missiles employ a warhead dispensing mechanism, called a post-boost vehicle (PBV or 'bus') to target and release the warheads.

The PBV maneuvers in space to achieve successive positions and velocities. It releases its warheads on trajectories plotted to attack the desired targets, which can be spread over a wide geographic area. Current U.S. MIRVed intercontinental missiles include the Minuteman III ICBM, and Poseidon (C-3) and Trident I (C-4) SLBMs. Two new MIRVed systems are under development: Trident II (D-5) SLBM and MX ICBM. The U.S.S.R. currently deploys three MIRVed ICBMs (SS-17, 18, and 19), and two SLBMs (SS-N-18 and SS-N-20). Press reports indicate the Soviets have at least one, and possibly two, MIRVed ICBMs and one MIRVed SLBM under development. Verification of limits on the numbers and capabilities of nuclear weapons systems became significantly more difficult with the introduction of MIRV capability around 1970. (See also Minuteman, MX, SS-17, SS-18, SS-19)

Multiple Reentry Vehicle (MRV) Ballistic missile reentry vehicles carried by one missile but not capable of independent targeting. A precursor to MIRV and MaRV, MRV systems had two primary objectives: (1) to distribute nuclear effects over a large area more efficiently, and (2) to present ABM defenses with multiple targets. The Polaris (A-3) SLBM was the first operational ballistic missile to employ MRV. On the Soviet side, a version of the older SS-11 ICBM carries a MRV payload.

Mutual and Balanced Force Reductions (MBFR) Negotiations between NATO and Warsaw Pact countries on-going since October 1973. The agreed objective of the negotiations is to contribute to more stable relationships in Europe by reducing the concentration of NATO and Warsaw Pact conventional forces in Central Europe. A long-standing 'data dispute' over the actual number of Warsaw Pact forces in the area continues to be a major impediment to concluding a treaty. The Eastern bloc estimate has 150,000 fewer troops than the NATO estimate. Verification is acknowledged to be difficult, and both sides now recognize the need for cooperative measures such as on-site inspection, checkpoints for observing troops entering and leaving the area of reductions, and the exchange of information on forces and activities. After more than ten years of continuous negotiation, the MBFR talks were suspended by the Soviet Union on December 15, 1983, in the wake of the NATO deployment of cruise and Pershing II missiles in Europe. The talks were resumed on March 16, 1984. (See also Cooperative Measures)

Mutual Assured Destruction (MAD) A term describing the strategic nuclear deterrent policy of the U.S. since about 1963. The policy remains controversial and the term is usually used by its critics. In the mid-1960s, defense officials in Washington concluded that because of the size and nature of the Soviet nuclear arsenal, as well as the inherent limitations of U.S. BMD capabilities, the United States could not establish a strategic superiority over the Soviet Union sufficient to prevent unacceptable damage to itself in the event of a nuclear exchange. The U.S. decided, therefore, not only to target enemy military installations, but also enemy population centers to maintain, as stated by Secretary of Defense Robert McNamara in 1965, a 'convincing capability to inflict unacceptable damage on an attacker.' The policy of the United States, as contained in recent presidential directives, reportedly increases U.S. response options, no longer targets population centers per se, and places increased emphasis on military and industrial targets. Since many of these targets are located in Soviet cities, the effect would appear to be the same. Among the several proposed alternatives to this policy are: (1) a longer-term policy seeking superpower stability under a regime where offensive nuclear arms are reduced to mimimum deterrent levels; and (2) a defense that relies on anti-ballistic missile systems to perfectly protect U.S. cities and military installations, assuming that such a shield is, in fact, possible. (See also BMD, Deterrence, SDI)

MX Missile (Missile Experimental) An advanced MIRVed ICBM whose deployment has been proposed as a way to modernize U.S. strategic nuclear forces. The missile, which would be land-based, has four stages (three solid fueled, the last liquid fueled) and would carry ten Mark 21 nuclear warheads, seven more than the Minuteman III, which is currently the most modern U.S. land-based ICBM. The deployment plan, based on the April 1983 recommendation of the President's Commission on Strategic Forces (The Scowcroft Commission), calls for the placement of 100 MX missiles in Wyoming and Nebraska in existing Minuteman silos hardened against the effects of nuclear blasts. The MX is larger, heavier and more accurate than Minuteman III and it is also launched differently. The MX is 'canisterized', which allows it to be cold-launched and its silo reused. In 1984, the Reagan Administration was locked in a struggle with the U.S. Congress over the number of MX missiles to be funded and whether their deployment should be connected with Soviet willingness to resume the START talks. (See also ICBM, MIRV, Cold-launch, START)

N

National Security Council (NSC) Created by the National Security Act of 1947, the NSC is the principal national security policy making body in the U.S. government. Statutory permanent members are the President, Vice-President, and the Secretaries of State and Defense. The Director of the Arms Control and Disarmament Agency, the Chairman of the Joint Chiefs of Staff and the Director of the Central Intelligence Agency are statutory advisors. Occasionally, the Attorney General and others attend as advisors. Among its many functions, the NSC acts as a high-level decision making body on verification issues by setting requirements and requesting analyses. (See also Intelligence Community, Verification Community).

National Technical Means of Verification (NTM) First defined in SALT, NTM is the means used to monitor compliance with treaty provisions, which are under the national control of individual signatories to an arms control agreement. NTM can include photoreconnaissance satellites, aircraft-based systems (such as radars and optical systems), as well as sea- and ground-based systems (such as radars and antennae for collecting signals). (See also Collection Strategy, COMINT, Compliance, HUMINT, ELINT, In-Country Verification, Photoreconnaissance, Reconnaissance, Seismological Detection, Remote Sensing, SIGINT, Verification)

Negotiation The process of discussion and bargaining to reach an agreement or compromise that is acceptable to all the participants. Arms control negotiations attempt to reconcile the individual national security needs of nations while striving to enhance international security by reducing the threat of nuclear war. (See also INF, Protocol, SALT, START, Treaty)

Nonproliferation Treaty (NPT) A multilateral agreement signed in 1968 which aims to control the spread of nuclear weapons while ensuring the availability of the benefits of commercial nuclear power. The Treaty was ratified by the U.S. in 1969 and came into force in 1970. The principal verification-related feature of the NPT is its reliance on IAEA safeguards to guarantee non-nuclear weapons state compliance. The IAEA carries out on-site inspection of facilities engaged in peaceful uses of nuclear power. (See also Proliferation, Plutonium 239, Uranium 235, IAEA)

NPT (See Nonproliferation Treaty)

NSC (See National Security Council)

NTM (See National Technical Means)

Nuclear Free Zone Areas in which the production and stationing of nuclear weapons are prohibited by mutual agreement. The Antarctic Treaty, signed in 1959, was the first of these 'non-armament' treaties. Other areas made nuclear-free by treaty include outer space (the Outer Space Treaty, signed in 1967), Latin America (Treaty of Tlatelolco, signed in 1968), and the seabed (the Seabed Treaty, signed in 1971). Current proposals for nuclear free zones include Scandinavia, the Balkans, and the Indian Ocean.

Nuclear Weapons Freeze In its broadest form, the freeze proposal calls for a mutual and verifiable halt to the production, testing, and deployment of nuclear weapons and their means of delivery. The freeze would stop the modernization of nuclear arms, regarded by the proposal's adherents as one of the principal driving forces of the arms race, and ban the production of nuclear warheads and new weapons-usable fissionable material. This proposal is also the basis of a political movement active in the 1980s. It is a relatively simple and comprehensive approach to limiting nuclear arms: halt then reverse the arms race. Opponents to the proposal in western nations argue that halting now could permanently establish Soviet leads in certain weapons categories. The proposal's verifiability is a contentious issue. Some aspects of the freeeze proposal appear to be less verifiable than others. Critics point to these as indications of major weaknesses in the proposal. However, like the comprehensive test ban (CTB) proposal, this proposal has the advantage that if just one of the activities prohibited by a freeze agreement were detected, it would constitute an unambiguous violation. Proponents in the U.S. assert that all of its important provisions are readily verifiable and, in any event, there is a margin of safety since any covert Soviet action of strategic importance would be readily detected before the U.S.S.R. could gain any significant advantage. (See also Build-Down, CTB.)

O

Observable Differences (ODs) Design features, observable by NTM, used in SALT II to distinguish between those heavy bombers covered by the treaty and those not. ODs differ from FRODs in that they do not have to be related to the ability of a weapon system to perform specific functions. (See also Commonality, FRODs)

On-Site Inspection (OSI) The monitoring of compliance by using inspectors or sensors from one country to examine or monitor the other party's installations and/or activities. OSI is by its nature an intrusive means of verification. Provisions for OSI are included in the Peaceful Nuclear Explosions Treaty (PNET) which the U.S. has not ratified. (See also In-Country Verification)

Outer Space Treaty According to this Treaty, nuclear or other weapons of mass destruction cannot be placed in orbit around the earth, installed on the moon or any other celestial body, or otherwise stationed in outer space. It also limits the use of the moon and other celestial bodies exclusively to peaceful purposes and expressly prohibits their use for establishing military bases, installations or fortifications, testing weapons of any kind, or conducting military maneuvers. Verification is carried out by space tracking systems. The Treaty, signed by the U.S., U.S.S.R. and 87 other countries, was ratified by the U.S. in 1967. The Outer Space Treaty, like the ABM Treaty, places limitations on the deployment of space weapons. (See also ASAT)

Over-the-Horizon (OTH) An air defense radar used to locate air-breathing missiles, such as cruise missiles, and bombers. The system makes use of the atmospheric reflection and refraction phenomenon to extend its range of detection beyond line-of-sight radar. Forward scatter OTH is now in operation but the advanced technology OTH-Backscatter system, with coverage to 1,800 miles, is currently close to deployment. (See also Frontscatter and Backscatter)

P

Pave Paws Radar A phased array radar system. It has the dual purpose of protecting the U.S. from submarine-launched ballistic missiles over a 3,000 nautical miles (nm) range and monitoring satellites in low earth orbit. Pave Paws is currently operational in the northeast and northwest sections of the U.S. New sites are under construction in the southwestern and southeastern parts of the U.S. (See also Phased Array Radar)

Payload For missiles, the total weight of the warhead(s), shroud, penetration aids, post-boost vehicle (if MIRV or MRV system), and activating devices. (See also Bus, ICBM, PBV, Throw-Weight)

PBV (See Post-Boost Vehicle)

Peaceful Nuclear Explosions Treaty (PNET) A treaty governing all nuclear explosions carried out at locations outside the weapons test sites specified under TTBT. The yield of the explosions may not exceed 150 KT. The verification arrangements include NTM as well as the exchange of information and access to the sites of explosions. PNET was signed in May 1976 and submitted to the U.S. Senate in July 1976. It is as yet unratified. (See also Seismic Detection)

Penetration Aids (Penaids) Devices employed by ICBMs, SLBMs, and penetrating bombers to neutralize defenses. Both missiles and bombers employ penaids such as decoys, chaff and electronic countermeasures to mislead or confuse enemy radars. (See also ICBM, SLBM)

Pershing II A new, single warhead, U.S. intermediate-range ballistic missile (IRBM). One hundred and eight of these missiles began to be deployed in West Germany in December 1983 as part of the NATO INF modernization. These missiles are replacing the older Pershing IA short-range ballistic missiles (SRBMs). The Pershing II is mobile, extremely accurate and has a range of about 1,800 km. The NATO rationale for deploying the Pershing II was the need to counterbalance the Soviet SS-20 IRBM, which was first deployed in 1977. (See also INF, SS-20)

Phased Array Radar A radar system with no moving parts. Tracking elements are rotated electronically rather than mechanically, allowing for improved accuracy and data collection. Used for tracking missiles and satellites. U.S. types include Cobra Dane, Cobra Judy and Pave Paws radars. Soviet phased array radars are part of the Hen House early warning and tracking network. (See also Cobra Dane, Cobra Judy, Pave Paws)

Photoreconnaissance The photographing of the earth from specially outfitted satellites and planes. Photoreconnaissance has military, intelligence and verification uses. (See also NTM)

Plutonium 239 (Pu-239) A fissionable plutonium isotope produced in reactors through the transformation of fertile U-238. More than one plutonium isotope is produced in reactors, and only fissile Pu-239 is useful for nuclear weapon fabrication. The higher the concentration of Pu-239, the greater the suitability of plutonium for nuclear weapons. If the concentration of the Pu-239 isotope is 93% or higher, then the plutonium (which includes the other isotopes) is commonly known as 'weapons grade.' However, plutonium containing smaller amounts of isotope 239, such as may be produced in a commercial nuclear reactor, may also be 'weapons-usable' material. (See also Uranium 235, NPT, Proliferation)

PNET (See Peaceful Nuclear Explosions Treaty)

Polaris The first class of U.S. ballistic missile submarines carrying the first generation of SLBMs (UGM-27 or A-3). Each submarine carries 16 missiles. Decommissioning of Polaris class submarines began in 1980. (See also Poseidon, SLBM)

Post-Boost Vehicle (PBV) Sometimes also called a 'bus', the PBV is that part of the payload of a MIRV or MRV ballistic missile that carries the reentry vehicles, guidance package, fuel, and thrust devices for altering the ballistic flight path so that reentry vehicles can be dispensed sequentially toward different targets. (See also Bus, MIRV, MRV)

Poseidon The class of U.S. ballistic missile submarine that carries the first generation multiple warhead SLBM. Each submarine carries 16 SLBM launching tubes. At present 19 Poseidon SSBNs are armed with the Poseidon C-3 missile, a MIRVed weapon carrying 6 to 14 warheads. The other 12 Poseidons are armed with the Trident I (C-4) SLBM carrying 8 MIRVed warheads. (See also Polaris, Trident)

Production The manufacturing stage of a particular weapon system or device. It follows the development and testing stages.

Proliferation The spread of nuclear weapons capability beyond the five nations that now possess it. Non-Nuclear Weapons States (NNWS) could acquire this capability through a weapons transfer from a Nuclear Weapons State (NWS) or by diverting a peaceful nuclear program to a weapons effort. This is sometimes referred to as 'horizontal' proliferation, as opposed to the increasing number of nuclear weapons possessed by NWS, which is known as 'vertical' proliferation. (See also Nonproliferation Treaty, Plutonium 239)

Protocol An international agreement that is usually less formal than a treaty. It is often used to supplement, elucidate, or qualify a treaty. A protocol enters into effect when signed by heads of state, but in the U.S., if a protocol is ratified, it is given the force of a treaty. A number of very important international agreements, such as the 1925 Geneva Protocol restricting biological and chemical weapons, have been entered into in the form of protocol. (See also ABM Treaty, SALT II, Ratification Process, Treaty)

Q

Qualitative Limitation Restrictions on the capabilities of a weapon system. These are distinct from quantitative limitations which restrict numbers of weapons. For example, in SALT II, such qualitative limitations included prohibitions on more than one new type of ICBM, restrictions on missile launch-weight and throw-weight, and limitations on the number of reentry vehicles a missile may carry. (See also SALT I, SALT II)

Quantitative Limitation Limits on the number of weapon systems in certain categories. An example in SALT II is the various aggregate limits on weapons. (See also SALT II).

R

Radar (Radio Detection and Ranging) The use of electromagnetic energy for the detection and location of objects. A radar installation operates by transmitting high frequency radio waves (microwaves) toward an object. When the microwaves are reflected back to the transmitter, they are compared to the originally transmitted signal. The result is information on the size, distance, etc., of the object being monitored. Radar penetrates cloud cover and also dry earth to varying depths. For example, radar imaging has detected dry river beds under deserts. (See also Line-of-Sight Radar, NTM, Over-The-Horizon Radar)

Radar Cross-Section The image produced by radar signals reflected from a target's surface. The size of the radar image is determined by the target's size, structural shape and the refractory characteristics of its material. (See also Backscatter)

Rapid Reload The capability of a launcher to be reloaded and fire a second missile within a short period after the initial firing. The term 'rapid' varies with the system under discussion. It could be measured in hours or days depending on the type of system. (See also ABM, Cold-Launch, ICBM, Silo)

Ratification Process The process, and final step, by which a country agrees to adhere to a treaty and make it part of its law. For some countries (e.g., the U.S.) ratification is a crucial step in domestic acceptance of a negotiated agreement. For others (e.g., the U.S.S.R.) ratification is merely a pro forma step following the signing of an agreement. If the U.S. does not ratify a treaty with the Soviet Union, the Soviets will withhold their approval. After a treaty is signed by the President of the United States, it is usually sent to the U.S. Senate. The senators debate the merits of the treaty among themselves, after bringing in experts to comment on the substance of the treaty. The Senate, exercising its advice and consent power, then either recommends ratification of the treaty, asks for renegotiation of the treaty's terms, or rejects it. Finally, if ratification is advised (i.e., the Senate approves by a two-thirds majority), the President ratifies the treaty (i.e., exchanges documents of ratification with the other treaty signers). (See also Agreement, Protocol, Treaty)

RC-135 The designation for a U.S. air-based radar system reportedly used to assist in early warning and Soviet missile test data collection, among other functions.

Reconnaissance The use of radar, listening posts, satellites and aircraft to survey the territory and activities of one nation as part of the intelligence collection process of another. (See also NTM, Photoreconnaissance, Satellite Surveillance)

Reentry Vehicle (RV) That portion of a ballistic missile that carries the nuclear warhead. It is called an RV because it reenters the earth's atmosphere in the terminal phase of the missile's flight. (See also Bus)

Remote Sensing A type of unilateral verification that does not require the physical presence of observers on the territory of another nation. Sensing is usually done by electronic means. (See also NTM)

Resolution The capability of a sensor to distinguish the individual parts of an object, closely adjacent optical images or sources of light, or events occurring at nearly the same time. For example, the resolution of a particular radar system is the minimum separation at which two objects can be distinguished by the radar. In the context of verification, resolution is the capability of an imaging system to make an area distinguishable in sufficient detail to ensure detection, recognition, identification and, if possible, description of whatever weapon system or facility is of interest. (See also Photoreconnaissance, Radar, Seismology)

Rhyolite-Chalet These U.S. satellites are in geosynchronous orbit at an altitude of 22,300 miles over the Soviet Union. They collect Soviet missile telemetry. (See also High Altitude Satellite)

RV (See Reentry Vehicle)

S

SALT (Strategic Arms Limitation Talks) Bilateral negotiations between the U.S. and U.S.S.R. which began in Helsinki in 1969 following preliminary discussions between President Johnson and Premier Kosygin at Glassboro, N.J., in June 1967. The aim of the SALT process was to move towards lower numbers of nuclear weapons by first establishing parity in forces and equal aggregate totals then moving to reductions in arsenals. Throughout the SALT negotiations, verification issues played a key role in determining the final outcome of many of the provisions (e.g., MIRVs, testing air defense systems in an ABM mode, and cruise and mobile missiles). (See also Deliberate Concealment, SALT I, SALT II, Vladivostok Accord)

SALT I This first set of strategic arms limitation talks produced two major agreements which were ratified in 1972, one permanent (the ABM Treaty with five-year reviews by the U.S. and the U.S.S.R.) and one of five years duration (Interim Agreement) limiting offensive arms. These were followed by an accord signed at Vladivostok in 1974 setting the framework for the SALT II negotiations. (See also ABM Treaty, Interim Agreement, Vladivostok Accord)

SALT II This Treaty, which was signed in 1979 and was to last through 1985, set limits on the number of U.S. and Soviet strategic offensive nuclear missiles, warheads, launchers and delivery vehicles, and constrained the deployment of new strategic offensive arms on both sides. The SALT II agreement was signed by President Carter and General Secretary Brezhnev in Vienna on June 18, 1979. President Carter transmitted it to the Senate on June 22, 1979, for its advice and consent to ratification. Because President Carter withdrew SALT II from consideration, Senate consent has not been given, but both the U.S. and U.S.S.R. have declared that they will adhere to the terms of the Treaty. (See also SALT I, Build-Down, Vladivostok Accord)

SAM (See Surface-to-Air Missile)

SAR A sensing device called synthetic aperture radar. (See also SLAR)

Satellites (See Close Look Satellites, NTM, Search and Find Satellites, Thermal Infrared Detectors)

SCC (See Standing Consultative Commission)

SDI (See Strategic Defense Initiative)

Sea-Launched Cruise Missile (SLCM) A cruise missile launched from a surface vessel or submarine. New U.S. SLCMs under test can be launched from standard torpedo tubes, which complicates an already difficult verification problem. Currently deployed Soviet SLCMs are older, of shorter range, and less accurate, although reports in the press suggest a new, more sophisticated, longer range SLCM may be under development. A new Soviet submarine (Oscar class) is reported to be a nuclear-powered cruise missile submarine. (See also Cruise Missile)

Search and Find Satellite These satellites are designed to cover large areas of land and ocean. They operate at altitudes over 100 miles. Some take television pictures and photographs which are then sent back to earth in film pods for analysis. Others provide 'real time' enhanced color and infrared television pictures as they pass over the earth. Since these satellites have multispectral capability (the ability to form images in several bands of visible and infrared light) they are able to distinguish features not apparent in normal light. These satellites have the ability to stay in orbit well over a year. (See also NTM, Satellites)

Seismic Coupling A measure of the fraction of the total energy released in an underground explosion that is transformed into seismic waves in the earth. The greater the coupling of a particular explosion, the greater the seismic waves. Longer seismic waves make the detection of an explosion and the discrimination from an earthquake (which has a different seismic signal) easier. The detonation of a nuclear explosion in a large salt cavity or other appropriate medium can 'decouple' the energy release from the earth's mantle. It has been theorized that such decoupling, which would make detection and discrimination more difficult, could permit evasion of threshold test limits and may be a barrier to verification of a comprehensive test ban. Recent seismic research suggests that with a network of in-country seismic sensors, the decoupling possibility would not impede detection of detonations down to about 1 KT or lower. (See also Compression Waves, Seismic Detection, Seismology, Shear Waves)

Seismic Detection In the context of verification, this method is used to detect and measure the yields of underground nuclear explosions. (See also NTM, Seismology, Seismic Coupling)

Seismology The study and analysis of seismic or earth vibration phenomena and signals. In the context of nuclear explosion limitations agreements, seismological instruments detect the underground event, and seismologists characterize and identify the event according to parameters that describe various source types (e.g., earthquake or explosion). The identification method is a discrimination process that attempts to determine if the event was an earthquake, a nuclear explosion, a chemical explosion, a rockburst or some other seismic phenomena. (See Acoustic Detection)

Sensors (See In-Country Verification, Infrared Scanners, NTM, Remote Sensors, Seismology, Thermal Infrared Detectors)

Shear Waves Seismic waves that are slower than compression waves (P waves), but still vibrate through the solid body of the earth. They are called S (for shear or secondary) waves because they are created by the shearing motion characteristic of an earthquake. An earthquake generates predominately S waves because it is produced when two blocks of the earth's crust rapidly slide past each other along a fault. (See also Seismology, Compression Waves)

Side-Looking Airborne Radar (SLAR) or Synthetic Aperture Radar An image-forming, high resolution radar carried on aircraft. SLAR is capable of surveillance beyond national borders and is largely unaffected by weather conditions, such as cloud cover or rain. (See also Radar)

SIGINT (See Signal Intelligence)

Signal Intelligence (SIGINT) The interception, processing, analysis, and dissemination of foreign electromagnetic (radio, radar, etc.) signals. This is an umbrella term for communications intelligence, electronic intelligence, and foreign instrumentation signals. (See also NTM)

Signature In the context of verification, the total set of characteristics (shape, radar image, electronic 'noise' emitted, wake, etc.) which are specific to a particular weapon or system. (See also NTM, Verification)

Silo A fixed, vertical structure either above ground or now more usually in the ground housing an ICBM and its launch support equipment. A silo includes the power supply, communications equipment and environmental control equipment, all of which have been constructed to withstand the effects of nearby nuclear explosions. (See also Hardened Silo, ICBM, Launcher)

SIR A sensing device called synthetic-aperture imaging radar. (See also SLAR).

SLAR (See Side-Looking Airborne Radar)

SLBM (See Submarine-Launched Ballistic Missile)

SLCM (See Sea-Launched Cruise Missile)

Soviet ASAT Weapon This three-ton Soviet system consists of an explosive anti-satellite warhead and its maneuvering engine (together known as the interceptor) launched from a modified SS-9 ballistic missile (the predecessor of the SS-18). The mode of attack of the Soviet ASAT system is called co-orbital interception. The interceptor is boosted into an orbit that is about the same as the target and, after a process that can take up to several hours, it closes in on the satellite to be destroyed. When the ASAT is close enough, the non-nuclear warhead explodes, firing a shotgun-like blast of metal pellets toward the target. Because the Soviet ASAT is ground-based, it must wait until the earth turns to bring the target over the launch site. The highest altitude a Soviet interceptor has reached is reported to be 1,400 miles, and thus high orbiting satellites are beyond its range. Since the Soviet ASAT booster is used to launch other space payloads, some experts believe that it would be easy for the U.S.S.R. to switch payloads to an ASAT weapon, making an ASAT weapons ban difficult to verify. (See also ASAT, U.S. ASAT Weapon)

Space Object Catalogue A North American Aerospace Defense Command (NORAD) intelligence facility that records the identity and current orbits of all space objects (several thousand in all). (See also ASAT)

Spacetrack A world-wide radar and optical system run by the U.S. Air Force for the detection, tracking, and identification of all objects in space.

SR-71 A sophisticated U.S. photoreconnaissance aircraft newer than the U-2. (See also Photoreconnaissance, U-2)

SS-17 A cold-launched, fourth generation Soviet ICBM with high accuracy that became operational in 1975. The SS-17 can carry four MIRVed warheads although there are some single warhead SS-17s. The missile has a range of about 10,000 km, and has targeting flexibility. There were 150 deployed as of April 1984. (See also ICBM, SS-18, SS-19)

SS-18 A very accurate, cold-launched, fourth generation Soviet ICBM. The SS-18 has a range of 11,000 km and can carry 10 MIRVed warheads. As of April 1984, there were 308 deployed. (See also ICBM, SS-17, SS-19)

SS-19 A hot-launched, very accurate, fourth generation Soviet ICBM that became operational in 1974. With a range of 10,000 km, the SS-19 can carry 6 MIRVed warheads. It has targeting flexibility enabling it to be aimed at either North America or Eurasia. As of April 1984, there were 360 deployed, some with single warheads. (See also ICBM, SS-17, SS-18)

SS-20 The newest Soviet MIRVed (three warheads) intermediate-range ballistic missile (IRBM). Currently, over 300 of these accurate missiles, first deployed in 1977, are stationed in the U.S.S.R. These IRBMs are primarily deployed west of the Ural mountains and are targeted on Western Europe. Some are also deployed in the eastern Soviet Union with Asian targets. It was the deployment of SS-20s that led to the NATO INF modernization decision in 1979. (See also INF, Pershing II)

SSB (See SSBN)

SSBN (See Sub-Surface Ballistic Nuclear [Missile Submarine])

SS-N- The general designation given to Soviet submarine-launched ballistic missiles (SLBMs). The designation would precede a number (e.g., 18) to identify a particular missile. The Soviet SLBMs deployed include: SS-N-5 with one reentry vehicle (RV) and a range of approximately 700 nm; SS-N-6 with one or two RVs and a range of approximately 1,300 nm; SS-N-8 with one RV and a range of approximately 4,300 nm; SS-N-17 with one RV and a range of from 1,300-1,600 nm; SS-N-18 with one-to-seven MIRVed RVs, a range of from 4,000 - 8,000 nm; SS-NX-20 with six-to-nine MIRVed RVs and a range of approximately 8,300 km.

SS-N-18 One of the newer Soviet submarine-launched ballistic missiles. It is deployed in three versions -- MIRVed (seven and three warheads) and a single warhead version. It has ranges of 6,500, 6,500, and 8,000 km respectively. (See also SS-N-, SLBM, Typhoon, SSBN, MIRV)

Standing Consultative Commission (SCC) A bilateral body established in SALT I as a forum for resolving compliance issues. The SCC consists of two commissioners (one from the U.S. and one from the U.S.S.R.), each accorded ambassadorial status, and their staffs. The U.S. Commissioner reports to the Arms Control and Disarmament Agency. The U.S. delegation includes representatives from the offices of the Secretary of Defense, the State Department, the Joint Chiefs of Staff and the intelligence community. The SCC, which convenes in Geneva twice a year, has mandated functions concerning compliance and verification issues, and weapons dismantling. It also treats questions related to the strategic balance, treaty amendments and arms control proposals. (See also SALT I, SALT II)

START (See Strategic Arms Reduction Talks)

Star Wars Name given in the popular press to the concept of a space-based ABM system designed to protect the U.S. by destroying Soviet ballistic missiles after they have been launched. The name is associated with President Reagan's speech of March 23, 1983, in which he called for the development of the means of rendering nuclear weapons 'impotent and obsolete.' (See also SDI)

Strakelets The FROD chosen by the U.S. to distinguish cruise missile-carrying B-52s from other B-52s, as required in the SALT II Treaty. Strakelets are rounded farings where the wing meets the fuselage. They are observable by NTM. (See also B-52, FRODs).

Strategic A term usually used to denote those weapons or forces capable of directly affecting another nation's war-fighting ability, as distinguished from tactical or theater weapons or forces. In the context of arms control treaties and verification, the term strategic is applied to specific long-range missiles and bombers. (See also SALT, START)

Strategic Arms Reduction Talks (START) Bilateral negotiations between the U.S. and U.S.S.R. seeking reductions, as opposed to limitations, in the strategic arsenals of both sides. These talks, which superseded SALT, were initiated by President Reagan in June 1982 and were suspended by the Soviet Union in December 1983. The U.S.S.R. stated that developments in the INF deployment by NATO required the Soviet Union to re-examine the issues under discussion in START. (See also INF, SALT)

Strategic Defense Initiative (SDI) A long-term research program of land- and space-based advanced anti-ballistic missile technologies. The program will provide development of options from which a president may choose in the 1990s. It is similar to previous ABM research with substantially greater funding. Candidate technologies include both kinetic energy (e.g., interceptor missiles and hypervelocity gun systems) and directed energy (e.g., space- and ground-based laser systems, and space-based particle beam) weapons. Other elements of the research program include development of surveillance, acquisition, and tracking capabilities, as well as technologies needed for the battle management/command, control and communication systems. Great technical problems must still be overcome before actual systems are proven effective. The purpose of the program differs from earlier efforts in that it now is directed towards a presidentially-stated goal and strategic concept that breaks with the previous premises of the U.S. and Soviet strategic relationship and with that of the ABM Treaty. In contrast to the mutual deterrence policy of the past 20 years, the goal is now 'eliminating the threat posed by (U.S.S.R.) strategic missiles', thereby providing complete protection of U.S. (and allied) strategic nuclear forces, territory and population. Some experts doubt that a BMD system can be developed to provide the degree of protection set forth by President Reagan in his March 23, 1983, 'Star Wars' speech. Others think that such efforts may further stimulate the arms race, destabilize the nuclear balance between the superpowers, and be more costly than production of the numbers of offensive weapons needed to overwhelm the defense. (See also ABM, BMD, Star Wars)

Submarine-Launched Ballistic Missile (SLBM) A ballistic missile carried by and launched from a submarine. (See also Polaris, Poseidon, SS-N-, Trident)

Sub-Surface Ballistic Nuclear [Missile Submarine] (SSBN) The Navy designation for nuclear-powered, ballistic-missile-carrying submarines used by the U.S., U.S.S.R., and U.K. Similar submarines used by the Soviets, that have diesel engines, are designated SSBs. (See also Delta, Hotel, Polaris, Poseidon, Trident, Typhoon, Yankee)

Surface-to-Air Missile (SAM) A ground-launched air defense missile. The U.S. no longer deploys SAMs for continental air defense, though the Pentagon has proposed the development of the SAM-D. Older systems are the Nike Ajax and Hercules. The U.S.S.R. has some twelve different SAM systems, of varying missions (from low altitude defense to high altitude defense) and age (some are upgrades of older systems). (See also Air Defense)

Surveillance Satellites (See Close Look Satellites, NTM, Search and Find Satellites, Thermal Infrared Detectors)

Synergism The cooperative interaction of discrete elements or bodies so that the total effect is greater than the sum of the effects of individual elements acting independently. In the context of verification, a group of complementary sensor systems acting together can produce more confidence in verification capability than sensors acting independently. In some circumstances, getting sensors in the right places requires cooperation among parties. (See also NTM)

T

Tactical Relating to battlefield operations, as distinguished from theater or strategic operations. Tactical weapons are not designed to reach an opponent's rear area as are theater or strategic weapons. (See also Strategic)

Talon Gold The potential pointing and tracking component of the space-based laser system being developed as part of the Reagan Administration's Strategic Defense Initiative. It is scheduled to be tested in the late 1980s. (See also SDI)

Teal Ruby A new U.S. surveillance satellite designed to detect aircraft from space and scheduled to be launched from the space shuttle in 1986.

TEL (See Transporter-Erector-Launcher)

Telemetry In the context of verification, data electronically transmitted from sensing instruments on a weapon system being tested to personnel conducting the test, who monitor the functions and performance parameters. 'Listening to' this telemetry by NTM is a principal means of verifying that performance-related restrictions are being complied with, as specified in arms control treaties. (See also Encryption, Ground Surveillance, NTM)

Test Range Locations and facilities, stipulated in SALT, where ABM and ICBM testing activity may take place. For the U.S. the missile launch points are at Cape Canaveral, Florida, and near Santa Maria, California, and the ranges are at White Sands, New Mexico, and Kwajalein in the Pacific. For the U.S.S.R. they are Sary Shagan, Kapustin Yar, Kamchatka Peninsula, and the areas near Tyuratam (in Southwest Russia) and Plesetsk (in the Northwest section of the Soviet Union). The ranges may extend across the continent, as is usually the case with the U.S.S.R., or out over the ocean, as is the case with the U.S. Kwajalein range. Notification of future launch points and test ranges takes place in the SCC. (See also Declared Facility, SCC)

Theater Nuclear Weapons A nuclear weapon, usually of longer range and larger yield than tactical nuclear weapons, that can be used in theater operations (e.g., Europe or Asia). Many strategic nuclear weapons can be used in theater operations, but not all theater weapons are designed for strategic use. The Soviet SS-20 and the U.S. Pershing II are usually considered theater nuclear weapons.

Thermal Infrared Detectors Sensors included in the payload of early-warning satellites which measure the radiated energy of the hot plume of a missile during its boost phase. (See also NTM)

Threshold Test Ban Treaty (TTBT) A treaty which sets a maximum limit of 150 KT on the yield of underground nuclear weapon tests. Signed in July 1974 and sent to the U.S. Senate in July 1976, the Treaty is as yet unratified. Soviet compliance with the TTBT is an ongoing issue. (See also Seismology)

Throw-Weight The maximum weight of the warheads plus the guidance unit and penetration aids which can be delivered by a missile over a particular range and in a stated trajectory. (See also Bus, Payload, PBV)

Titan II A liquid-fuel, two-stage U.S. ICBM, with a single 8 to 10 megaton reentry vehicle. Deployed in the early 1960s in substantial numbers, the Titan force is currently being deactivated. As of March 1984, 33 Titans were deployed in hardened silos in Arizona and Arkansas. (See also ICBM, Minuteman, MX)

Transporter-Erector-Launcher (TEL) A ground-based, wheeled vehicle that can carry, position and fire land-mobile ballistic missiles. TELs are currently used by the U.S. Pershing IA and Pershing II and the Soviet SS-20. (See also Launcher).

Treaty A formal agreement entered into between two or more countries. The treaty process includes negotiations, signing, Senate approval, exchange of ratification documents, publishing and proclamation, and treaty execution. A treaty having only two signatory states is called bilateral, one with more than two parties is multilateral. A treaty may expire at the end of a specified time period, when certain conditions have been met, or by mutual agreement. It may have regular review periods (e.g., every five years) after which if the parties agree that the treaty is still useful, it will continue in force until the next review. In the U.S., all treaties are negotiated under the direction of the president. A treaty must be approved by a two-thirds vote in the Senate, followed by presidential ratification. Increasingly, American presidents have come to depend on executive agreements rather than treaties. In a political sense, a treaty is the highest form of agreement between countries, but in a legal sense, there is no difference in the binding nature of executive agreements and treaties. (See also Agreed Statement, Common Understanding, Executive Agreement, Ratification Process, Unilateral Statements)

Trident The U.S. Navy's newest and largest nuclear-powered, ballistic missile-carrying submarine. Designated the Ohio Class, the Trident has 24 missile tubes capable of launching Trident I (C-4) or Trident II (D-5) missiles. Twenty Trident submarines are planned by 1998. (See also SLBM, SSBN, Trident Missile)

Trident Missile The most modern U.S. submarine-launched ballistic missile. The Trident I (C-4), with eight warheads, is currently deployed, while the larger and more accurate Trident II (D-5) is proposed for deployment in the late 1980s. The D-5 will have more warheads (approximately ten) and better accuracy than the C-4. (See also MX, Polaris, Poseidon, SLBM, Trident)

TTBT (See Threshold Test Ban Treaty)

Type Rules Treaty limits that restrict a weapon system, once it is deployed, to the same function it performed when being tested. For example, a ballistic missile, if tested as a single warhead ICBM, must be deployed as such and not as a multiple warhead ICBM. (See also SALT II)

Typhoon The newest class of Soviet nuclear ballistic missile submarine. It is equipped with 20 missile launch tubes and carries the Soviet SS-N-18 and SS-N-20 MIRVed SLBMs. (See also Delta, SLBM, SSB, SSBN, SS-N-18, SS-N-)

U

U-2 A U.S. photoreconnaissance aircraft that is also used to monitor Soviet ICBM tests by intercepting missile telemetry. (See also Photoreconnaisance, SR-71)

U.S. ASAT Weapon This interceptor, known as the Miniature Homing Vehicle (MHV), is carried into space on a two-stage rocket launched from an F-15 fighter plane. The MHV is a small cylinder (about one foot in diameter) that uses direct ascent interception to destroy its target. The MHV is launched from the F-15 and is propelled into space by its booster rockets.

After these boosters fall away, the interceptor follows a ballistic trajectory until it approaches the target. The infrared homing device within the cylinder then guides the vehicle into collision with the target. The entire process takes 10 to 20 minutes. Because the U.S. ASAT is plane borne, interception of a satellite can take place anywhere. Currently, the MHV is only able to reach low-orbiting satellites. The small size and launching technique of the U.S. ASAT weapon makes it more difficult to verify than its larger Soviet counterpart. (See also ASAT, Soviet ASAT Weapon)

Unilateral Statements Policy statements made by one party to a treaty on the course of action that party proposes to follow with regard to one of the treaty's provisions. A unilateral statement is communicated to the other negotiating party for its information and guidance. Unilateral statements by one side are not binding on the other. They are sometimes incorporated into the statements and understandings attached to the treaty. (See also Treaty)

Uranium 235 (U-235) The only fissile isotope naturally occurring in quantities large enough for a practical chain reaction. Weapons materials (those made of uranium) normally consist of 90% of this isotope, whereas commercial nuclear power reactors use uranium having a maximum of 3% U-235. Nuclear weapons can be made from U-235 or Pu-239. (See also Plutonium 239)

V

Vela U.S. Satellites reportedly used for detection of above-ground nuclear explosions and early warning detection of ICBM launches. It operates at an altitude of about 60,000 miles.

Verification The technological and intelligence process involving both monitoring and evaluation that establishes the fact of compliance with arms control agreements. (See also Confidence Levels, NTM, Signature)

Verification Community The main agencies and committees with responsibility for managing, analyzing and evaluating the information provided by verification systems. It includes the National Security Council, ACDA, the Department of State, the Office of the Secretary of Defense, the Joint Chiefs of Staff and the intelligence community, the Senate Foreign Relations Committee, House Foreign Affairs Committee and the Senate and House Armed Services Committees. (See also Intelligence Community)

Vidicon Camera Essentially, a color television camera. A vidicon camera is placed on a satellite to take color photographs of the earth.

Vladivostok Accord A framework for a SALT II Treaty agreed to at a meeting in Vladivostok between Gerald Ford and Leonid Brezhnev in November 1974. Important concessions were made at this meeting, including the Soviet acceptance of equal ceilings of strategic weapons launchers and deferral of the issue of American forward-based systems -- weapons based on the periphery of the Soviet Union. In return, the U.S. deferred discussion of the controversial Soviet Backfire bomber. The Accord, an executive agreement later endorsed by the U.S. Congress, was expected to lead to the speedy completion of Salt II, possibly in 1975 or 1976. However, two factors impeded progress: the lack of agreement on cruise missiles, and growing resistance in the U.S. to negotiating with the Soviets and to the SALT process. (See also Backfire, Executive Agreement, Protocol, SALT I, SALT II, Treaty)

Y

Yankee A class of Soviet nuclear ballistic missile submarine. It is deployed in two versions. The Yankee I has 16 missile launch tubes; the Yankee II has 12 tubes. They carry the SS-N-6 and SS-N-17 SLBMs respectively. (See also Hotel, Typhoon)

IV Selected Bibliography

Chapter One

1. **Arms Control and Disarmament Agreements.** Washington, D.C.: U.S. Arms Control and Disarmament Agency, 1982, 290 pp.
   A comprehensive guide to the texts and histories of negotiations of the arms control treaties the U.S. has signed.
2. Aspin, Les. "The Verification of the SALT II Agreement." **Scientific American.** Vol. 240, No. 2, February, 1979, pp. 38-45.
   U.S. Representative Les Aspin concludes that "the multiple and duplicative methods of detection at the disposal of the United States are sufficient to reveal any cheating on a scale adequate to threaten this country militarily." Aspin also thinks that the verification standards of SALT III would have to be lowered significantly as a result of technological advances in cruise missiles and transferable MIRV payloads.
3. Buchan, Glenn. "The Verification Spectrum." **Bulletin of the Atomic Scientists.** Vol. 39, November, 1983, pp. 16-19.
   Buchan examines three schools of thought on verification (substantive, legalistic and metaphysical), and discusses their meaning in the SALT/START process.
4. Krepon, Michael. **Arms Control: Verification and Compliance.** Headline Series, No. 270. New York: Foreign Policy Association, 1984, 64 pp.
   This monograph presents the basic concepts of verification and illuminates current compliance controversies. It examines both the politics of and Soviet views on verification. Two chapters deal with treaty compliance and "compliance diplomacy."
5. **Verification: The Critical Element of Arms Control.** Washington, D.C.: U.S. Arms Control and Disarmament Agency, 1978, 35 pp.
   A concise report dealing with the different political, ideological and technical aspects and consequences of verification in past, present and future agreements.

Chapter Two

1. Aspin, Les and Kaplan, Fred M. "Verification in Perspective." In **Verification and SALT.** Edited by William C. Potter. Boulder, CO: Westview, 1980, pp. 177-192.
   In this chapter, the authors attempt to put the issue of verification of strategic arms agreements into perspective. They discuss the term "adequately verifiable" and stress "that levels of confidence and margins of error are inevitable...the important questions are how high can we make the levels of confidence and how narrow the margins of error."
2. Buchheim, Robert W. and Caldwell, Dan. **The US-USSR Standing Consultative Commission: Description and Appraisal.** Center for Foreign Policy Development, Brown University, Working Paper #2, May 1983.
   This paper describes the general functions of the SCC, outlines its past role in SALT and appraises its future.
3. Einhorn, Robert J. "Treaty Compliance." **Foreign Policy** No. 45, Winter 1981-82, pp. 29-47.
   This article reviews Soviet compliance in implementing the Strategic Arms Limitation Talks I, The Threshhold Test Ban Treaty, and the Biological Weapons Convention.It surveys problems in developing verification procedures for arms control agreements.The author stresses the need to promote confidence in the bureaucracy, in Congress, and among the people that the agreements are functioning well and that U.S. interests are being protected.

4. Farley, Phillip J. "Verification: On the Plus Side of the SALT II Balance Sheet." In **Verification and SALT**. Edited by William C. Potter.Boulder, CO: Westview, 1980, pp. 221-228.

   In this chapter, the former deputy director of ACDA attempts to answer the questions what is "adequate verification?" and what are the military and political dimensions of "the success or failure of verification?" The author stresses the contribution of SALT (particularly SALT verification agreements) to U.S. intelligence capabilities and to increased confidence in strategic stability.

5. Fisher, Roger. **Improving Compliance with International Law**. Charlottesville, VA: University Press of Virginia, 1981, 370 pp.

   Fisher's study includes an assessment and several examples dealing with military treaties and how to approach and respond to an incident of noncompliance in accordance with the international legal system.

6. Goldblat, Jozef. "Verification and Enforcement of Arms Control." SIPRI, London: Taylor and Francis, 1982, pp. 285-316.

   This chapter outlines the role of verification in arms control agreements. It explains how bilateral and multilateral agreements are monitored, and addresses the issues of treaty violations and institutional structures for verification.

7. Harris, William R. **A SALT Safeguard Program – Coping with Soviet Deception Under Strategic Arms Agreements**. RAND Report, P8388, September, 1979.17 pp. Also in **Verification and SALT**. Edited by William C. Potter. Boulder, CO: Westview, 1980, pp. 129-142.

   The author presents a skeptical view of the relative importance of verification while stressing the need for warning of Soviet "breakout" (attempts to upset the balance of nuclear deterrence). Harris asks the question whether SALT would "help or hurt the United States in obtaining strategic warning, including timely breakout warning?"

8. Katz, Amrom. "The Fabric of Verification: The Warp and the Woof." In **Verification and SALT**. Edited by William C. Potter. Boulder, CO: Westview, 1980, pp. 193-220.

   In this updated and abridged version of the author's report for the Heritage Foundation, the former head of the Verification and Analysis Bureau in ACDA presents an outline of the role of verification in arms control agreements by using historical examples and emphasizing the limitations of verification. Katz stresses that possible Soviet covert deployment of strategic forces has not been given adequate attention and poses a major problem for verification.

9. Kruzel, Joseph J. "Verification and SALT II." In **Verification and SALT**. Edited by William C. Potter. Boulder, CO: Westview, 1980, pp. 95-110.

   The author emphasizes that arms control agreements depend upon confidence in compliance. He uses SALT II as a case study in determining "how much confidence is enough."

10. Lowenthal, Mark. "U.S. Organization for Verification." In **Verification and SALT**. Edited by William C. Potter. Boulder, CO: Westview, 1980, pp. 77-94.

    In this chapter, the author outlines the formal structure of U.S. SALT verification efforts. Lowenthal emphasizes, however, that the "formal structure described here is but a general framework within which verification is handled and that the actual functioning of the system will not always correspond to this structure."

11. Meyer, Stephen M. "Verification & Risk in Arms Control." **International Security**, Vol. 8, No. 4, Spring 1984, pp. 91-110.

    Meyer attempts to develop a complete understanding of the fundamental relationship between verification in arms control and risk to U.S. national security. He does this by examining the assumptions and premises of those who contend that a less than 100% verifiable treaty cannot be in the national interest.

12. SIPRI. "A Role for Satellites in Verification of Arms Control Agreements." In **World Armaments and Disarmament: SIPRI Yearbook 1980**. SIPRI. London: Taylor and Francis, 1980, pp. 187-208.

Summarizes the proposal for an International Satellite Monitoring Agency and provides several extensive tables describing U.S. and Soviet satellite systems. In addition, it provides a brief description of several categories of U.S. and Soviet satellites.

13. "The Soviet Approach to Arms Control." In **Challenges for U.S. National Security**. Report prepared by the staff of the Carnegie Panel on U.S. Security and the Future of Arms Control, Carnegie Endowment for International Peace, Washington, D.C., 1983, pp. 1-24.

This section notes and briefly analyzes the relative Soviet indifference towards verification.

14. "Strategic Arms Limitation: The Soviet View." **Survival**. Vol. 20, May-June, 1978, pp. 121-127.

A Soviet commentary (from the February 11, 1978 issue of **Pravda**) reflecting the Russian view in the arms control process. It includes a section on verification where the author claims any U.S. questions on Soviet compliance are designed to sabotage the agreement. In addition, the author asserts that "When it signs an agreement, the Soviet Union strictly and unswervingly observes its commitments."

15. Wallop, Michael. "Soviet Violations of Arms Control Agreements: So What?" **Strategic Review**, Summer 1983, pp. 11-20.

The U.S. Senator from Wyoming thinks that the debate over Soviet violations of arms control agreements is primarily quibbling over technicalities.The fundamental issue concerns U.S. national security after decades of arms control efforts. Wallop believes that arms control should be viewed in terms of its effects on U.S. military strength and not vice-versa.

Chapter Three

1. Blair, Bruce and Brewer, Garry. **Verifying SALT Agreements**. ACIA Working Paper #19. Los Angeles: Center for International and Strategic Affairs, UCLA, 1980, 61 pp. Also in **Verification and SALT**. Edited by William C. Potter. Boulder, CO: Westview, 1980, pp. 7-48.

The authors provide a detailed and technical description of U.S. verification capabilities based upon unclassified sources. Their report "is a survey of the relevant technical means of verification and a description of the strengths and weaknesses of each in the context of SALT II verification requirements."

2. Hafemeister, David. "Advances in Verification Technology." **Bulletin of the Atomic Scientists**, January, 1985, pp. 35-40.

This article discusses several advances in satellite monitoring technology and data processing. It concentrates on image enhancement methods such as digital image processing and charge-coupled devices which assist analysts in extracting maximum information from satellite photographs.

3. Hafemeister, David; Romm, Joseph; and Tsipis, Kosta. "The Verification of Compliance with Arms Control Agreements." **Scientific American**, Vol. 252, No. 3, March, 1985.

The authors report that military activities in the U.S.S.R. can be unilaterally monitored by the U.S. with the aid of a wide spectrum of remote-sensing technologies, including high-resolution satellite photography.

4. Krepon, Michael and Blechman, Barry. "America's Global Lie Detector." **Popular Mechanics**, February, 1984, pp. 86-89.

An overview of U.S. surveillance technology and intelligence-gathering methods.

5. Richelson, Jeffrey. "The Keyhole Satellite Program." **The Journal of Strategic Studies**, June, 1984, pp. 121-153.

This article discusses the U.S. photographic reconnaissance satellite program known as "keyhole." It begins with an overview of the sensors deployed on the satellites and their utility.The main body of the text is devoted to a historical examination of the program and the capabilities and uses of the various satellites.

6. Richelson, Jeffrey. **The U.S. Intelligence Community**. Cambridge, MA: Ballinger Publishing Company, 1985, 358 pp.

A comprehensive portrait of the U.S. intelligence-gathering organizations.It charts the evolution of the U.S. intelligence agencies, explains the interrelationships between them and examines their role in U.S. national security.

7. Scoville, Herbert J. "Verification of Soviet Strategic Missile Tests." In **Verification and SALT**. Edited by William C. Potter. Boulder, CO: Westview, 1980, pp. 163-176.

The author illustrates the importance for arms control verification of U.S. efforts to monitor Soviet strategic missile tests.He gives a detailed outline of U.S. methods for monitoring Soviet strategic programs and explains (using the ABM Treaty and SALT II as examples) how observation of Soviet missile tests are essential for the verification of strategic arms agreements.

8. SIPRI. "Verification of the SALT II Treaty." In **World Armaments and Disarmament: SIPRI Yearbook 1980**. SIPRI. London: Taylor and Francis, 1980, pp. 285-315.

This article discusses the various procedures used to monitor ballistic missiles and flight tests which enhance verification. The author concludes that the inadequacies of SALT II are due more to political shortcomings than to deficiencies in NTM.

9. Tsipis, Kosta; Hafemeister, David; and Janeway, Penny. **Arms Control Verification: The Technologies That Make it Possible**. Elmsford, NY: Pergamon-Brassey, 1985.

This work addresses some of the broader verification and compliance issues and concentrates on NTM technologies.

Chapter Four

1. Brown, Paul S. et. al., Editors for **Energy and Technology Review**, Lawrence Livermore National Laboratory, May, 1983, Special Issue on Treaty Verification.

"This special issue...is devoted to the Laboratory's efforts relating to nuclear arms control negotiations and treaty verification measures." The contents are "The Test Ban Treaties: Verifying Compliance"; "Negotiating With the Soviets"; "The Regional Seismic Test Network"; "Peaceful Nuclear Explosions in Soviet Gas Condensate Fields"; "Ionospheric Detection of Explosions"; and "Seismic Verification of a Comprehensive Test Ban."

2. Sykes, Lynn R. and Evernden, Jack F. "The Verification of a Comprehensive Nuclear Test Ban." **Scientific American**, Vol. 247, October, 1982, pp. 47-55.

This article provides a technical explanation of how networks of seismic instruments could detect even small clandestine explosions and could monitor a comprehensive test ban with high reliability.

3. U.S. Congress. Senate Committee on Foreign Relations. Subcommittee on Arms Control, Oceans and International Environment. **Threshhold Test Ban and Peaceful Nuclear Explosion Treaties: Hearings**. 95th Congress, 1st Session, 1977, 159 pp.

A variety of viewpoints, ranging from the confidence of the director of the Arms Control and Disarmament Agency to the guarded optimism of the director of the Los Alamos Scientific Laboratory, are presented regarding the verification of any test ban treaty.

Chapter Five

1. Garn, Jake. "The SALT II Verification Myth." **Strategic Review**, Vol. 7, Summer 1979, pp. 16-24.
   Senator Garn believes that the U.S. ability to verify SALT I is insufficient, and the qualitative provisions of SALT II are beyond current U.S. unilateral capabilities of verification. Garn thinks that the U.S. should consider additional verification steps such as reciprocal territorial monitoring and on-site inspection.
2. Greb, Allen G. and Heckrotte, Warren. "The Long History: The Test Ban Debate." **Bulletin of the Atomic Scientists**, Vol. 39, August-September 1983, pp. 36-41.
   The article reviews the "long and complicated history of the negotiations to achieve a complete (nuclear weapons) test ban." The authors conclude that the test ban is an issue that is unlikely to fade away although the possibility of finding a way to bring about such a ban remains an unanswered question.
3. Kemp, Jack F. "Congressional Expectations of SALT II." **Strategic Review**, Vol. 7, No. 1, Winter 1979, pp. 16-25.
   Congressman Kemp believes that the qualitative properties of today's increasingly sophisticated weapons are becoming progressively more difficult to monitor. Kemp thinks that existing intelligence systems can be misled by Soviet deceptions and many aspects of the SALT II agreement cannot be verified with high confidence.
4. Seaborg, Glenn T. **Kennedy, Khrushchev and the Test Ban**. Berkeley: University of California Press, 1981, 320 pp.
   Seaborg, the former chairman of the AEC during the LTBT negotiations, presents an intricate history of the negotiations strategic and diplomatic techniques leading up to the signing and ratification of the 1963 Limited Test Ban Treaty.
5. Smith, Gerard C. **Doubletalk: The Story of the First Strategic Arms Limitation Talks**. New York: Doubleday & Company, 1980.
   In this definitive account of SALT I, Ambassador Smith provides a detailed picture of the negotiations within the U.S. administration as well as those with the Soviets. He also relates the role that verification played in the failure to reach a MIRV ban in SALT I.
6. Talbott, Strobe. **Endgame: The Inside Story of SALT II**. New York: Harper and Row, 1979.
   Talbott presents a detailed account of the SALT II negotiations, including their political backdrop, verification issues, and others.
7. U.S. Congress. Senate Select Committee on Intelligence. **Principal Findings on the Capabilities of the U.S. to Monitor the SALT II Treaty: Report**. 1979, 5 pp.
   The report concludes that the United States may monitor the SALT II Treaty with high to moderate confidence. In addition, it notes that without the Treaty the Soviets would be free to engage in unrestrained concealment and deception measures which would significantly hinder verification.
8. Wolfe, Thomas. **The SALT Experience**. Cambridge: Ballinger, 1979, 405 pp. (See also Rand Report R-1686-PR September 1975. **The SALT Experience: Its Impact on U.S. and Soviet Strategic Policy and Decisionmaking**.)
   In this broad historical and analytical study of the SALT process, Wolfe shows how verification issues have played an increasingly important role.
9. York, Herbert F. "Bilateral Negotiations and the Arms Race." **Scientific American**, Vol. 249, No. 4, October, 1983, pp. 149-160.
   A historical review of the negotiating positions of the U.S. and the U.S.S.R. for several major arms control talks. It describes the special problems each side has had in dealing with the other.

Chapter Six

1. Arms Control Association. **Analysis of a Quarter Century of Soviet Compliance Practices Under Arms Control Commitments: 1958-1983.** Washington, D.C., October 11, 1984.
   Background and analysis is given for each of the assertions put forward in an October 1984 report by the U.S. General Advisory Committee on Arms Control and Disarmament regarding Soviet noncompliance over the past 25 years.
2. Federation of American Scientists. **The General Advisory Committee Report**. Washington, D.C., 1984.
   An analysis and detailed evaluation of the General Advisory Committee on Arms Control and Disarmament Report is given. The Federation of American Scientists concludes that the intent of the General Advisory Committee was simply to discredit arms control rather than to report on it.
3. Hamm, Manfred. "Soviet SALT Cheating: The New Evidence." **Heritage Foundation Report**, No. 31, Summer, 1983.
   Hamm presents charges of repeated Soviet violations of the ABM Treaty provisions of SALT I and calls for the U.S. abrogation of that Treaty "unless Moscow can refute the evidence that its radar and weapons programs are not designed for an ABM role..."
4. Klass, Philip J. "U.S. Scrutinizing New Soviet Radar." **Aviation Week and Space Technology**, August 22, 1983.
   The author reports that U.S. intelligence officials are concerned that a new Soviet ballistic missile detection radar in central Siberia is a violation of the ABM Treaty.
5. McClure, James A. **Congressional Record – Senate**. April 14, 1983, pp. S4640-S4648.
   The senior U.S. Senator from Idaho details alleged Soviet violations and circumstances of arms agreements. He argues that the U.S. should not be kept from modernizing its strategic nuclear forces by an unratified treaty (SALT II) which, according to McClure, the Soviets have repeatedly violated.
6. **President's Report to the Congress on Soviet Noncompliance with Arms Control Agreements**. White House, Office of the Press Secretary, January 23, 1984, 6pp.
   The President's Unclassified Report to the Congress on Soviet Noncompliance with Arms Control Agreements. White House, Office of the Press Secretary, February 1, 1985.
   The General Advisory Committee on Arms Control and Disarmament. **A Quarter Century of Soviet Compliance Practices Under Arms Control Commitments: 1958-1983**. Washington, D.C.: U.S. Arms Control and Disarmament Agency, October 1984.
   The Reagan Administration's unclassified reports on possible Soviet violations of existing arms control agreements. The two White House reports list current issues of contention, the Soviet obligations, and the Administration's findings. The General Advisory Committee's report covers 25 years and a range of issues.
7. **Report to the Congress on U.S. Policy on ASAT and Arms Control**. White House, Office of the Press Secretary, March 31, 1984, 16 pp.
   The unclassified version of a detailed report by the Reagan Administration on its policy on anti-satellite arms control.
8. Smith, R. Jeffrey. "U.S. Experts Condemn Soviet Radar." **Science**, March 22, 1985, p. 1142.
   Smith writes that most U.S. experts agree that the Krasnoyarsk radar violates the ABM Treaty, but they differ on its strategic significance.
9. U.S. Department of State. Bureau of Public Affairs. **Verification of SALT II Agreement**. Special Report No. 56, August, 1979, 6 pp.
   In an update of the 1978 report, the document assesses the consolidated provisions of the SALT II Treaty and concludes that any significant Soviet violation would be detected. It also notes that what the U.S. lacks in verification, it makes up for in flexible weapons development.

10. "The United States Violates its International Commitments." **News & Views from the U.S.S.R.**, Soviet Embassy, Information Department, Washington, D.C., January 30, 1984, 6 pp.

The Soviet response to the Reagan Administration's noncompliance report. It details five areas where the U.S. has allegedly violated its international commitments.

11. Wilke, John. "Seismic Verification." **Bulletin of the Atomic Scientists**, Vol. 39, No. 3, March, 1983, pp. 4-5.

Wilke concludes that in spite of current suspicion of Soviet violations of the Threshhold Test Ban Treaty and doubts about U.S. ability to monitor Soviet compliance with it, the Soviets have not violated the Treaty, and the U.S. would detect it if they did.

12. Longstreth, Thomas K.; Pike, John E.; and Rhinelander, John B. **The Impact of U.S. and Soviet Ballistic Missile Defense Programs on the ABM Treaty**, A Report for the National Campaign to Save the ABM Treaty, March, 1985.

13. Boutwell, Jeffrey and Scribner, Richard A. **The Strategic Defense Initiative: Some Arms Control Implications**. AAAS, Publication No. 85-9, 1985.

Chapter Seven

1. Colby, William E. "Verification of a Nuclear Freeze." **The Nuclear Weapons Freeze and Arms Control**. Center for Science and International Affairs, John F. Kennedy School of Government, Harvard University, 1983, pp. 73-75.

Colby concludes that U.S. intelligence capabilities are sophisticated enough to adequately verify a nuclear freeze.

2. Cohen, Stuart A. "SALT Verification: The Evolution of Soviet Views and Their Meaning for the Future." **Orbis**, Vol. 24, Fall 1980, pp. 657-683. Also in **Verification and SALT**. Edited by William C. Potter. Boulder, CO: Westview, 1980, pp. 49-76.

The author examines the evolution of Soviet thinking in regards to strategic arms limitation and verification and concludes that a variety of factors are responsible for Soviet recalcitrance in verification. In addition, he notes the virtual nonexistence of detailed Soviet studies on verification.

3. Forsberg, Randall. "A Bilateral Nuclear Weapons Freeze." **Scientific American**, November 1982, Vol. 247, No. 5, pp. 52-61. Also, "Stopping the Nuclear Arms Race: Defining the Possible." **The Nuclear Weapons Freeze and Arms Control**. Center for Science and International Affairs, John F. Kennedy School of Government, Harvard University, 1983, pp. 170-176.

In this exposition of a nuclear-weapons freeze, Forsberg argues that it is possible to verify such a freeze. The author believes that the more comprehensive the freeze, the easier it would be to detect a violation of it. Also, a cutoff of the production of fissionable material would be verifiable.

4. Garthoff, Raymond L. "Soviet Perspectives." In **Cruise Missiles: Technology, Strategy and Politics**. Edited by Richard K. Betts. Washington, D.C.: The Brookings Institution, 1981, pp. 339-358.

The author presents Soviet views on the effects of cruise missiles on arms control efforts. Garthoff reveals Soviet concern that cruise missiles will present difficulties for verification that will hamper or "even preclude arms limitations."

5. Kincade, William H. "Arms Control: Negotiated Solutions." In **Cruise Missiles: Technology, Strategy and Politics**. Edited by Richard K. Betts. Washington, D.C.: The Brookings Institution, 1981, pp. 309-338.

In this article dealing with the arms control aspects of cruise missiles, the author raises the issue of whether the military benefits of cruise missiles are short term in comparison to the longer term arms control difficulties they generate. Kincade analyzes the impact of cruise missiles on the strategic environment—particularly in how they affect stability. Verification problems and possible approaches to solving them are also explored.

6. Pike, John. "Anti-Satellite Weapons and Arms Control." **Arms Control Today**, December, 1983, pp. 1 and 4-7.
   Pike explains the development and uses of U.S. and Soviet ASAT weapons and the possibilities for controlling them through negotiation. He concludes that an "agreement limiting ASATs can be adequately verified."
7. Quester, George H. "Arms Control: Toward Informal Solutions." In **Cruise Missiles: Technology, Strategy and Politics**. Edited by Richard K. Betts. Washington, D.C.: The Brookings Institution, 1981, pp. 275-308.
   This article covers some of the verification problems posed by cruise missiles. The author also looks at potential new methods of monitoring weapons systems.
8. **Report to Congress on U.S. Policy on ASAT and Arms Control**. White House, Office of the Press Secretary, March 31, 1984, 16 pp.
   The unclassified version of a detailed report by the Reagan Administration on its policy on anti-satellite arms control.
9. Scoville, Herbert Jr. "First Steps Toward a Freeze." **The Nuclear Weapons Freeze and Arms Control**. Center for Science and International Affairs, John F. Kennedy School of Government, Harvard University, 1983, pp. 75-80.
   The author outlines a possible structure for a freeze on nuclear weapons and addresses the issue of verifying a freeze. Scoville argues that overall U.S. verification capabilities would be enhanced by a freeze.
10. Sharp, Jane M.O. "Exploring the Feasibility of a Ban on Warhead Production." **The Nuclear Weapons Freeze and Arms Control**. Center for Science and International Affairs, John F. Kennedy School of Government, Harvard University, 1983, pp. 80-87.
    The author examines the impact of verification concerns on the feasibility and acceptability of a nuclear freeze.
11. SIPRI. **Outer Space — A New Dimension of the Arms Race**. SIPRI. London: Taylor and Francis, 1982, 423 pp.
    This book, containing several essays assessing weapons and satellites in space, also contains several sections calling for the creation of an International Satellite Monitoring Agency which would contribute to the discovery of violations and would make concealment more difficult.
12. Slocombe, Walter. "Verification and Negotiation." **The Nuclear Weapons Freeze and Arms Control**. Center for Science and International Affairs, John F. Kennedy School of Government, Harvard University, 1983, pp. 80-87.
    The author examines the impact of verification concerns on the feasibility and acceptability of a nuclear freeze.
13. Stoetz, Howard Jr. "Monitoring a Nuclear Freeze." **International Security**, Vol. 8, No. 4, Spring 1984, pp. 91-110.
    A former U.S. intelligence analyst discusses the verifiability of a nuclear freeze. The article examines verification methods and measures to improve monitoring confidence.
14. Von Hippel, Frank and Levy, Barbera G. "Controlling the Source: Verification of a Cutoff in the Production of Plutonium and High Enriched Uranium for Nuclear Weapons." In **Arms Control Verification: The Technologies That Make it Possible**. Edited by Kosta Tsipis, David Hafemeister and Penny Janeway. Elmsford, NY: Pergamon-Brassey, 1985; and von Hippel, Frank; Albright, David H.; and Levi, Barbara G. "Stopping the Production of Fissile Materials for Weapons". **Scientific American**. September, 1985.

The authors argue that a cutoff in the production of plutonium and high enriched uranium is verifiable. They present extensive technical analysis to support their conclusion.

15. Weiler, Lawrence D. "Strategic Cruise Missiles and the Future of SALT." **Arms Control Today**, Vol. 5, No. 10, October 1975. Reprinted in **Negotiating Security: An Arms Control Reader**. Edited by William H. Kincade and Jeffrey D. Porro. The Carnegie Endowment for International Peace, 1978, pp. 85-88.
    Verification problems resulting from the development of a new nuclear delivery vehicle, the strategic cruise missile, threaten to preclude future arms control agreements.

Chapter Eight

1. Kincade, William H. "Arms Control in the 1980s." **The Annals of the American Academy of Political and Social Science**. September, 1981, pp. 145-163.
    This article considers the motivations for arms limitation talks. Reviews the technical, institutional, and political problems that must be solved in negotiating an effective arms control agreement.
2. Kincade, William H. "Challenges to Verification: Old & New." **Arms Control**, Vol. 3, December, 1982, pp. 14-30.
    The author discusses future verification necessities and reviews past strategies and changing technologies.
3. Schear, James A. "Verifying Arms Agreements: Premises, Practices and Future Problems." **Arms Control**, Vol. 3, December, 1982, pp. 76-95.
    This article traces past verification debates and presents three future challenges: the strategic environment, verification and public trust and diplomatic pressures. These need to be met by a widespread approach rather than a single-minded solution.
4. "Verification." Chapter 2 in **Challenges for U.S. National Security**. Report prepared by the staff of the Carnegie Panel on U.S. Security and the Future of Arms Control, Carnegie Endowment for International Peace, Washington, D.C., 1983, pp. 25-68.
    This chapter on verification "reviews the basic methods used in verification and in intelligence generally, examines some of the controversies over verification of past and proposed agreements, and assesses the impact of verification on the likely scope of future agreements."

V Index

D

E

F

G

L

M

N